D1798329

Solomon on Leadership

Dr. Solomon Kimuyu

Library of Congress Control Number: 2009907491

Cover Design and Masinga Reservoir Photograph
By Dr. Solomon Kimuyu
First Edition, 2009

PUBLISHED BY:
Solomon Center For Leadership
10239 Deermont Trail
Dallas, Texas 75243 USA

AUTHOR:
Dr. Solomon Kimuyu

JUNE 2009 PRINTED BY:
Brentwood Christian Press
4000 Beallwood Avenue
Columbus, Georgia 31904 USA

December 2009 Print On Demand By:
Lightning Source, INC., U.S.
246 Heil Quaker Blvd.
La Vergne, TN 37086 USA

Solomon on Leadership

Dr. Solomon Kimuyu

Dedication

I dedicate this book to Protasia Shileo, my wife, for bearing with me those many endless days and nights; for her support and encouragement to complete the project, and to my beloved children: Respid (Spido), Victoria and Mark, whose exceptional behaviors contributed to an exemplary family. They were also our first paid employees with Solomon Home for Children, Inc., Abilene, Texas.

Dad

Acknowledgments

I owe a considerable gratification to several people who made it possible for me to take upon myself the mission of writing my first book on Leadership.

Protasia Shileo, my wife, friend, and partner for life, for her encouragement, moral support for my first candidature in Kenya general elections, December 27, 2007 and to put my thoughts with ink on paper for a leadership book.

My mother, who was responsible for giving me life.

Tom McMillan, a missionary to Tanzania, he was my pastor, teacher, friend, and responsible for my advance degrees in North America. He has since left this life.

Will J. Roberts, a missionary to Kenya, my long-time confidant who encouraged me to consider postgraduate studies. And Mark and Beth Hill, Christ Centered, for moral support and their heaviest financial support for the establishment of "Solomon Center For Leadership," where the book will be used to reach many for Jesus Christ.

First Baptist Church, Sweetwater, Texas for funding my BBA degree, Hardin Simmons University and to all former Southern Baptist missionaries who served in Kenya and Tanzania who taught me at Mombasa Baptist High School and Baptist Seminary of East Africa; now Mount Meru University, Arusha, Tanzania.

A moral authority of a Leader is Honesty and Integrity
www.muumandu.com

Jo Scales, my High School English teacher, now a retired missionary, edited and made suggestions. And Keith and Peggy Oliphint, for their financial support for the establishment of "Solomon Center For Leadership", Muumandu, Kenya.

Dr. Steve Christopher, Director of Discipleship at Our Savior in Livermore; with Lutheran Ministries, California, who granted permission to incorporate some of his unpublished work in my book for the benefit of developing leader(s).

Respid (Spido), our first born for supplying my writing instruments and for making sure my computers were in good repair and Victoria, (daughter) for financial support for publishing Leadership.

Roy and Ginny Pool, members of a Sunday School class I taught at First Baptist Church of Garland, Texas, who proofread my manuscript and made numerous suggestions. They did an exemplary job; and for their financial support for the establishment of "Solomon Center For Leadership", Muumandu, Kenya.

And Ms. Lila Kathryn Farmer, a retired missionary to Kenya with Campus Crusade for Christ, International, a family friend of many years and one who had the final task to proof the pre-press proof.

"That I may publish with the voice of thanksgiving, and tell of all thy wondrous works." Psalm 26:7

Foreword

I have been a follower of Jesus Christ since I was a child, accepting Christ as my own personal Savior on November 30, 1965, and am a member of a Baptist church. While I had many exhortations to keep a personal business journal as part of my responsibility as father, business man and an educator, I never did it. Part of my disobedience to this important counsel was that I thought I could not find the time and the resources to pen down my thoughts and convictions on leadership.

Now I truly believe that everybody should write an account of his sojourn of his life experience here on earth. I wish I had personal records of my ancestors who left us only with fragments of some oral traditions – mostly about how they conducted their barter business.

My father died during my early teenage years. I looked for older adults as mentors and did not find it easy. I learned at an early age that if I was to succeed in life I had to have good common sense and wisdom. I learned how to trade and made money by selling fish I caught from a nearby river. It was a very risky business for a teenager to fish on an African river. Hungry crocodiles would often have one of the local children for their weekly meal. Somehow I managed to survive that ordeal in spite of my many fishing expeditions. The Lord was looking out for me even back then. After a day's catch I sold my fish in my neighborhood door to door. I bought shoes and other incidentals from my fish sales. And of course the best thing is I hadn't been eaten.

When I graduated from grammar school I moved on to high school. I started a new business of selling the extra food I had for lunch to the other boys at the school. By the week's end, the boys would be lined up to pay what they owed me. Looking back on it, it was funny that you could make a business out of something so simple.

After graduation I moved with my entrepreneur spirit to a Baptist Seminary at Arusha, a small rural town located at the foot of Mt. Meru, Tanzania, East Africa. Every seminarian was allocated a quarter of an acre to grow vegetables for our upkeep. I rented my portion of the land to the highest bidder during the entire time of my seminary years. I worked hard. I bought my first butane cook top. I also bought my first used car -- a Volkswagen Beetle. When the first weekend rolled around I wanted to surprise my girlfriend Protasia, now my wife. Unfortunately, my beetle never made it to its destination due to an engine knock. Obviously, I had no experience checking for engine oil. I never forgave myself until years later when we bought our family car.

We moved to North America for my postgraduate education. Now with our quiver full of a family of five, I had to think business. This book is about my business experience in America. Sometimes I made bad business decisions for which I paid a high price. In most cases I made good business decisions which resulted in God's blessings and prosperity. This is my story.

Solomon Kimuyu
Dallas, Texas
www.muumandu.com

A moral authority of a Leader is Honesty and Integrity
www.muumandu.com

About the Author

Dr. Solomon Kimuyu is a focused, task-oriented leader. He knows exactly where he wants to go with his life and persuades other people to come along with him. He has strong convictions about life and family. He has managed to keep his wife and children on his team, by keeping a zealous fervor and to have them take an active part. This is a desire for every family man, for no man can claim to be successful when his family is not supportive of him.

I met Dr. Solomon Kimuyu in 1976 when he was doing his pastoral apprenticeship at Nairobi Baptist Church. He was attending Baptist Seminary of East Africa, Arusha, Tanzania. He later attended Daystar Communications Institute, now Daystar University. He was senior pastor at Athi River Baptist Church [1976-1982]. During his time at Athi River he undertook many projects to assist the poor members of the church. Thirty years later the church still remembers Dr. Kimuyu's leadership and vision. At the start of 1977 Solomon and his wife, Protasia joined the staff of Campus Crusade for Christ, International. Dr. Solomon and Protasia were translators for CCCI educational materials and books, and audio recordings they developed are still in use in East Africa.

Dr. Kimuyu mobilizes people. He was the General Secretary of the Baptist Convention of Kenya for many years and Vice President for All Africa Baptist Union. He is also a great organizer and administrator. He implemented administrative structures, which are still the backbone of the administration of the Baptist Convention of Kenya. He is an educator and entrepreneur. Solomon is a board member of the Grace Evangelical Theological Seminary of Nairobi. He believes the purpose of education is to change beliefs, attitudes, and value systems and to form them to be more Christ oriented. He is Founder/President, Solomon Home for Children, Inc., Dallas, TX and Solomon Center For Leadership, Nairobi, Kenya. He ran

A moral authority of a Leader is Honesty and Integrity

for Machakos parliamentary seat December 27, 2007. Solomon was defeated due to voter irregularities and a tribal euphoria that was sweeping his tribal area.

This book is a great contribution to leadership development, especially in Africa. It is a book born in the right season. Africa is experiencing an unprecedented leadership crisis. This book is a must-read for all leaders and potential leaders, especially in Africa.

Wellington (Willy) Kyalo Mutiso
First Baptist Church Athi River, Senior Pastor,
Athi River, Kenya
Grace Evangelical Theological Seminary, Director
Evangelical Alliance of Kenya, General Secretary

Why I Wrote *Leadership*

The *Leadership* book has been a life time experience in numerous ways. It took many months and thought to put down on ink and paper my thoughts. At last the topic crystallized which forced me to follow six specified paths of thought. My writing is about my life seen in different windows of life, I am grateful for the blessings God has afforded my family and me to be able to travel the world at a time when it was not possible for my ancestors, and even today a few who are not privileged to travel to distant places. Missionaries who had a profound impact on my family and my spiritual journey gave me the courage to put pen to paper my thoughts on the way I saw the crumbling leadership in Kenya.

The purpose of *Leadership* book is to educate you with tested managerial techniques to help you make informed decisions, to challenge you, and inspire you with biblical principles about leadership, and ultimately to help you to be more like Jesus. The Leadership Seminar will equip you with managerial skills to help you become a better and more effective leader than you may have thought possible. You will learn how to lead purposefully, efficiently and effectively with a better understanding of goal setting. You will learn how to exert influence in a better way than ever before. A successful leader continues to work at becoming an exemplary leader.

The book *Leadership* is designed for anyone in church leadership, public administration, politics, education, human resources/personnel management, and entrepreneurship.

A moral authority of a Leader is Honesty and Integrity
www.muumandu.com

Biblical leaders have been used as examples of men and women who were very instrumental in leading God's people. Moses, in particular, is a great example of a godly man in leadership. The book is fully researched on the subject matter, presenting the great Philosophers of our time, with discussion on theories and practices on Leadership.

The book can be utilized as a textbook, in seminars, camp retreats and resource material on leadership. The examples used, compare leadership in the developing nations of the world and industrialized nations of the north.

This is a story about a man who has done it all. Former missionary/pastor in East Africa, years in public service in Texas, an educator in colleges in Texas, established entrepreneur, and the pursuit of politics in Kenya in 2007, afforded the author to write *Leadership.*

The *Leadership* was written covering the span of years between August 2006 – February 2009 purported to capture the outcome of Kenya general elections on December 27, 2007 and the America general elections of November 4, 2008. *Leadership* captures the highlights of Barack Obama's first senatorial campaign whose late biological father had Kenyan roots. He announced his second tier of his presidential political career on the cold morning on the steps of the State Capital of Illinois. Obama ran a magnificent campaign that led to the inauguration on January 20, 2009. He made history as the 44th President and the first African-American President of the US and the leader of the free world.

Rev. Jesse Jackson, the first African-American presidential front runner, and the founder of RainbowPUSH Coalition, Inc. wrote, "Mr. President, your future, vision, strength and courage will take America and the world a long way. We have made it through the primary season, the engagement party in Grant Park on November 4th, and the wedding on January 20th, we are entering into marriage—the final stage, one that is full of challenges."

America is facing high rising cost of education, housing, and health care for the uninsured. Jackson further wrote, "It is high noon in our politics, where hope abounds, but it is midnight in our economics. We are in a time of the worst economic crisis of the last half century, and amid expanding wars and conflicts in Iraq, the Middle East and Africa".

Obama's success to the Oval Office also came with great challenges of his presidency, one that will be mired with expectations of fulfillment and perhaps the eradication of century old racially-slurred differences between Blacks and Whites of the southern states.

During the first 100 days in office, Obama signed a bill into law allowing women and minority the right to sue for equal pay. The bill was a milestone for the realization of African-American into the utopia of the American dream.

He is faced with the challenges of his own African roots with some expectancy for the continuation of the Millennium Development Goals. Obama administration will HAVE to continue to embrace and prioritize the MDGs through the Africa Foreign Policy. MDGs remain the only force behind Obama's greatest impact on Africa.

The Islamic world is not alone; his middle name identifies ties to the Islam faith, expecting Barack HUSSEIN administration to end wars on terrorism in their own midst. All in all, Obama, with his rich heritage of "half this and half that," also may find the White minority who helped him ascend to the presidency; they too, will WANT to have their share and perhaps greatest influence in his daily administration.

...Will Obama Presidency have an effect on his African roots? Only time will tell.

Extra-judicial Killings:

A U.N. Rapporteur was appointed in February 2009 to investigate; Kenya's special security forces, alleged of carrying out extra-judicial killings, which claimed more than 500 lives since December 2007... Coalition government has never been able to bring the murders and the killers to justice. Ω

Preface

The author's goal for this book is to present both Bible-based teachings on leadership and leading-edge business principles on the subject. The author desires that persons in leadership will be encouraged to apply the materials presented here, both for themselves and for the people they lead.

The selection of persons for leadership positions has become a subject tainted with increasing dishonesty in the following areas: church leadership, academic institutions, business enterprises, governments, not-for-profit organizations, and politicians on all levels.

United Nations (Sept 6, 2000)[1] Independent Committee published its twelve months report which disparaged United Nations - Secretary-General, the Security Council and a few member states who aided large-scale smuggling.

The preface forlornly revealed years of United Nations inefficiency, corruption within the UN itself, as well as corruption within agency senior personnel in the field.

The preface suggested four basic principles of leadership (1) Creation of a Chief Operating Officer, (COO) to administer United Nations hiring practices based on talent comparatively to political expediency or family association. (2) Creation of an Independent Audit Board (3) Establish harmonization between

[1]U.N Independent Inquiry, Management Oil-for-food Program

the United Nations agencies. (4) United Nations Security Council refines its program's purpose and criteria.

In the final analysis, the responsibility rests upon United Nations leadership which appears to be engulfed with managerial weakness, dishonesty, and ethical lapses.

Therefore, it is the responsibility of a proven leader to help restore honesty, integrity and to help stem the deteriorating leadership crisis we see today in so many of the world's developing democracies.

Once these basic principles of leadership are observed people can begin to elect/hire a true leader(s). The book is a road map recommended to anybody in a leadership role.

Dr. Solomon Kimuyu
January 2009

The book uses American-English expressions and wit.
The New American Standard Bible and Revised King James Bible are used unless otherwise referenced.

Solomon on Leadership
Faith ∞ Politics ∞ Governance

Table of Contents

ONE: *Foundation of Leadership*

Table of Contents, cont.

A moral authority of a Leader is Honesty and Integrity

Table of Contents, cont.

Table of Contents, cont.

A moral authority of a Leader is Honesty and Integrity
www.muumandu.com

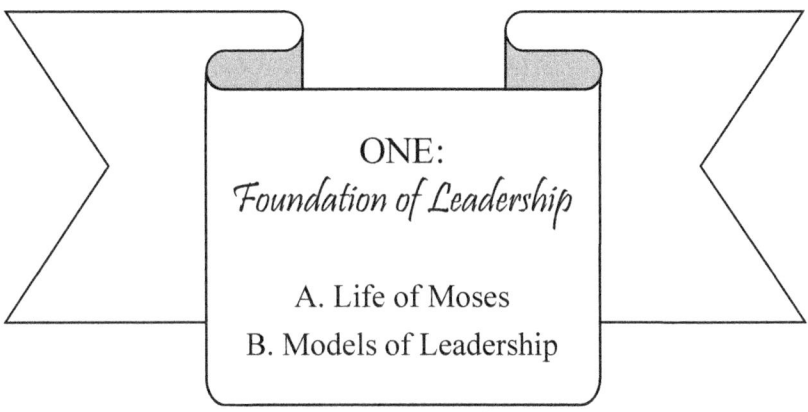

ONE:
Foundation of Leadership

A. Life of Moses
B. Models of Leadership

ONE: *Foundation of Leadership*

A. Life of Moses
Introduction

While there are many books on leadership, a Christian leader must always look to God's Word to see what the Lord wants in a leader. This brings us to possibly the greatest human leader of all time – Moses. For hundreds of years the Hebrews had come to Egypt for refuge and for food. During the summer months the Nile River rises from the torrential rainfall from the mountains and hills of East Africa. From Jinja Falls, Uganda the Nile River embarks on its 4,000 mile journey headed northwards. It joins the Blue Nile southwest of Abyssinia Hills, pushing billions of gallons of water through the flat lands of the Sahara Desert, Sudan and Egypt and dumps its rich soil with nutrients into the delta basin, then finally to the Mediterranean Sea. This causes the Nile to overflow to allow irrigation without the rainfall. The soil, rich with nutrients is good for wheat, corn, barley, and perishable produce. During bad economic indicators, a country becomes aware of the immigrants who take up jobs and use the country's resources. Like in many parts of the world, Egypt had concerns on the status of the rising Jewish immigrants. Egypt was the bread basket for the Babylonians, Rome, Palestine, Syrians and other smaller city and states.

The Man Called Moses: The Egyptian name for water is **"Mo,"** a name given to the baby infant Moses by Pharaoh's sister, because he had been rescued out of the banks of the River Nile. Pharaoh's sister had been married and sadly barren. So it came to pass when she was bathing in the River Nile, she saw the baby infant, she gathered the baby infant into her bosom and probably declared "this is my baby, Mo." Moses' sister, having witnessed the drama, she offered Pharaoh's sister, to look for a nurse among the Hebrew people. Without knowing, Pharaoh's sister gave Moses to be nursed by his biological parent.

Moses was by birth a Hebrew son and by adoption an Egyptian Prince. Moses was the seventh generation in succession from his Hebrew ancestors. He was raised as one of the princes of Pharaoh. As an Egyptian prince, Moses was educated by the best tutors and philosophers under Egyptian culture. He learned Greek, the trade language and the diplomatic languages of the nations outside Egypt.

Since then, the name Moses remained a house hold name to the Jews and many religions of the world outside the Holy Bible. Moses is the main character in the book **Solomon on Leadership** and the foundation of which leadership principles are herein.

After the death of Joseph, Pharaoh made Hebrew slaves to build stores of grains and pyramids for the Pharaoh's tombs. Moses' parents risked their lives in saving baby Moses; he never stopped being a Hebrew just because he was raised in Pharaoh's court. God in His divine plan made Moses a leader to lead His chosen people out of the bondage of the Egyptians.

His actions and intelligence found favor in Egypt, as he was hard-working and successful in all he did. Perhaps he would even have become one of the pharaohs of Egypt. One day his life in Egypt came to a sudden end when he killed an Egyptian guard; therefore Pharaoh sought to kill him. Moses ran for his life alone through one of the worst deserts of North Africa. As he fled, the scriptures tell us that Moses found refuge with a loving

Midian family who took him in.

Moses was called to be a leader and equipped to be a leader by God Himself. One day when Moses was tending the flocks, he saw a bush that burned but was not consumed. When he approached it, God spoke to him and told him to take his shoes off because he was on Holy Ground.

Moses' eminent degrees of success are as: Prince of Egypt under Pharaoh's Leadership, prudent organizer, politician, lawgiver, deliverer and most of all an interpreter, and author of the Torah, the first five books of the Old Testament. My desire in **Leadership** is to introduce such a man of great intelligence and wisdom, one who gave the world a recipe of the basic organizational chart used in every leadership level, from a mother and father of Hebrew immigrants to the greatest nations of the world.

Moses the Politician: God instructed Moses that he was to go back to Egypt and lead the Hebrews out of bondage. Initially, Moses tried to talk the Lord out of it, claiming he was not a good speaker. The Lord replied: *Who makes man's mouth? Who makes him to speak? Is it not I, the Lord?* So God chose Moses as a leader, even though Moses was like you and I, we don't think we're up to the task either. But God is able to make us up to the task.

Moses the Lawgiver: So Moses obeyed the Lord and returned to Egypt. Through many miracles, God proved that He was with Moses and with the last plague of the death of the first-born of all of Egypt. Pharaoh relented and let the Hebrews go. Moses led about two million people on a forty-year journey in the desert. Can you imagine the challenges of leading that many people where there is no ready food or water? Often there were those who rebelled against Moses' leadership (in spite of the obvious fact that God was with him) and Moses met these rebellions always in a godly manner. He had become the leader that God intended for the task.

Moses the Servant-Leader: The Bible does not discuss every detail regarding what happened at Mt. Sinai, but we know that somewhere on that mountain, God talked face to face with Moses, giving him the great Ten Commandments that have withstood the test of time. From this encounter, Moses' face glowed with such a brilliant radiance, that he had to wear a veil in order to protect the Hebrews who looked at him. The Bible says when Moses came down from the mountain people were afraid to approach Moses. *"...the skin of his face shone because of speaking with Him. From that day on ...Moses would replace the veil over his face until he went in to speak with Him."* Exodus34:29(b), 35(b).

The evidence that Moses was truly a great godly leader is seen when Jesus goes on the mountain of Transfiguration. In the Gospel of Matthew 17:2-4, the Bible says, *"And He was transfigured before them; His face shone like the sun, and His garments became as white as the light. And behold, Moses and Elijah appeared to them, talking with Him. Peter said to Jesus, "Lord, it is good for us to be here; if You wish, I will make three tabernacles here, one for You, one for Moses and one for Elijah."* From the Egyptian palaces of Pharaoh, through the Moab deserts, back to Egypt, and through the deserts for forty years, including Mt. Sinai, Moses was an ordinary man chosen in the plan of God to become the liberator, the lawgiver, and the leader of the nation of Israel.

What is Leadership? Leadership involves three important elements: (1) the ability to combine ideas, material resources, human resources, and (in the Christian environment) faith to achieve a mission objective for the organization; (2) the ability to persuade individuals to participate in your endeavors; and (3) the ability to motivate one or more people to actively share your vision. When ideas and vision are exchanged and accepted, leadership can take place. The key element of leadership is the ability to get things done through others.

Who are Leaders? They are not usually supermen; they are typically just ordinary human beings. They may come and go with times of age; they may retire or even get fired by their board of directors. They are subject to make mistakes that sometimes may affect the lives of their families, and even millions of people depending on the span and scope of their leadership. There are many leaders from hundreds of communities of the world whose leadership remains an icon to the local community and even to the world at large.

Who Can or Should Lead? Just about anybody can lead, as long as one has a desire to lead, and a readiness to ask God for the ability and strength to lead. Once in that position, a leader must ask: "What is my responsibility? What am I supposed to do?" "How can I best serve God in my leadership position?"

What is Charismatic Leadership? Charismatic leaders can be found in many positions of leadership. While charisma is often associated with effective leadership, that is not always the case. A charismatic leader in most cases is a person with an unusual ability to persuade and draw large crowds of people to himself. In this case the charisma can be used for both good purposes and bad. While charismatic leaders can draw large crowds and tend to receive respect from their followers, charisma itself should never be viewed as a prerequisite for a leader.

Some examples of charismatic leaders within the political realm are: Nelson Mandela, first Native President of South Africa; Winston Churchill, Prime Minister of England; Indira Gandhi of India; and Martin Luther King JR, who championed the civil rights of minorities in the United States of America; and Adolph Hitler, the despotic leader of Germany who annihilated millions of Jews. As you can see, most of these leaders used their charisma for good, but Hitler used his for terrible evil.

Idi Amin, a former dictator of Uganda who once called himself a son of Africa, declared himself a president-for-life of Uganda. He expelled tens of thousands of Indian-Asians who had controlled Ugandan economy for decades dating back to British Colonial rule to exile. The country's economy plunged into economic bedlam.

During his military rule he had murdered more than 500,000 people who are believed to have been thrown into the River Nile and some bodies were usually fed to hungry crocodiles. Amin was the worst dictator the continent of Africa had ever known.

Jimmy Carter, President of the USA, said that Amin disgusted the entire civilized world[2]. Amin was known to have said that Hitler was right when he burned six million Jews. Amin's eight years' reign came to an end when his army failed to annex parts of his neighbor nation of Tanzania. He was never tried or charged for his atrocities.

[2]The Associated Press, 2003

A moral authority of a Leader is Honesty and Integrity

Idi Amin is an example of a tyrant, and terror dictator whose leadership was evil. He died poor in exile. Some charismatic leaders in the spiritual realm are: Moses himself, King David, Elijah, the Apostle Paul, and Billy Graham, the great American evangelist who presented the Gospel of Christ to over 210 million people in live audiences in 185 countries. Of course the Leader of our souls, our Savior Jesus Christ, was very charismatic, drawing large crowds wherever He went (even to the cross).

Moses' Organization Chart: Jethro (also known as Reuel), the Priest of Midian, was a descendant of the sons of Keturah; one of the three wives of Abraham. They settled east of the Dead Sea and south of the Sinai Peninsula, modern South Arabia. They were nomads, shepherds, and caravan traders. That makes Arabs and Jewish people good traders. When Moses fled from Pharaoh after killing the Egyptian slave driver, his first encounter in Midian was at a watering hole. There he drove back other herdsmen who were refusing to let Jethro's daughters draw water from the well for their livestock. They invited Moses to their home and he was welcomed into their fellowship.

Not long afterward, Moses married one of Jethro's daughters, Zipporah. For forty years, Moses worked as a hired shepherd for Jethro, building a life for himself among the Midianites. God was preparing Moses to lead the Israelites out of slavery in Egypt. Moses did this, first being their spiritual leader and second being their national political leader through many years of wandering in the wilderness before entering the Promised Land of Canaan.

Jethro was temporarily reunited with Moses during the wilderness travels. He recommended to Moses a method of leadership that would help him. Up to that time, all types of cases were brought only to Moses for ruling; healthcare, military, personal disputes, worship, etc., were all Moses' responsibility. The task was too much for Moses to undertake alone. Jethro advised Moses to focus on his main calling – to be the voice of God to the people. He should teach the Lord's statutes and laws and the way to honor God.

Jethro suggested that Moses divide up the responsibility for decision-making among trusted men. Some would be responsible for a thousand, some for a hundred, some fifty and some ten. They would handle all low level issues and only the harder and most important ones would be brought through the leadership ranks to Moses. Moses agreed. This was Israel's first system of self government and is the model for the court systems in all civilized nations of the world. Also in Figure 2, we see the additional leadership layer of the single family. Here the father is the family head of household and brings this important leadership role to any family in the church, and to society as a whole. The organizational chart(s) depicts an orderly system of governing whereby authority is assigned to subordinates. This system has shown to typically result in peace among the people, in honesty, in obedience, in respect for government, and (when the Lord is considered in the nation's values) in the fear of God.

Traditional Organizational Chart

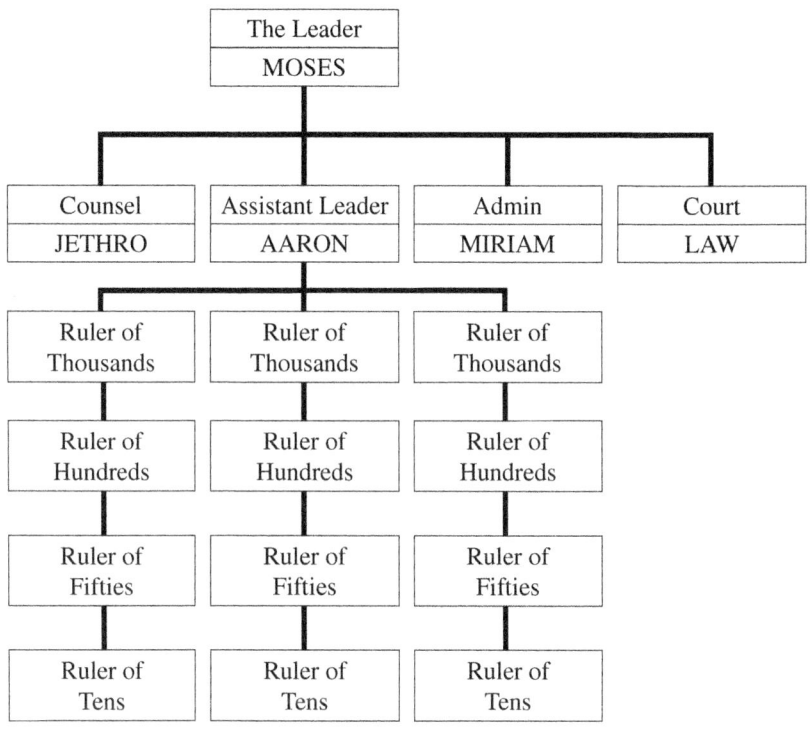

Jethro advised Moses to remain the intermediary of Israel before God. Moses was to teach statutes, laws and the way to honor God. Moses listened, he selected able men out of Israel and positioned them as leaders of thousands, hundreds, fifties, and tens, from that day on Jews formed a system of self governing. [Exodus 18:19-25]

Figure 1. ©Kimuyu 2008

A moral authority of a Leader is Honesty and Integrity
www.muumandu.com

This organization chart is used in business, church, institutions, government and a single family household.

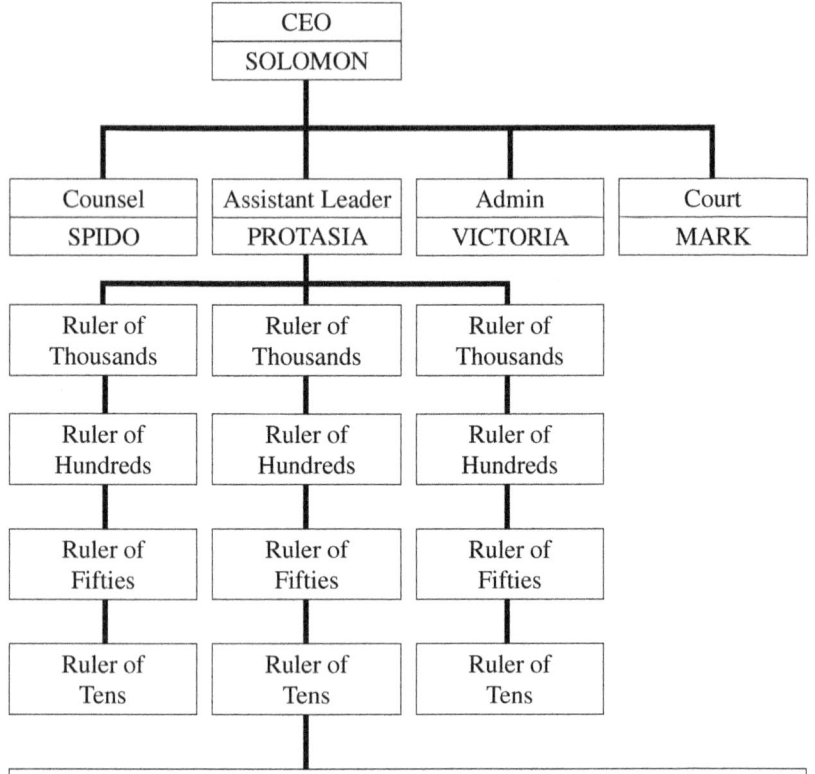

HUSBAND HEAD OF SINGLE FAMILY HOUSEHOLD

Figure #2 adds additional leadership layer of single family signifying an important leadership role of any family in the church and the society. Moses' organization chart produced an orderly system of governing which resulted in: Peace among people, Trust-worthiness, Honesty, Obedience, Respect and Fear of God. "Unity is a link in the great educational movement inaugurated by Jesus Christ; our objective is to discern the truth in Christianity and prove it. The truth that we teach is not new; neither do we claim special revelation or discovery of new religious principles. Our purpose is to help and teach mankind to use and prove the eternal truth taught by the Master." Filmore. ©Kimuyu 2008

A moral authority of a Leader is Honesty and Integrity
www.muumandu.com

B. Models of Leadership

Born or Made? You may have heard the phrase "born and not made". This phrase came out of an old study on leadership more than half a century ago. The study was an extensive survey to determine the traits of successful leaders. If the research was able to find and categorize these traits, it would have been a way to determine who should be appointed in positions of leadership.[3] However, after more than 50 years of leadership research, there is no hard evidence that a person's traits alone produce a successful leader. The word "Trait" comes from the Latin word *tractus*. This means a person with an intelligent mind or a person of integrity. Leadership researchers shifted their studies from human traits to situational approaches to leadership. With studies of traits, considering situational leadership, we can begin to answer the old question, "Is a leader born or made?"

While one can *be* born to be a leader (such as an heir to a throne), no one is born being a leader. Some of the child kings in the Bible did not actually lead until they developed some maturity and began to use the skills and power that had been bestowed on them. However, some skills essential to leadership may be noticed at an early age in an individual. What a child learns during developmental years may change in later years. That is why often in a family of two or more; one member may develop a different career and vocation from their other siblings.

[3]Samuel C. Cert, Principles of Modern Management, WMC. Brown Company Publisher, 1983. Dubuque, Iowa. Pp 319

A moral authority of a Leader is Honesty and Integrity
www.muumandu.com

Once a person is elevated to a position of leadership it is wise for *him* to continue to learn through continued education. Leadership seminars, management courses, books and online classes are a few ways to increase one's leadership skills. There are many management institutes in many parts of the world that are sponsored by governments or The United League of Nations through its divisions of education. A leader can also learn by reading business journals, observation and modeling other successful leaders.

In the United States of America all medical doctors and many practitioners from a number of professions are required by the laws of the state or federal government, or by their own by-laws, to stay current in their profession. They have to stay up to date in technology, new discoveries and other aspects of their profession. Hence, to be excellent at what one does, learning is and should be, a life-long journey. In light of this, a leader should explore and create new opportunities for growth, and challenge his followers to high self expectation by inspiring a moral commitment of excellence.

When opportunities of growth and learning are made available to employees of an organization, it may result in a desire within those employees to strive to be their best. One area a leader needs to stay current is local and international politics. These can change day-to-day affecting global trade balances between nations of the world. Thus a wise leader stays up on these issues as it often affects the people under his leadership. Did you know that when ostrich eggs are in danger of fire, an ostrich immerses itself in water and then runs to its eggs and shakes drops of water around its nest? Why? Protection! Did you know that a house mouse always takes the same path as it tries to escape from danger to its home? It follows the same route even if there is an obstacle in its path. It is amazing. Just imagine a house mouse that always takes the same route. Is it a good leadership model? Should leaders ask their future community leaders to think about animal traits? Would that make them good leaders? Would they want their leaders to consider animal traits as good leadership traits? Can leaders learn from animals? Choose five animals of your choice. Make a list of animal traits. Explain their traits.

Types of Leaders: The following are some types of leaders - they are not in any particular order, but are a collection of the general types of leaders who are out there leading as: school administrators, church leaders, business leaders, and elected public officials. These people provide some type of leadership on a daily basis for the purpose of governing. The reader can make his/her own judgment as to the type of leader he/she chooses to endorse.

1. Autocratic leader – a "single leader" (as opposed to a leader as a part of a leadership group). This person may get his authority from the organization he leads. An example might be stockholders designating a leader (CEO). The stockholder does not exercise any power or have daily contact with workers. The power is invested to one person, such as a director or CEO. All management decisions are made from the top management downward. The employees must follow the rules and policies of the organization. An example of autocratic leadership is the top general of armed forces around the world.

Autocratic Leadership: One advantage of the autocratic style of leadership is that things can get started quickly and orderly. The disadvantage of the autocratic style is it results in poor employee morale. In this style of leadership, often the only way to complain to management is by employing union shops. Many large corporations and governments are examples of the autocratic style of leadership. Leadership in the autocratic system is judged by the efficiency of the total organization. When the profit margin is affected by the employees poor output the leader is often the one to blame.

2. Equalitarian leader – one who makes decisions based on the degree and efficiency of the whole organization. Under this leadership people are motivated because they feel a part of the decision – making process.

Equalitarian Leadership: The advantage of the equalitarian style is that it allows for communications and interactions between the leader and the subordinates. The disadvantage of this model in the Church setting is that the pastor/leader may find it difficult to dismiss an ineffective subordinate. The equalitarian leadership style is used extensively in many North American churches because the model is analogous to American democratic systems. It is recommended that leaders should learn to adapt their leadership style when operating with different people from various walks of life.

3. Team Player – a leader, who listens, respects, supports and welcomes ideas of others. This type of leader has a desire to involve other people in the decision-making process. When individuals under this leader have a say-so in the activities, they typically give full support to the endeavor. And when the leader makes the final decision, the group supports it since they have already had a chance to give their input.

4. One-Man-Show – a selfish leader who refuses to welcome suggestions from anyone. This leader hinders progress by refusing to let others make suggestions or offer alternatives. This type of "leadership" usually accomplishes very little and is often quite detrimental to the people that are being led.

THE WEAKNESS OF ONE-MAN- SHOW

The year 1984 is considered the year of the personal computer industry; I was in my second year in college of business. The first original IBM personal computer was rolled out in 1981 from the assembly line. The original PC had two floppy drives and used an Intel 8088 microprocessor which ran at 4.77 MHz which was quite fast at the time of its début. All Business majors were enrolled in computer introductory courses, and two computer assembly languages. The world witnessed the development of numerous sub-industries, which were: hardware, software, systems, printers, terminal workstations, data communications, semiconductors, CAD/CAM, office automation, service/leasing distribution, and forms/supplies. Furthermore, the computer industry was only a part of layer information—processing system which included office equipment and other related communications industry firms. The information—processing industry had over 500 computer hardware manufactures and over 5,000 software companies and over 430 communications. (Business Weekly, July, 1984, pp. 24-30)

IBM had produced a series of personal computers ranging from mainframes; the production of PC Jr. was the big joke for Big Blue. It was a machine that came with many limitations, poor performance, insufficient market testing, and it was poorly marketed, and yet, it sold between $3,000 and $7,000. It was an atrocious and totally fatal business decision on the part of IBM leadership.

The history of IBM is one of the best examples of a **ONE-MAN-SHOW.** IBM had been tainted with certain points of weakness which had plagued its profitability and future investments in the early 1980's. When a customer bought a machine or equipment from IBM, the customer was left to his/her own devices when it came to customer support. IBM failed to satisfy tens of thousands of its customers' needs. IBM was known for versatile and dependable machines, but their PC computers were not among the fastest or the most powerful. IBM charged exorbitant prices for their low end personal computers which were not equal to the price they charged. For example, the IBM desk top computer, the Ps/2 was introduced to the market too late; other computer manufactures had flooded the market with clones that were more powerful and less expensive and affordable. Apple and other small computer companies had garnished a fair portion of the PC market share up to this day.

IBM let the cost of the original PCs run away and failed to take advantage of its dominant research powerhouse. The IBM leadership did not think anyone could beat them—they were a monopoly for business machines since the 1920's. Charging high prices allowed small companies to develop compatible computers which were more powerful than IBM's, at a fraction of the cost. IBM top management leadership had a serious impact on the early misfortune of its original PC line. It is all because of one human being, Thomas J. Watson, who ran IBM like a monarch over a country. He made the decisions, no matter how trivial. He led IBM bureaucratic bottlenecks, whereby the right hand did not know what the left hand was doing. The paperwork necessary was astronomical. Therefore, IBM did not suggest a workable solution for meeting customer needs and satisfaction.

Watson nurtured IBM operations through The Great Depression until his death, June 19, 1956; he had made IBM an international force. "From a handful of little factories that made meat slackers, grocery store scales, time clocks, and primitive tabulations promoted as 'business machines', Watson sermonized into existence the explosively expanding enterprise that has produced the tools and technology to compound and multiply man's world--- or escape beyond it to the stars." (Think, Autobiography of Watson, 1969, pp. 108)

Watson's future CEO, John Akers was caught off guard; he failed to realize that computer information technology would be crucial for future business. He was masked in the heaps of IBM routine; policy and procedure that failed him to embrace the change in the information system technology from day one. He failed to identify the niche of PC that would dominate the future information technology systems of the twenty-first century. Watson failed to plan for the PC which would control and influence future CEOs' decision making process.

The tides of changing from large mainframe, that occupied rooms of 12'x12' or larger, to perform tasks that the PC was capable to do from a desktop. IBM enjoyed the long, good reputation for its technological breakthrough, leadership, semiconductors, in storage communication, communication architecture, that had become a template for emerging worldwide standards. The personal computers had revolutionized the decision making process from top management, line-managers, and supervisors down to the customer service specialist.

In the early 1980's, the implications for computer makers were clear. Steve, at Apple Computer and other computer gurus of the day had seen what the PC would do in business, industries and in the marketplace; entrepreneurs jumped right into the game and surpassed the sleeping giant, IBM, under John Akers' leadership. The spread of networking computing changed forever the way business decisions were made by CEOs. The PC innovation benefited largely small industries over big companies, because of its high performance, such as Apollo, Sun Microsystems, both made powerful workstations used by scientists and engineers of the day.

The law makers turned to the educators in universities, colleges and the nation's schools to write computer curriculum that would prepare graduates on the use of computer information systems in business, industries and the marketplace. Because of the One-Man-Show, IBM lost the ability to dominate the PC market share.

The lesson learned from monopolies like IBM and AT&T was that big corporations tend to ignore early warning signs of new business opportunities when top leadership refuse to acknowledge advice from their subordinates when calling for a change in market strategy. Both leaderships were blindfolded by their monopoly dominance in their respective market share for many years. IBM lost the race in the PC market share while AT&T lost the race in local and long distance telephone services.

Comparison of Leadership Models

AUTOCRATIC	DEMOCRATIC
Direct	Shared
Commands	Suggests
Dictates	Solicits
Negative re-enforcement	Positive re-enforcement
Leader's needs	Majority's needs
One good idea	Several good ideas
Leader's one way	We are the bosses

© Kimuyu, 2005

I believe that every right implies a responsibility; every opportunity an obligation; every possession a duty –JD Rockefeller

INTEGRITY: The word "integrity" has received little attention from the philosophers. However, Aristotle is one of the forerunner users of the word integrity in his writings. Integrity was introduced in western societies by the Christian movement in the first century as they sought purpose of life and solitude. Integrity remains a central concern to all major religions of the world. Saint Thomas Aquinas and John Wesley agreed the virtue of obedience has more praiseworthiness than other virtues. Judaism lay emphasis on the study of the Torah — reveals the rules under which man is expected to live by [Ten Commandments]. Integrity encapsulates the significance of wholeness and perfection, when these conditions are met they yield moral values, honesty and sincerity in life of the person. Integrity is wholeness of an undivided life in harmony with the divine [Supreme] power of

God. Therefore, integrity remains central in all major religions of the world. The Christians are upheld by the beatitudes to be pure in heart for they shall see God. (Mathew 5:2-11)

Integrity Formula:
Wholeness 100/100 + Perfection = Integrity

Integrity requires three major conditions:

- (1) Give verdict on what is right and wrong

- (2) Act on discernment of right and wrong

- (3) Articulate openly on judgment of right and wrong

Integrity implies intrinsic obedience that dictates the wisdom of right and wrong. Your life must be consistent, controlled by the sense of good judgment. You were born a perfectly innocent child; you remained innocent until when you were old enough to know the difference of right and wrong. Owing to nature of the first sin of Adam you were not pure. You began to acquire guilt of sin until the day you accept Jesus Christ as Lord and Savior. Thus, your sinful nature was removed by the blood of Jesus Christ. It is possible to have honesty without integrity; a person may state honestly his opinion on corruption, graft and bad governance.

If a person fails to take a stand, act and speak publicly on right and wrong, the conditions of integrity have not been met. Moses' life and leadership would be a perfect example of living integrity. As an expert in several fields of study from the colleges of arts and sciences and business, I am in agreement with social psychologists who advocate that it is a human phenomenon to refuse to think independently. Such irrational behaviors tend to result in mob violence.

Integrity 2: It is easier to know what somebody else believes on certain issues of right and wrong, than taking part to help bring a change. Many leaders and politicians all over the world tend to give promises during their campaign trails; once they occupy the office they often fail on their promises. This is not about a political speech, it is a world inhabited by public-spirited citizens to learn about the tenets of good leadership, governance and what integrity is all about. We are called as leaders of our communities to preach a message of hope and forgiveness while denouncing the evils of corruption, graft, stealing and deceit in our communities and entire nation. This is the price we must pay to live a life of integrity.

Integrity 3: It is the hardest of the previous discussed steps. To live a life of integrity is a personal choice. A person who decides to live with integrity may sometimes reach a conclusion that may differ from the mainstream. Once that decision is reached it becomes an aspect of the wholeness *(100/100 + perfection)* in which integrity exists in the presence of the Lord.

During the reign of Emperor Caligula, he ordered General Petronius to erect a statue of the emperor in the temple in Jerusalem; tens of thousands of unarmed Jews risked their lives in protest in the streets of Jerusalem. They said that they would rather die than to have a statue erected in their holy temple. General Petronius was moved seeing the multitude in protest without weapons. After a long time of diplomatic negotiations with the Jewish leaders, General Petronius wrote a letter to the Emperor of

Rome, Caligula saying "the honor would not allow him to erect a statue in the holy temple." Both the general and the Jewish leaders met the conditions of integrity: When the Jews protested and when the general's refusal to carry out the orders of the Emperor Caligula was considered treason. The story of the Roman general clearly illustrates a life of integrity so inspiring that it caused the transgressor to change his intention to do evil.

There are biblical examples of men who lived lives of integrity, they are: Moses for choosing to return to face the brutal Pharaoh, Abraham who was ready to sacrifice his son, Isaac. Job, who refused to abandon his faith in spite of the loss of his wealth, family and his terrifying torture. In New Testament the stoning of Stephen, and the tens of thousands of men and women who have been persecuted over the centuries in the name of our Lord Jesus Christ.

Proverbs 11:3 reads, "The integrity of the upright will guide them, but the falseness of the treacherous will destroy them." King Solomon wrote the proverbs to show how Integrity is part of wisdom and the ownership of the upright. When Proverbs say that the upright shall guide them, it means living with Integrity is self-denial toward the good and the truth. Integrity in itself becomes a "Journey rather than a destination," this is a concept consistent with the act of duty that forms the integral basis of Integrity.

Is Violence a Mode for Change? I have a rich entrepreneurial leadership experience of many years from industrial societies of the west, developing leadership, management, honesty and integrity. I will not promise what I cannot deliver. I bring leadership on the table while politicians and leaders are only thinking of the next election. I know with empowerment by the people no child will ever be left behind in education, no family should go hungry waiting for the rain seasons to fill the seasonal river banks and creeks, no able-body should sleep on a floor for a bed with rain over head. Leaders should find new ways to prosper as we have never done before.

The population of the third world democracies is growing at a high rate, but the quality of leaders is not keeping up with the new breed of citizens. Most people of the third world democracies will never have the opportunity to rise above the standard into which they were born. Many people starve to death, while some families can afford food or clothes for their children. Only good leadership, honesty and integrity can bring a change in the lives of men, women and children.

It is true the third world democracy is changing, but for some in Kenya the changes have not been good enough. I propose that elected leaders should cuddle integrity and honesty as their major stakeholder in the adventure of bringing a change to society that only offers a lasting hope. The message is how to get rid of corruption, abuse of power in the hands of the elected few politicians, and administrators. I urge the citizens of the third world democracies and especially in Kenya to vote for God fearing men and women of integrity who represent the best interest and will of the people. For the last several decades I have been convinced the only way to bring a change to the society is to change one person and one constituency at a time.

The nations of Africa are blessed with many tribes who represent a rich source of history and culture. Tribalism, similar to racism in the west creates physical, social and emotional barriers. As large as these barriers are the battles waged in the minds and hearts of men and women with children who are caught in crossroads of the sickness of poverty and HIV, the greatest battle in Kenya and the rest of Africa is a spiritual one.

Dag Hammarskjöld was a former UN Secretary General, before he was killed while on a peace mission in Belgian Congo, said, "I see no hope for world peace. We have tried so hard and failed so miserably. Unless the world has spiritual rebirth, within the next few years, civilization is doomed." The Secretary General never lived to witness the atrocities against humanity that happened in Congo and Rwanda where tens of millions of men, women and children were murdered by their own countrymen. This was a time the universal church and world governments watched from the sidelines while citizens of Congo and Rwanda butchered each other like a lion digging its claws into a running zebra. Unfortunately, Kenya like Darfur is not an exception; they failed to learn from their neighboring central African nations.

Tribal clashes in Kenya are not something new. It goes back to the first and second Presidents of the Republic of Kenya. During British colonial rule in Africa, land was taken by force from the original tribes and given to white settlers. These lands were given to grow farm goods for export. When Kenya received her independence in December of 1963 from Great Britain, it was widely believed that all land taken by the colonial rule would be returned to the rightful land owners under the leadership of the first President of the Republic of Kenya, Jomo Kenyatta. White settlers who were not sure of the future of the new Kenya were encouraged to sell their farms to the incoming new government of Kenya. While a neighboring state Tanzania simply nationalized most all white settlers' farms. A few financially able natives of Kenya bought some of the farms from white settlers as ranching cooperative societies.

The majority of the original land owners who could not afford to buy back their ancestral lands lost to a few wealthy, greedy natives who were then incoming young politicians and powerful government administrators. **The natives never forgot!** As years went by politicians misused their power — they took much of the remaining Government reserve land and protected forest. Exploitation, deforestation and land grabbing continued during the reign of Moi, the second president of Kenya.

It is widely believed that Jomo Kenyatta awarded the majority of the Rift Valley lands to his Kikuyu tribe as a reward for fighting in the Mau Mau uprising which resulted in Kenyans' independence. Jomo Kenyatta died during his third term in office. His predecessor, Moi, who comes from Rift Valley made no attempt to settle land dispute during his entire 23 years of rule. Tribal clashes in Kenya have been discussed in depth in previous parliaments even resulting in commission investigation yet no political solution has ever been reached, because some of the land grabbers are one and the same government leaders and powerful politicians.

For months preceding Kenya general elections there are reliable reports indicating Muslim extremists linked to opposition parties threatened that if certain election conditions were not met prior to the December 27, 2007 general elections, a mass action would be called. After the disputed presidential elections violence and ethnic killings blossomed. I saw televised images of violence long before the polls closed; followers of the opposition parties created the perfect storm with elements — coming together of the natives who never forgot about their land and with close ties to the Memorandum of Understanding of 2007 with National Muslim Leaders Forum orchestrated much of the riots.

Destruction, violence, death, burning churches, homes, schools, business and government properties were inevitable in the storm. After the failed leadership I witnessed tens of thousands of men, women and children slain and displaced from their homeland. Mobs hungry for revenge marched freely into villages, slums and rural towns of Kenya for a killing spree. It is unfortunate, in the aftermath some of the politicians would request that amnesty should be extended to the perpetrators. Violence for many Kenyans and other leaders of the world appeared to justify violence as a paradigm for change. In an article published by the late former president of Ghana states "when a social system becomes a disease…a point is reached where the only alternative to constitutional change is a violence resolution" Rhodesia/Zimbabwe 1971-77 The American Ambassador to Kenya made the comparison that United States became one strong nation after the American Civil War. *Leadership* disagrees with the above sentiments, violence results to more killings of innocent people. It took world leadership under the former United Nations General Secretary Kofi Annan to solve political and leadership crisis in Kenya through a coalition government to calm the storm. Therefore, a servant-leader holds the faculties of integrity, and has the power and the ability to discern and do the will of God. Ω

Principles of Leadership
1. Lead by the Golden Rule *The old rule, treat others with respect* 2. Keep away from tendencies of favorites *Respect other styles of leadership* 3. Follow your own rules *Make rules that you can keep* 4. Lead by example *The world is watching you* 5. Keep people informed *Create a two way communication* 6. Leader – Act like a Leader *Remember your commitment* 7. Seek for counsel *A few heads are better than one* 8. Keep positive constructive criticism *Remember the last time you made a mistake* 9. Always tell the truth and keep your word *Would you like to be told a lie?* 10. Prepare someone else to take your place *You may not be here tomorrow*

From the time a leadership position is assumed, a Leader must adopt an attitude to train someone else for the incumbent position. The rule # 10 ***you may not be here tomorrow*** guarantees a continuum of leadership.

A moral authority of a Leader is Honesty and Integrity

TWO:
*Leadership &
Management Functions*

TWO: *Leadership and Management Functions*

Leadership and Management Functions

What inherent general characteristics of a good leader come to your mind? The following list gives some common traits that many successful leaders exhibit. It would be wise for us to incorporate as many of these into our standard way of leading others as possible. Recently, I came across a study that really surprised me. A school of business at Indiana University conducted the study. The purpose of the study was to compare successful and unsuccessful organizational leaders. The study concluded that successful leaders were those who had majored in business, read business journals, *read the Bible,* watched the evening news, placed a high priority on moral standards and integrity, and showed fairness to others.[4] Indeed, when the principles of the Bible become a core-value for transactions of business deals, and God is honored, the fruits of that business should grow into 100 fold with blessings running over the whole operation.

The History of Organization: As long as there have been people, there have been organizations, societies and institutions. Organization is as old as people themselves. The construction of great pyramids of Egypt, temples and ships had to have been built by well organized organizations of the day. The evidence of their ingenuity can be seen in ruins located all over the world.

[4]Samuel C. Certo, Principles of Modern Management. WMC Brown Company Publisher, 1983, Dubuque, Iowa. Pg 319

The business leaders wrote basic principles of business, marketing, philosophy; literature and architecture that worked well for them, these principles are still the hallmarks of the business world today.

At the dawn of the 20th Century a French man, Henry Fayol, director of a large coal mining company in France described the five basic functions of business: planning, organizing, commanding, coordinating, and controlling. He further directed managers how to solve business problems of mining. In 1938 during the WWII, Chester Bernard, an American with Bell Telephone in New Jersey, wrote the organization "system of goal-directed cooperative activities." He believed that managers function better with formulation of objectives and acquisition of resources. He strongly emphasized communication as a better process in acquiring cooperation at the work place. In 1964 Alfred P. Sloan, CEO of General Motors Corporation, wrote that a top management team must rely on what lower management tells them.

It was the beginning of the "upward" communication between top and lower management; compared to the traditional "downward" communication. In addition, he believed that lower management should be allowed to think independently to better improve the quality of GM business model. What works well today in a business may not work tomorrow; however, the principles are still with us.

In the early 1950s Foundation for Research on Human Behavior was formed. The mission of the new organization was to support business and government to advocate for a scientific approach, such as behavioral sciences, psychology, anthropology and sociology to be injected into the work place. They envisioned that scientific procedures would validate practice. Behavioral science became a major tool for improving productivity. Behavioral science researchers predicted that future leaders and managers would rely on scientific description reports to draw informed and accurate data on employee input and output of widgets.

And so the majority of us would agree that organizations infuse the society and our skillfulness provides organizations with manpower. Throughout history enormous organizations of great empires like Alexander the Great, King Solomon, king of Israel, Roman Empire and Roman Catholic Church and a host of other ancient state governments in modern Europe; and especially the last two organizations, church and state, required excellent application of administration, organization and leadership.

The Roman Catholic Church, in collaboration with the modern Vatican City, the RC international headquarters still operates as church organizations. Business historians have said that "the real secret of the greatness of the Romans was their genius for organization." Why? The Romans used creative organization principles that enabled them to coordinate their massive worldwide Empire at a time when there were no telephones and sophisticated military artilleries.

In my opinion, without endorsing the church doctrine, beliefs and practices; The Roman Catholic Church is one of the oldest most successful organizations that is known to man today; which has withstood and weathered internal changes of Papal reign at all times.

The key to their success has been **consistency, continuity** and **commitment** with sound business principles that have worked well for the College of Cardinals and the Pope. Successful business leaders of the day left us with fragments of business literature on how they planned and executed their business models of the ancient times. Future leaders and managers should learn from the records of history from all fields of study to continue to perfect our institutions for generations to come.

The Management Wheel

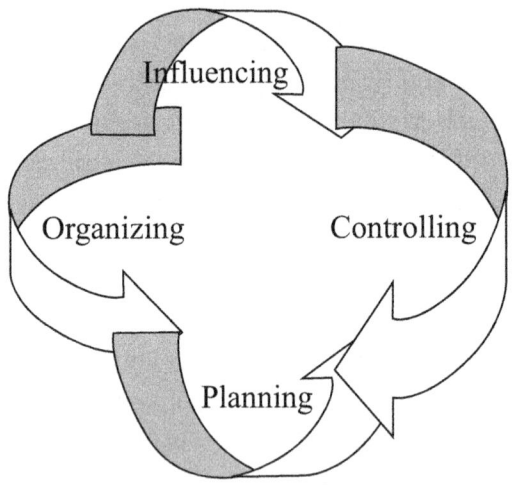

The Management wheel is an important tool for every person in Leadership positions; managers and supervisors. The approach to organizational leadership involves the four famous management functions first introduced by Henry Fayol as mentioned earlier are illustrated by the leadership wheel: *Planning, Organizing, Influencing* and *Controlling.* Hence, the text will discuss briefly these management functions shown in the diagram of the Leadership Wheel. Remember, management skills are necessary everywhere leadership is provided from our homes, our churches, institutions, governments and businesses. For detail read books on management.

An architect opens up his drawing kit and draws a blue print for a new office. A housewife gets up early in the morning, takes inventory from her pantry and makes a grocery list. She finds a run to the store is a must if she is to have food on the table that evening. She determines she must make this run to the store after 5 PM on her way home. Businessmen have discussions about new government contracts (nyama choma) sometimes even taking place at out of office settings like a golf course. A student talking on his new cell phone while walking home has his thoughts interrupted by advertisements on billboards to buy various products. All these individuals are employing some of the elements of the Leadership Wheel.

PLANNING is a process that empowers a leader with a clear sense of direction, enabling him to focus on the goals and objections of the organization. This process applies to all men and women in leadership positions on all levels of government, church, big business and small companies. Planning takes time, but planning saves time in the long run. To **fail** to plan is to plan to **fail**. It is wrong to suggest that management skills are limited to only professionals such as architects and businessmen in the corporate world. Indeed, management skills are vital to individuals in many settings and especially when considering the leadership positions of the New Testament Church and her associated institutions.

Organizational church leadership structures tend to use the essential management skills as the basis of their leadership foundation. In spite of this, some pastors/leaders believe that their job is to control the members of the fellowship as if they were their own personal property. Compared to the business world, Leaders of the New Testament Church have even more responsibility. For the first time in the history of mankind we are communicating 24 hours a day due to the invention of the Internet. Leaders must rethink new ways to reach and educate our complex society with the Gospel of Jesus Christ. It is logical that this new thinking should include shared vision. Life in the 21st Century continues to become more complex in the management of our shrinking world resources, especially considering the impact of diseases and the explosion of the world population.

In 1823, King George IV was receiving his morning briefings from his colonial officers about the brutal war machines – the Zulu people of southern Africa. They were advancing to the Cape and threatening the British installations there. After his briefing the king looked out through the window and asked, "What do you see falling, Lord Henry?" "Rain sir," the officer answered. "What do our colonies represent for us, Lord Henry?" "Sunshine Sir." King George IV said, "Precisely, safeguard our sunshine."

That was in the 1800's. We should learn from the British who refused an alliance with the Zulu kingdom. They also rejected to cooperate with the thirteen American colonies, which eventually led to the demise of the United Kingdom as the leading world power. The British took more than a century to realize that they were fighting a much stronger enemy – the growth of civilization itself. Today these same questions apply to everyone, because nations have intermingled with each other through marriage, and displacement of nationalists groups have taken place in most of the continents of the world. There are no owners of a particular continent as it once was. The world has become one large family.

ORGANIZING: The August 2005 issue of Forbes magazine published an article entitled "The death of artificial Intelligence." The article predicted that by 2020 nano-technology will be so advanced that nanobots will be built to the microscopic level of human blood cells. Billions of nanobots will be capable of traveling through human blood streams like a submarine in the deep sea, sending wireless messages to a local network via an internet. The article proclaimed that these nanobot's machines will be able to demolish cancer cells and remove unwanted elements in the blood. They would also be capable of correcting human DNA with a likelihood of reversing disease and even the aging process of human beings. Supposedly, these nanobots will also be able to go into human brain capillaries and communicate with biological neurons. They will replace signals from real human senses by providing a virtual reality within the human nervous system. Practitioners will be able to plug into a computer and experience what it feels like to be another person. While this all is one group's view of the future, it cannot be simply dismissed as unthinkable.

The lesson we can learn from the article is to realize the seriousness of good leadership in all levels of business, government and especially the church as an institution. Leaders at all levels must be prepared to find solutions to solve the problems of human health and the growing world population. If nano-technology proposes to have found a solution for human health, what about the issue of the increases in the world population?

INFLUENCING is part of the responsibility of a leader to organize and positioning business and or the country resources to handle the society's wants and needs for the current physical year and decades ahead. Business leaders and politicians alike must find ways to influence the government to protect the environment and the future business interests. In most western democracies politicians require millions of dollars to finance a political campaign. Interest groups manipulate and influence potential candidates with financial incentives to protect their business interests when passing laws. In Kenya, politicians take all to themselves.

Business leaders in developing societies use different methods, to corrupt government officials to relax by manipulating the nation's laws for their business whether illegal or legal. In third world democracies, politicians have a significant influence over the presiding Government. However, in recent years the United Nations passed a resolution to put economic sanctions on nations that fail to abide by the accepted code of international financial conduct. A politician's job is to legislate and pass laws for the good of the nation. Most all candidates promise to legislate change. Often, one must organize and influence opposing parties to pass the desired laws that will protect the interests and the will of the people. In most third world nations their pockets come first and the people's business come second, if any resources are left!

The New Testament church has even a greater responsibility to educate the faithful to fill leadership positions with able men and women who will represent the needs of the people. They will need to consider the local constituency, national and international issues that affect the society's living standards such as: environment issues, global warming, health issues and graft and corruption. At this moment of Africa history of leadership deforestation and soil erosion affects flora and fauna the biggest natural disaster in the continent.

A leader should never compromise his leadership position for a bribe. Such compromising is what **Leadership** calls the "Goliath fall." The real Giant-man mentioned in the Holy Scriptures made threats/promises to young David when he saw his fighting gear of a few collected stones from a nearby creek. The story of Goliath, the Philistine's fighter has been told and repeated; most people have heard or read the story between the two men. Goliath said that afternoon, "I will give your flesh to the birds of the sky and beast of the field." [1 Sam. 17:44] The analogy of the story is to remind us all (leader) the power of serving people in honor and respect comes from those who put God first. A leader must learn to use the magic words "NO" and "YES" when appropriate. For the sake of his credibility and his respect and honor to God, a leader should avoid making promises that cannot be delivered or fulfilled. Goliath died that afternoon, he never fulfilled his promises. David killed Goliath and took with him his head as it was the custom after winning a national battle for people in Jerusalem to witness.

BUILDING TRUST: Human resource experts, psychologists and mental health counselors agree that trust is an essential ingredient between individuals undertaking an endeavor together. A leader must examine himself as to whether he has unsolved and unwanted personal conflicts in his life. What a person may have inherited as negative behavior from his family and friends may serve as an obstacle for that person in a leadership position. It has been said that we are our own worst enemy. Part of the healing process comes through self-understanding. Organizations that are led with a transparent leadership usually yield high profits and tend to prevail even when there are many storms in the life of the business.

Example: Lee Iacocca, a former chief executive of the Chrysler Motor Corporation, is a good example on trust and leadership. Chrysler was in dire financial trouble before Iacocca was hired. The Chrysler board of directors made an important decision to hire Iacocca as their new CEO. On his first day as CEO, he took inventory of the crumbling corporation. As he examined the situation, Iacocca had a vision as to how he would save Chrysler from folding. He went directly to the United States Congress. Never had a corporate CEO gone to the United States Congress to ask for a business loan. Mr. Iacocca, however, was not your ordinary leader. He presented his case to Congress and told them if Chrysler folded, thousands of American families would go without jobs. Congress was impressed with his plan and his boldness and accepted his proposal. The situation repeated itself in 2009 when both Chrysler and GM were bailed out by USA government.

In his continued service as their CEO, three (3) major outcomes resulted: (1) indeed, thousands of jobs were saved; (2) Chrysler paid its debt well ahead of time; and (3) Chrysler employees were motivated to work harder and to help save Chrysler from folding. Lee Iacocca (retired) remains one of the most trusted names in the history of the American automotive business. Not only did he save the corporation from the brink of bankruptcy, he also changed the way Americans transport their families when he introduced the first mini bus (van). For over 10 years Chrysler led the industry in sales in this type vehicle and practically every American family wanted a mini-van.

Church Leadership: Several years ago the pastor of a large Baptist Church in West Texas led his congregation with a directed study that involved every church member. The purpose of the study was to allow people to voice their ideas and opinions on how church programs and activities should be run. He wanted to find ways to bring positive change in the church worship, activities and other related matters for the body of Christ for the next five years.

He asked his congregation to voice and write down their suggestions during regular Sunday school classes. The project lasted several weeks allowing every member to have an opportunity to express their opinion as a member of the congregation. The church elders compiled all the ideas from the members in the order of priority and delivered their findings at the church business meeting. The church accepted the projects mentioned in the study without opposition. As you can see, each individual member felt included. There was a sense of unity among the members, probably for the first time in many years.

The results were so unifying, probably because every member of the church took part in the project. Many sister churches sent their elders to observe and learn from the church. When trust becomes a beacon in an organization, people will typically perform their duties successfully. Trust and delegation work hand-in-hand with good leadership.

Tribal Leaders: Before the British colonial rule in Kenya, the Akamba tribe was organized in many small clans for the purpose of governing. Their governmental system was very strong because elders were elected to the office of leadership by the virtue of their character and integrity. The clans never had a chief or a king, except a war chief in time of war. Their government can best be described as a government by agreement. In times of war and famine the clans had one large (parliament) council of the elders from every clan. They established rules and regulations to run the general council. During many of their council gatherings there was always one elder who stood out from among all the other elders, as one having outstanding oratorical ability, integrity, respect, physical presence and who was willing to be accepted as a leader in times of war with or against other tribes. This was the war chief, one always reliable and a person of good character. The elders were also the judges for their clans. The government was ruled by consensus. No elder or any other speaker was allowed to speak or address the council with a forceful tone of anger that would only weaken his point.

Qualities of a Leader
Ambitious Courageous Cooperative Moral Efficient Talented Optimistic Orderly Analytical Integrity Energetic Self-Disciplined Tolerant Intelligent Tactful Resourceful Progressive Foresighted Poised Perseverance Self-Confident

The tribal rulers ruled until they were replaced by the next incoming generation. This all changed with the arrival of the British Colonial rule in East Africa. Many tribes of Kenya were forced to abandon their tribal governments and they were required to work within the Colonial Office system of government in their tribal lands. By around the 1940s, most tribal governments had died out except a few remaining in the kingdoms of Uganda, Swaziland and West Africa.

Today many tribes of Kenya retain some of the tribal ways of leadership and customs from the distant past, even though nothing was ever written - it was transmitted by oral communication only. When we examine the successes of these clans we still find the elements of trust, commitment, and the willingness to serve others within the policies of the clans. These same qualities can be seen in a number of the military generals of the western civilization: Alexander the Great, Augustus Caesar, and Oliver Cromwell of England, George Washington of the Continental Army of the United Sates, and Napoleon of France are just a few that can be mentioned. These generals were trusted by their men and their countries, and fought their wars with integrity.

A **Vision** starts with a person; then more people often are drawn into the vision with time. A vision may not be realized immediately, because it takes time for a vision to take root in the minds of people. Vision is looking ahead and a leader must be willing to face up to the challenges to come.

> *"The power to perceive what the eye cannot see."* or
> *"natural intellectual shrewdness."*
> – Webster

Developing one's vision depends entirely on an individual's leadership style. It has been said that being a leader doesn't make you a visionary, but that a leader always has a vision. Ray Kroc, founder of McDonalds, envisioned that he could build a successful business through quality, service, and cleanliness. His vision was his beginning point for what would become a huge success.

He shared his vision to his employees and made McDonalds the leader in fast food sales around the world. As a result of one person's vision McDonalds now employs tens of thousands of men and women around the world.

The Bible tells us that Noah had a difficult time enlisting people to help build the ark that would later save his family and each species of the world's living creatures. These people could have been saved from destruction also if they had accepted the fact that God had given Noah a vision on how to save the whole world. With persistence, his sons also realized the vision and joined in with the work required to complete the vision.

The Bible says that on a Passover afternoon at Calvary the wonderful Son of God, Jesus the Christ, went into the depths of Hell to pay for our sins. The disciples fled and were scattered like wild fire, fearing that they too would be arrested and possibly even executed like Jesus.

However, the fear of the disciples was only temporary. The vision that had been planted in their minds continued to linger there, to be brought back to life when they later met the risen Lord. Judas Iscariot, the betrayer of Jesus was the first to abandon Jesus' vision. He hanged himself on a tree after feeling remorse for his betrayal. Thomas' faith and vision appeared to subside by the wayside. He told his fellow disciples that he could not believe until he had seen and touched his Master with his own hands.

On the evening of Jesus' arrest, Peter had denied Jesus three times, going so far as to curse before a girl to prove he was not a follower of Christ. After the resurrection, he ran to the tomb, only to find it empty. Jesus had risen and gone to Galilee, doing good and appearing to more than five thousand people. A few days later, Peter reconfirmed his faith in Jesus when the Lord prepared the disciples a breakfast of fish at the banks of the Sea of Galilee.

Fortunately, unlike earthly leaders, our Lord is forgiving and willing to forget our mistakes as we go forward with Him to complete His vision of saving the world. Like Jesus, a successful leader is one that shares his vision with his people. He creates credibility and respect within the organization. Every person within the organization should be aware of the organizational goals and objectives (the vision) and where the organization is headed.

Risks: Every time we step outside our door, even going about our daily lives, we take risks. There is risk riding in automobiles, flying in airplanes and even simply walking in our neighborhood. Risks are everywhere and one cannot completely avoid taking risks. In the business world entrepreneurs, salespeople and business people make daily business decisions with risks inherent in every decision they make. Sometimes the decisions fail, sometimes they have success, and once in a while they take a risk that pays off with enormous rewards. Where there is no risk there is no success.

A successful leader must often take risks. An example of this is Mr. Smith, the founder of Federal Express. In recalling how he hit upon success, he said that he was not afraid to fail, that he was willing to take a huge risk with his idea of overnight delivery. It was a shrewd business decision, as he risked millions of dollars of shareholders' money. His investors were sharing this risk with him, as they admired the boldness of his idea.

Mr. Smith's bold business risk paid off richly when he grew his delivery business into an empire with annual revenues of nearly $4 billion. Mr. Smith's philosophy of risk is affirmed in the Federal Express Manager's Guide, *Fear of failure must never be a reason not to try something different.* What comforting words for all employees of Federal Express – they are free to try new ideas without changing company goals and mission. Employees should never leave the task of reinvention of new ideas to the management team. Today FedEx Kinko's is the nation's office and print center of the world. "Make it. Print it. Pack it. Ship it."

A man called Saul (later to be Paul the Apostle) was armed with warrants to persecute the followers of Jesus hiding out in Damascus. On the Damascus road he met the Lord Jesus Christ. He was commissioned to be the Apostle Paul. His life was never the same again. He risked his life when he told the disciples that he had seen Jesus and that he was one of the followers of their Lord. At first the Disciples did not trust this man who had recently arrested Christians.

Meanwhile, the Jews hated Paul because he had become a traitor to them. Paul also risked his life when he made his famous missionary journeys. He was imprisoned, shipwrecked, beaten (2 Corinthians 11: 23) and even lowered in a basket before daybreak to avoid being stoned to death. Through it all Paul managed to write three-quarters of the New Testament, and become regarded as probably the most dedicated follower of Jesus of all time.

Early on an April morning in 1873, a boy who was keeping watch over David Livingstone alerted Susi one of David's companions, to come quickly. Susi hurried up to his master's tent and by candlelight, he found his master kneeling by his bedside.

His head was in his hands in a gesture such that one may speculate that he had died thanking God for his life, his companions and perhaps praying that the Good News of Jesus Christ might reach the rest of Africa.

In his final hours David Livingstone was basically alone. Two days before his death he wrote "Knocked up and remain—recover—sent to buy milch-goats. We are on the banks of the Molilamo"[5] suggesting that medicine or other medical help was not available to him. He had suffered many malaria attacks, and now he had suffered one final and fatal attack. He left a legacy of being the first white man who had traveled through the deep jungles of Africa to spread the Word of God and for scientific discoveries. I am grateful for his life of integrity and his service because the whole continent of Africa continues to be won to Christ, in large part due to the prayers of this man.

[5]Mrs.J.H.Worcester, JR, David Livingstone, Moody Press, Chicago, Illinois, pg 103

Ethics On: Graft, Corruption & Greed

More is stolen everyday with a flick of the pen than the point of a pistol
– paraphrased FBI

Understanding Ethics

E thics come from a Greek word *ethos* which means stability and permanence. It is best illustrated by a *boma,* a Swahili word for a homestead where people live together with animals in rural Kenya. Far away in a west Texas farm, a cowboy is putting his cherished horse in a *stall* keeping it safe from storms or getting loose and running away. Both the cowboy and the Kenya peasant have put down roots for many generations. These homes mean stability and permanence, because land does not move; it stays constant in one place.

It is hard for a west Texas cowboy to understand why genocide, deception and the torching of innocent people are massacred in Eldoret, Kenya while in their sacred places of worship. This was not the fictitious movie *Mississippi Burning;* it was the lives of real people burning! Is it because people are shaped by the culture by which they live or is it because of sin, greed and power? What ethical standards were broken? Perhaps these questions should be answered by the community leaders and politicians who committed these crimes against humanity and who are still at large.

Aristotle taught that human happiness comes from self-realization, a concept of being a good person. In addition, Kant wrote,

"Act as if the maxim from you which you act were to become through your will a universal law." We shall always be left with many unanswered questions. Did the burning of the innocent, powerless people help a few greedy and ruthless politicians achieve self-actualization of gaining power and leadership?

To contrast Aristotle and Kant's ethics on happiness with Christian teachings, the Bible says "blessed are the pure in heart for they shall see God." (Mathew 5:8 NASB) The philosophers sanctioned personal good deeds as the key to Happiness. Paul wrote, for him to die was gain, an indication that happiness in obeying God and dying in Christ was the greatest reward that man can ever realize. This is the notion that happiness is not based on personal achievement or material things. Therefore, ethics is a system of moral standards or principles by which we live.

The major part of the **Leadership** advocates honesty and integrity as the basis for the good conduct of a servant-leader. There are hundreds of definitions of communication in print in related subject matter by practitioners and scholars of the field – in the effort to depict and understand communicative phenomena. Some definitions of communication fall in the context of human relationships, and a preponderance of researchers mention the effects of a message on its beneficiary. These definitions may vary depending on individual scholarly interest.

Consequently, communication must be transmitted to the receiver who interprets the data and decides to take an action. A leader's relationship with his/her subordinates depends solely on the open communication of thoughts, feelings, touch, sending and receiving information. We send (encode) and receive (decode) gathered facts whether untrustworthy or genuinely true messages simultaneously.

Corruption and lying does not happen in a vacuum, it is a purposely deceiving message in the form of statements or gesticulation to another person. The majorities of people have been lied to or have lied to someone else for whatever reason may be.

Ethics in the Work Place: Ethics is a hot issue in today's society. It affects the fabric of our daily lives, the quality of services offered to customers, employees, and the public at large. Tens of billions of customers around the world transact business one to another. Since the advent of the Internet, technology has enabled online-business like, E-bay, Amazon and other online business to go worldwide.

Our homes are refinanced online, cars are purchased and airline travels booked. You name it and somebody will do almost anything to get your business. I was able to refinance a property located in North America online while on a safari to East Africa! It took less than 15 minutes to secure a notary for my signature from the American Embassy in Nairobi, Kenya and with a click of a send button my loan was completed and secure. Then I continued with my safari. With technology at work, my trust depended squarely on the ethics of the person located thousands of miles away.

Unfortunately, our confidentiality is at risk from the fear of being compromised by a few of our medical practitioners, accountants, finance institutions and other professionals who have direct access to our credit system. There are always ethical conflicts, doing what is right and doing wrong. One often hears the saying that politics is a dirty game — this is so because historically men associated with wealth, scandal and immoral lives end up in public offices.

Therefore, Politics and public services should be considered just like any other careers. Politics does not have to be a dirty business; it is the character and the behavior of people. Ethics is about everything we do, treating our employees, customers and public at large with respect. The following are 5 ethical practices that should be embraced by a leader:

1. Ethics on telling the truth will save one from future mishap. A leader is not worried about what was spoken yesterday or of twelve months ago.

2. In your personal ethics — there should never be a difference in identifying right from wrong.

3. Ethics on dependability, inform your people with current status of events, find solutions for problems and provide necessary support.

4. Ethics based on moral value, is about respect of the law of the land, professionalism, policy and procedures, written standards that may be inflexible and universal. These documents are guidelines to steer one to make ethical decisions if need be. Ethics is about personal ideals and aspirations.

5. Ethics on Integrity and Honesty refers to a person's wholeness, consistence, respect, and reliability. These are marks of a leader.

Ethics is about doing the right thing anytime to anyone and to everybody. During the writing of **Leadership** there were chilling twists to the Enron and Madoff sagas – epic tales of *graft, fraud, and greed in American history. Enron occupied the minds of many Americans including myself; taxpayers were the victims of Enron's collapse.

Ken Lay's death provided a shocking moral lesson to tens of millions of Americans. To describe the hatred by Lay's critics they could not believe that a simple heart attack took Lay's life, some critics, believed that he could have faked his death to escape his sentencing. Ken Lay's leadership was among the nastiest cases of leadership reported in graft and corruption anywhere in the world. The most important thing, someone with good moral standards within Enron Corporation blew the whistle, the United States law enforcement found its way into the deep guarded secrecy of Ken Lay's leadership.

Mid 2009, Bernard Madoff, another American, was convicted of scandalous investment fraud worth $65 billion. During cross examination he admitted to guilty as charged. Madoff repeatedly apologized for the harm he caused victims. He was sentenced to two life times, 150 years in Federal Prison. "More is stolen everyday with the flick of the pen than the point of a pistol," lying and cheating are one and the same, both having no respecter of gender or nationality; the act of lying has dominated humans since the dawn of civilization.

A Contrast of Two Neighboring States: All over the world people have become disillusioned and skeptical with clergy/religious, political and business leaders. Let us now examine a few cases that the public cannot prove to be right or wrong. In North

America the subject of abortion has never found a solution, neither am I trying to offer one. To further complicate the issues, in recent years cloning has surfaced. Both deal with human life, one has to do with the killing of an unborn baby and the other with human duplication. Why have we not found a solution to these major social cases that affect our lives? It is then no wonder the public is misinformed about the true nature of the subject matter.

Unlike the social problems that face Americans, there are parallels in third world democracies — corruption and deceit have become the norm of the day. Some government officers and politicians are dishonest to a point that deception has become relative. For example, during Moi administration, the second President of Kenya, one could rationalize bribing a poorly paid police officer in exchange for breaking the law of the land. It went on for so long until the society accepted bribery as norm. In my opinion and mine alone, Moi's twenty-four years of rule produced a generation with the mindset that endorses deception and dishonesty as a way of life.

I predict that it will take another full generation to fix what was done during his reign.

Capitalism in Kenya came at an early age for some leaders who had no idea of what capitalism/democracy was; it bred greed, tribalism, fraud and selfishness versus servant-leadership, which sacrifices self gain for the betterment of the society. Democracies of: Uganda, Ethiopia, Somalia, Rwanda, Burundi, and Congo have never been the same after the coups of the 1970s, 1980s and 1990s and Kenya's failed coup attempt of 1982.

In contrast, a neighboring socialist nation of Tanzania, under the rule of the former Julius Nyerere, adopted a **combination** of a socialist model of governing from the east with an African methodology system of **culture** that has existed for many years — at a larger scale in the form of a national government for the people. As a former teacher by his own right, he went to the Far East in search for a government model that would best meet the needs of his people.

Equipped with a new ideology, he nationalized firms, hospitals, schools and industries that had been under foreign ownership and declared that no citizen was allowed to have more than one property. As a devout Catholic, he remained consistent with his ideology and never acquired wealth for himself. He was ridiculed by his counterpart, the capitalists of his day, for the collapse of his social programs. However, history remembers Nyerere as the first President in Africa to refuse to be elected for another term as President of Tanzania.

In spite of the failed economic policies in Tanzania, it is an interesting observation for two neighboring states — Kenya adopted a capitalist model where land and tribalism became a national problem, while Tanzania followed the African socialist system model where land and tribalism has never been an issue. The critics would argue that under Julius Nyerere, economy suffered, while under Jomo Kenyatta, economy prospered. I say with a good economic policy any government can fix her economic lapses, but at the end of the day, it is the lives of men, women and children that count!

A Summer in Nairobi: It was the summer of 2003; I had just walked out of a bank on a busy crowded street of the city of Nairobi. Suddenly, I was horrified! Knowing I had just gotten cash out of a bank, I felt something pulling down my jacket. I heard a voice, "Mdozi," a Swahili word for master. I found myself looking down on a dirty, ragged, filthy little boy who was yanking on my jacket. I stopped. I noticed he was not alone. Now I realized I was in real trouble. I replied in Swahili, "What can I do for you my fellow Kenyans?" I saw they were street boys.

It is very common for street boys to approach a person for money and if not attended, they can smear feces on the unkind persons. Now that the situation was calm, I began to engage myself in a dialogue. One of the little boys said, "We are hungry, we have not eaten since morning." I asked how many they were. The little boy counted and said, "We are five." I could see they were five boys ranging between 8-10 years old. I was filled with empathy and pity when I saw it was as if they were covered with a black blanket of flies! I asked, "Are there more of you?" One of the bigger boys said, "Yes, Mdozi, but we are hungry. They will find for themselves their own food to eat."

By now I had drawn a crowd of street watchers. I was dressed in foreign clothes with American panache. Everyone around me could tell I was not one of the daily city commuters. I gathered my little boys and asked them to take a step forward, and elect one among themselves to whom I would give money for their lunch. The boys were very cooperative. They stepped aside and elected the oldest boy.

When asked why they chose the bigger boy, before I could get an answer, the little boy interrupted, "Mdozi," while pointing at the bigger boy, the young boy said, "He did not allow me to say anything." "Well," I told the boys, "Go back and agree who would get the money." This time they agreed on a little boy whom they said was the most honest among them! He was youngest and small in size compared to other boys but in essence, he was willing to stand up and be heard. I gave them lunch money as promised.

The moral of the story is – I gave money after the little boys had worked hard coming up with a system of election process. Second, they knew who among them was honest, and third, they could count up to five. I can only assume they shared equally among themselves. Unless somebody cares enough to provide them with education, food and shelter for their survival, otherwise they would die of hunger. These boys were potential Kenya voting members. I will never know if they survived during the killings of the disputed presidential elections of December 2007.

I could only imagine, some will make it through the cracks of the system or die for lack of basic needs. Giving money for lunch was a temporary solution. Later that evening, I was reminded by friends that those boys are bad, to the point that they can smear feces on your clothes and run away. Quite the contrary, the boys obeyed and followed my instructions. Not a day passes by that I do not remember the ordeal.

Orderly – a state in which everything is in its proper place and status, especially with reference to reason. A leader must initiate order and stability in his leadership style, by applying basic management principles of planning, organizing, influencing and controlling all the resources to the benefit of the organization.

Positive Attitude – This is one of the most valuable assets a leader can have. A leader must believe in himself and his organization to succeed, regardless of the challenges or set-backs that might arise. When some difficulty does occur, we must learn from our faux pas and move on with a positive attitude.

Several years ago in West Texas I dreamed of building a psychiatry facility where abused children from dysfunctional families would have a place to rehabilitate and be restored back to the communities they were born in. I had the architecture work done, bought land not too far from a small town of about 1,000 people and began to move forward with my project. To my surprise I was faced with very strong opposition from neighbors and ranchers of the area. It became media frenzy to the community, and the local TV network included it in their evening telecasts.

Since they were backed by substantially more money and a unified determination, the citizens decided that my project would not be built in their neck of the woods. They went to the streets and protested against my project. While I was advised not to approach the angry crowd, I very much wanted to do something about the needs of the abused children and the community at large. On that evening I appeared on the local TV network responding to the concerns of the citizens. Unfortunately, though I was disappointed, I respected the citizens' concerns and dropped the project.

The following day, I received a call from another community who wanted my project in their community, because it would bring jobs to their dying economy. The project was moved to the new community. The land in the previous community was later sold to become a ranch. Ω

The Difference Between Leaders
and Managers

YOU
KNOW

Leaders	Managers/Supervisors
Success	Good Organization
See the Horizon	Follow Instructions
Ethical	Facts on Products
Entrepreneurial Spirit	Daily Schedules
Innovative Mind	Expected to do what is instructed
See the Bird's Eye View	See one Tree at a Time

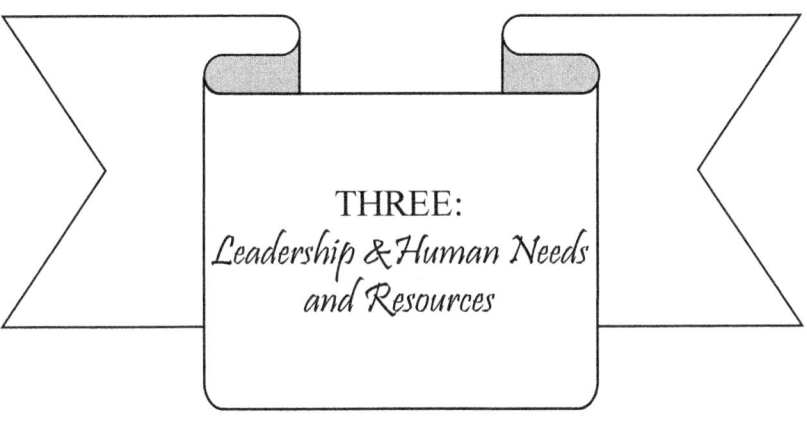

THREE:
*Leadership & Human Needs
and Resources*

THREE: *Leadership & Human Needs and Resources*

Historical Background of the Needs Theories

A braham Maslow was born in Brooklyn, New York, a son of Jewish immigrants, last of the seven children. He was a clinical psychologist who developed 5 tiers of basic human needs, established between 1943-1954 under a motivational personality that received extensive exposure in schools of clinical psychology and management around the world. However, Maslow himself admitted that his case study was developed from neurotic patients; therefore, he discouraged his case study to be applied to the general labor force. He acknowledged that he had sampling problems with the last tier - self-actualization.[6] Maslow's motivational personality needs have been paraphrased in a parable to assist a Bible reader to understand the relationship between human physical and spiritual needs of man within a Biblical context. *See the Need Grid diagram on page 74.

Limitation of the Needs Models: The section addresses the "NEED" issue as an integral part of man. Both Maslow and McClelland failed to determine the transition stages of "Need" theories. People may not move through the hierarchy stages as suggested by Needs theories, because various factors affect people living in different democracies of the world with different economic scales. Thus (food, shelter, affiliation and acceptance) identified in the structures in the Needs theory may not be universal, especially in agrarian societies; dominated by farming and rural living.

[6]Samuel C. Certo,Principles of Modern Management, WM C. Brown Company Publisher, 1983. Dubuque, Iowa. pp 343-48

However, the third tier of McClelland and Maslow may be applicable for those living in urban cities of any society. The Theory of Need was first coined by Henry Murray (1938) during the Great Depression, and the beginning of the Second World War. In 1961, McClelland popularized the Need theory to the practitioners. He advocated the Need for achievement, power and affiliations as the key principles to the NEED Theory.

He further argued that it is the "want" that drives a person's desire to be successful; which creates the "need" to receive positive feedback. Under the Need theory a person who performs challenging job tasks requires specialized skills. Maslow added to the Need theory additional layers to his original model. However, the original model continues to be used widely in schools of psychology. These individuals prefer to work alone or with other high achievers. In most cases these people tend to make good managers and supervisors as they are able to perform special projects which require accuracy with deadlines. However, when left alone to run a company or a special project, they exert high demands from their subordinates or followers, which may destroy morale by the low-risk performance.

A majority of these individuals tend to work long hours with little time for rest. They easily fall in the category of workaholics whose spouses with young children are usually at risk, because job tasks take center stage of their daily life, therefore, neglecting to spend time with their family.

The Need of Affiliation theory is similar to the third and fourth tiers of Maslow's hierarchy of needs. Persons in this category prefer cooperation, working in a group environment with less competition. They too, make good customer service agents at large call centers and other related job tasks. These individuals may not be effective managers and supervisors; they tend to have difficulty making business decisions, because they are afraid of making mistakes. If they make mistakes, they feel guilty and responsible.

The Need for Power: A person in this group wants power to be in charge at any cost. McClelland identified two types of Need Powers: High Need for Personal Power and High Need for Institutional Power. In most cases individuals mentioned in Need Power are identical. However, their difference in Need for Power is based on each individual cultural environment. Politicians realize immediate power after their political win.

Why People Form Groups: People form groups because they want a place to belong and want to interact with people who are their peers. In recent years a majority of Kenyans moved to Texas mainly for the good climate, similar to that of East Africa. Second, Texas does not have state income tax like most states in the nation. Third, wages are comfortably offset by a cheaper cost of living compared to other states.

Lastly, of all, Kenyans move to Texas because of the fact that a majority of Kenyans in America have chosen the State of Texas as their new home. There are a number of social organizations where a majority of Kenyans meet to socialize. On Sunday they have a select variety of churches scattered in the DFW metro area targeted to meet their desired tribal orientation. Thus, the desire for the needs satisfaction is a strong motivation that leads to a group formation within an organization.

The security, social, esteem and self-actualization needs are easily met by group association. The social needs provide people with a unique opportunity to interact directly with political and civic groups. In large corporations, government agencies and institutions of higher learning, union shops are very active. In most organizations based in third world nations — employees tend to form informal financial lending groups, whereby employees contribute to a kitty bank to meet the needs of a single employee at a time of family needs.

The common use of strikes has historically forced bargaining power with the management. This is the most effective method to date to force management to come to terms with the union demands. The great state of Texas is known as the "right to work state;" it discourages employees to form Union shops. During the ecommerce of the 1990s and 2000s many large and small businesses were attracted to move their business and services to the great state of Texas for that very reason. There are many reasons why people form associations and why people choose to belong to a group of one's choice.

Others form groups because of religious affiliation, the freedom of speech and worship in United States. Some groups choose to live in remote areas in mid and southwest states of North America. They build and live in a city like community with their own temples, schools and healthcare systems to cater to their social and religious needs, without outside interaction.

1. Physical Needs Model. This model represents the basic need for shelter, food, water, air, sleep and worship. When these needs are not met they affect a person's behavior and view of life in general. As soon as the needs are met, man tends to think of the next thing to do. The Bible says in Mark 6:34-44 that when Jesus saw masses of people, he met their physical needs (food) by feeding them with five loaves and two fishes.

A leader should first understand the needs of his people by rewarding those with fringe benefits for the job well done. Most businesses have designated break areas around their work place to provide employees with an area for snacks and soft drinks when they take breaks from the work they are performing. The purpose of such services is to discourage employees from leaving the work compound, which would lead to lower employee output.

Samaritan Purse is one of the many not-for-profit organizations that travel around the world providing aid to citizens of third-world nations. They give relief for basic physical needs, primary education for poor children, and medicine for under-nourished children and people suffering with HIV/AIDS and other diseases.

Maslow was aware that not all needs are intrinsic to humans; the notion that, not all needs take a center stage at one time. The WANT is related to basic needs, to a starving man or child in a third world, consuming food is a basic, necessary need. It is a no brainer; if the person does not eat he will eventually die of starvation. The governments of the millennial are entrusted with the responsibility to feed her citizens, supply clean drinking water, provide health care services, and the elimination of mortality. Once these physical needs are met, man must seek a way to satisfy the safety need.

2. Safety/Security Needs. This is the need for order, stability, and protection from violence or injury. Children raised by a single mother require moral support from the next of kin, otherwise, the majority of children who end up growing up in the dysfunctional families; require government law and order for protection, safety and free basic education to sustain themselves in a society.

When Paul wrote to the Romans (Romans 8:38-39), he affirmed that nothing can separate us from the love of God. One is guaranteed eternal safety if he knows the Lord Jesus Christ. It is the responsibility of national governments to protect, to provide a national health program and other social programs that maintain a quality life for their citizens.

Large corporations can often attract new employees because of their benefit packages. Because of their size they can offer health care plans, insurance, retirement plans and 401Ks. Most small businesses are not able to provide such benefits to their employees. As followers of Jesus Christ, we must first be concerned with the safety and security concerning the afterlife (salvation). However, that does not mean that we must deny ourselves and our family's worldly goods. We must not let worldly goods become a main desire in our lives and always use the things that God gives us for His glory, by being good stewards.

The need to feel safe and secure runs deep in a person, regardless of the society one lives in. Every person would like to be free from fear and anxiety. In our family residence in west Texas, we often never locked the front and back doors, much less the windows, except in the winter months, until we moved to Dallas, a metropolitan city of north Texas.

In sharp contrast, in Nairobi and the rest of rural Kenya, the majority of human dwellings are constructed with quarry stones.

All doors and windows are built with iron metal sheets, and on the outside are reinforced with metal steel bars. These homes are built strong, confined, like a North American incarceration facility.

In addition, a majority of city homes and large estate compounds have guard services available to those who can afford night/day watch guards. I could not help but to experience fear and anxiety when confronted with the imagination of the "what if" the house I was sleeping in would catch fire! The cities and villages are not equipped with volunteer fire brigades. These are some of the many things people living in North America take for granted.

The majority of Americans experience a different kind of death threats compared to third world societies. Although, one would argue that in every society there are constant fears and anxieties. The majority of fears in the advanced societies are Depression caused by loneliness.

3. Affection/Belonging/Love Needs. The need for affection and belongingness is found in civic groups, churches, gangs, and unions at work places, professional organizations, Rotary and other related community groups. People take positions of employment, because they have the skills and experience required to perform the job task. However, most people often stay with an organization, because of the love and affection needs being met by other colleagues.

A leader must create a friendly work environment to boost worker's morale. Employees work better when appreciated for their work and for what they contribute to the group. An employee who feels appreciated and cared for is one who will look forward to coming to work on Monday mornings.

As mentioned earlier, my wife and I operated a 24-hour residential facility for abused and neglected children in West Texas. I established a policy that stated that all employees would receive three-days-paid vacation if any of their next-of-kin died, and two weeks benefit to those who failed to take sick leave during any continuous 21 months of work. The policy was written in such a way that the benefit would be paid three days before the Christmas holidays.

I developed the policy because we had significant numbers of people calling in sick, making our facility run very inefficiently. With the new policy in place, the absenteeism for calling in sick dropped to almost zero. We then worked and performed more as a family. When a person is feeling secure, he seeks to satisfy the need of love and affection. Humans are by nature dire for the need to belong.

Everybody wants to experience the value of worthiness and appreciation for one's accomplishment in life. Many spend their lifetime seeking to fulfill the need for love and affection; sometimes by the use of influence of money, power, and gratification resources to fulfill the said need.

4. Self-Esteem Needs. This is the need for respect and approval. This need can be very important, dependent on your geographical point of reference. In most third-world countries, not everyone has access to even a basic elementary education. In these countries, one's education is seen as a statement of respect and prestige. Unfortunately, truancy in third world countries is a major problem for all ages of school children.

Therefore, some fail to obtain even a basic education, a benefit that is taken for granted by children of industrialized nations. On the other hand, the drop-out rate for high school in the USA remains relatively high when compared to other industrialized nations of the world. Truancy in the business realm is hard to understand – you have a job, why not work hard to hold on to it? Operating business outside major cities of America is as though business owners must find ways to encourage employees to remain employed.

A leader is forced to learn to adapt to his environment. A leader working in a third-world nation must learn to adapt his/her leadership style for that environment. The "Solomon Youth Centers" was based in Abilene within a twenty-two county radius of west Texas, USA. My wife and I were very frustrated as business owners; we found it difficult to find Texans for hire as employees who had a high school education, yet, we had to fulfill the state wage-law requirement. Operating business in a rural industrialized nation, I had to learn patience and still maintain my vision.

5. Self-Actualization/Self Fulfillment. This need is for a person to realize his/her full potential. It is the ultimate satisfaction of a human need as it relates to a career, knowledge, peace and self-fulfillment. In the context of a leader, it does not mean that a leader has arrived at his/her ideal state. Rather, a leader should continue to attempt to get better and better at his/her leadership role. It may require that a leader stop and evaluate his past performance - what areas of leadership weaknesses need to be strengthened before forging on with the affairs of the organization. Leaders with successful businesses in many industrialized nations and at least in North America have developed policies and procedures as part of their company's goals for yearly evaluation.

It is a tool for communication between the top leadership and their employees and customers. For example, suggestion boxes placed in business places outside their offices, often with fly-ers with prepaid postage for employees and customers to give their feedback to management. This is one effective way to hear directly from customers who consume your product. Leaders should take their employee and customer report cards seriously. When they do, they are usually rewarded handsomely.

Historically, customers tend to give honest responses when their own privacy is protected. They can do it without fear of retali-ation. On one of my many international trips to Africa, I was traveling through London. I took a shuttle bus from one London airport, Gatwick, to the other London airport, Heathrow. I was seated up front near the driver.

Half way into my destination I noticed that the driver was dosing off at the wheel! I told the man seated next to me that our driver was dosing off. For some reason, this did not seem to bother this person. Clearing my throat, I decided it was about time that I did something. In a loud voice I shouted to the driver, "Wake Up! Otherwise you are going to kill us all." As soon as I did this, everyone on the bus echoed my words to the driver. The man seated next to me promised that he would report the behavior of the driver to the company (customer feedback). I don't know what happened after that, but at least we all made it to Heathrow Airport safely.

Once the need is realized, a man continues with the final stage of Self-Actualization, it is a need that sometimes may never be accomplished due to the frustrations that man and society faces on a daily basis. Sometimes frustrations may be caused by job career loss, inflations, sickness, death of a loved one, and other unwarranted situations. For some who feel they have arrived… tend to suffer destine lifelessness, the feeling of arriving empty. It would be good if many would look around and appreciate that so much has been made available to them by the Creator.

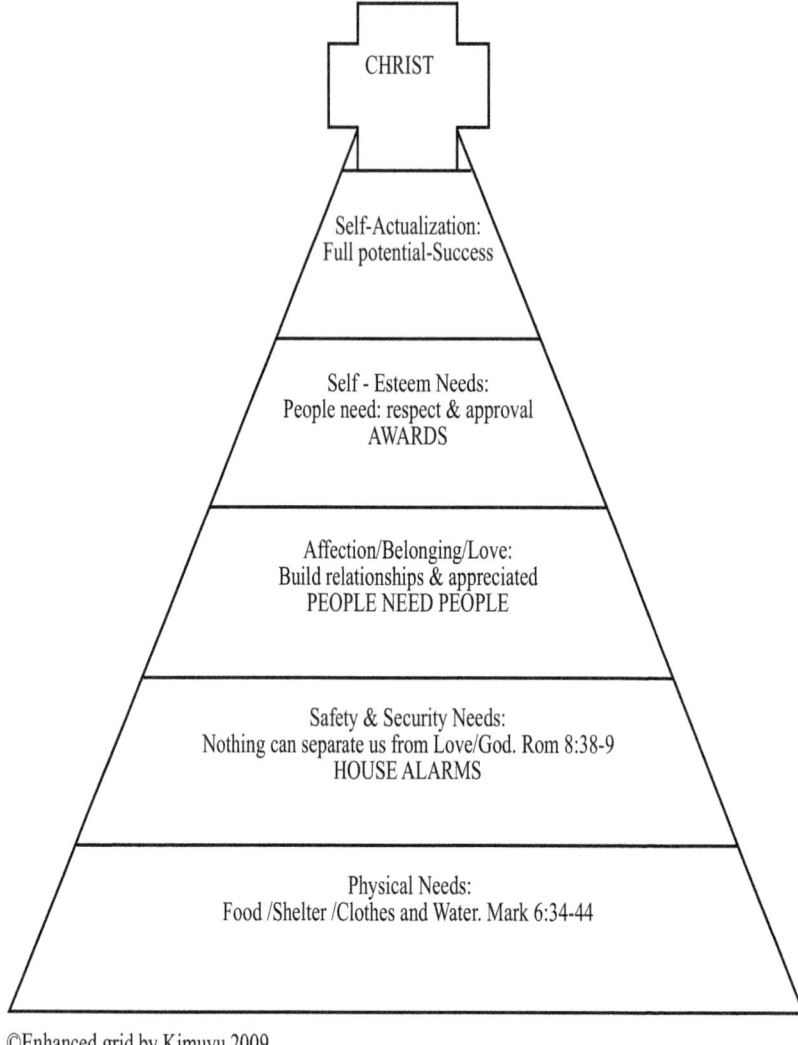

CHRIST

Self-Actualization:
Full potential-Success

Self - Esteem Needs:
People need: respect & approval
AWARDS

Affection/Belonging/Love:
Build relationships & appreciated
PEOPLE NEED PEOPLE

Safety & Security Needs:
Nothing can separate us from Love/God. Rom 8:38-9
HOUSE ALARMS

Physical Needs:
Food /Shelter /Clothes and Water. Mark 6:34-44

©Enhanced grid by Kimuyu 2009

The needs grid diagram is used to help a leader identify the different levels of human basic needs that can affect human behavior. The Maslow grid should be viewed as a tool to enable a leader to address and find ways to facilitate help to people in various categories of human needs.

A moral authority of a Leader is Honesty and Integrity
www.muumandu.com

Organizational Climate Atmospheres of an organization are created by the management team. The prevailing atmosphere established by the management team can be described as two major categories: (1) the supportive climate and (2) the defensive climate. The **supportive climate** promotes open communication, encourages new ideas, and allows interpersonal relationships to grow. It results to strong leadership built throughout the organization. Subordinates in such an organization are comfortable asking questions and presenting their opinions to their peers and to management in non-confrontational ways.

Other characteristics of a supportive climate are that workers can express various attitudes and beliefs without fear of retribution from management. Through unions (trade unions) in particular, they can challenge company policy and procedures, even the goals and mission of the organization. There should be healthy discussions between management and workers to benefit the overall organization. Once these discussions are completed and agreed upon by both sides; management can change its policies and procedures to line up with the organization's goals and the mission.

The other major organizational climate in business is the **defensive climate.** The defensive climate is one where open communication is discouraged. Managers in this climate will typically not support suggestions and ideas from the general worker. Workers do not feel they have a say in this climate since orders and directives come from the top with little regard for what the working level employees feel. Workers in this climate feel the leaders are telling them "just do your job and keep your mouth shut." This obviously leaves the working level employees unsatisfied in their work.

Organizational Culture is defined as "meaningful orders of persons and things." (Marshall Sahlins 1950) Organizational culture is achieved by implementing a set of common beliefs, values and ethics. The manner in which we speak to one another and the actions we take will cause us to react in different ways.

Organizations take on cultures of their own. In most organizations workers are expected to be good at what they do in the organization – to perform their work adequately. However, many organizations implement policies and procedures that stress excellence in the workplace. In such an organization, you feel you want to perform at the top of your game, because the other workers are also striving for excellence.

Some organizations such as health care, law enforcement and the armed forces require a dress code that helps in promoting a team atmosphere and aides in identifying management levels. While some individuals find such an environment restrictive, many find it meets their need for an orderly way of approaching their work.

The cultural environment within an organization often has a profound impact on the workers. In a family-like or team-built culture, workers may have formal or informal gatherings. They may hold parties and cerebrate co-workers birthdays, promotions and awards. In a healthy organizational culture such as this, employees are allowed to build personal relationships with each other and even with managers. They allow employees to share personal goals, successes, or even work related challenges, as well as expressing their feelings about their work.

By contrast, an organization where the culture is built on fear of one person, the boss (leader) is viewed as all-powerful and as more intelligent than anyone else. The notion exists that there is only one true method of doing things. We can expect trouble in organizations where relationships among subordinates are not encouraged. Subordinates with poor morale produce substandard widgets.

Organizational Power (leadership authority) is a force to be reckoned with, whether this power is acquired legitimately or illegitimately. It is assumed the leader has all the traits of a leader, since he/she has legitimate power as indicated within the organization rank and structure. A perceived power resource involves respect, power, and control. There is no doubt that a manager/supervisor has the power to hire, fire, and discipline and demote. Once power is realized the boss/leader has it all.

Conflict Management Resolution is a "struggle to resist or overcome; contest of opposing forces or powers; strife; battle. A painful tension set up by a clash between opposed and contradictory impulses." Dictionary Definition

People from all walks of life, regardless of economic background may have conflicts occasionally enter into our lives. The conflict originated from the Garden of Eden, where mankind once walked on the face of the earth; he consulted daily with his creator God. Dr. Barclays, a Scottish, New Testament interpreter said it best when he said, "When God created man, he implanted in him his affections and his dispositions; and then, all, and he enthroned the sacred, ruling mind."

It is there at the Garden of Eden after series of events; Adam and Eve disobeyed God. Soon after, the disagreement between two brothers led to the first physical fight which led to the first death. Adam and Eve became the first family to experience physical and spiritual eternal death. When evil attacks the desires of the mind, the outcome follows with evil desires. Conflict causes the majority of people a great degree of distress, exasperation, frustration, depression, and anguish. Jewish Rabbis believed that evil desire was found in an embryo in the womb, before a man was born. The evil desire was a person's ruthless enemy, the second personality.

The study of multiple personality has been carefully studied by psychologists for many centuries. It is a behavioral disorder that is severely destructive to self and other surroundings. Occasionally, a development of normal personality and behavioral functioning may surface. Today in North America and other developed nations, people with multiple personality are treated with prescribed medicine and many chronic personalities are admitted into mental state institutes for the rest of their earthly lives.

The Rabbis were the guardians of the Torah and overseers of the affairs of the Jewish community. The Jews were not too far from the truth of multiple personalities. They believed that no man should remain a prisoner of the evil desire. A man had a choice.

Paul went further; he spoke of conflict, as an experience of the mind, the "inward man," one who is possessed with self. When outside chemicals are added to the body, the results are measured differently from a normal person. Therefore, a man is born of the flesh and the will to control his actions. The person with multiple personality sometimes sees a window of normalcy, an opportunity to exercise his/her free will and to allow treatment to be administered to them. There are those individuals whose personalities are completely damaged; these end up in state mental institutions as previously narrated. Consequently, the reign of flesh is absolute and undeniable over man; it is not until a person is born again that he possesses the "inward" that Paul mentions in [Romans 7: 22] than conflict becomes a possibility.

Conflict is an expressed struggle between two interdependent parties who perceive incompatible goals, scarcity of resources, and interference from each other in achieving organizational goals. Organizational conflict is an ongoing battle between two leaders, managers, or subordinates in an organization. Sometimes the expressed struggle can be viewed as the desire to have revenge against another leader. It is important to point out that organizational conflict reveals many mismatched goals between two individuals.

Therefore, the two are interfering with the achievement of each other's goals. It is most unfortunate when one party considers conflict as war with one winner and one loser, that middle ground is inconceivable. This attitude usually limits healthy and productive conflict where a middle ground is expected to resolve issues in a professional manner. When one opponent refuses negotiations, an attempt to misuse power may be realized. One opposing party may apply intimidation, threats, and violent tactics. Anger is intensified, because a leader may not realize that the fear of losing is often a primary emotion that takes charge of a person's behavior. This management technique is common with high-D personality types and is characterized by the use of overt anger and intimidation.

Threats or intimidation may surface at a moment's notice. As a result, the creativity and self-esteem of subordinates are often crushed. Relationships are secondary to the task at hand and productivity eventually suffers due to low morale. Managers in conflict situations using this style view themselves on opposing sides of the negotiating table with the object of the conflict in the middle. A more productive view of conflict is that the problem is on one side of the table with the two conflicting parties sitting together attacking the problem, not each other.

My wife and I owned and operated a state sponsored residential treatment center for neglected and physically and mentally abused children of the United States. We treated neglected children ranging between one year old to seventeen years old; who had been placed in various treatment facilities by the state child protective and regulatory services for treatment programs like "Solomon Youth Centers." Most children were severely abused, burned, cut, chocked, sometimes nearly beaten to death.

Others were left by their parents or guardians unsupervised at home. The children left home alone have access to unauthorized substance abuse, alcohol, guns and other unauthorized narcotic substances of the day. Once these substances are consumed by the child (ren), it alters their chemical balance in their brains to the point where they cannot differentiate between right and wrong. A few who survived in homes unnoticed for a number of years become mean and dangerous to themselves and the society.

When these children reach adulthood, they roam in life as ruthless people with no respect of human life. They continue in life under the influence of alcohol, drugs and other substances, whereby their evil impulsive minds lead to destruction, which in turn leads to thousands of homicide deaths in North America.

There are similar cases for children living in the cities' slums of the third world nations. Thousands of children are exposed to malaria, unsafe drinking water, contaminated produce, with polluted environments unfit for human dwellings. Children of the cities' slums of Africa play with a sea of water sewage as ponds where they can cross and sometime fall into human feces. Now, which is worse, a child living in North America or a child living in the cities' slums of Africa? The answer is left to the reader. It is about taking responsibility on the part of adults and the political system of these societies.

When children of the cities' slum crack into adulthood and come into the society, their value of life in general is dysfunctional; they become unemployable, have no basic education, and their capacity to reason is based on the background he/she managed to grow out off. Prophet Amos says, "As if a man did flee from a lion, and a bear met him; or went into the house, and leaned his hand on the wall, and a serpent bit him." Amos 5:19 AKJV

Therefore, as young adults, they become agents and carriers of narcotic drugs and illegal substances from slums to the city streets of the nation's towns, and institutions of higher learning. In the end, a small group of young men and women are capable of contaminating the whole society within a short time with the evil desire of their minds.

During the last general elections in Kenya, it was alleged that men carried out mass killings of innocent children, and women in churches and villages by the night when they could find men in the villages. They claimed their motive of the killings was revenge to a system that had not helped them find jobs.

Conflict comes about from different phases of life - needs, values, dissatisfactions, prejudices, discriminations, unemployment and loss of a loved one. Conflict may not be a problem in itself - it is rather what we do with the unsolved conflicts that come to haunt us and our societies. We cannot escape conflict; yet, we should look at conflict as a way to prepare ourselves as the citizens in the world we live and for a greater spiritual warfare as good soldiers of our Lord Jesus Christ.

It is imperative as a people of the world, we must respect the dignity and the sanctity of life; we must be prepared at all times to fix any unresolved conflict between those we lead and work for. The problem of conflict resolution has never been an easy task for all humanity. But to achieve a peaceful solution requires a meeting of minds; first to agree to disagree and be willing to enter into conflict solution between men and women, tribes against other tribes and nations against nations.

However, there is a natural pendulum swing; more nations of the world have passed laws requiring protection of the rights of women and children. This is one area Conflict resolution is past due for ordinary men and women of many societies. In recent years leaders of the industrious nations of the north with collaboration with United Nations agencies have made it mandatory for third world nations to address the issue of women and children as one of the eight Millennial Development Goals, a paradigm of the twenty- first century; the protection of women and children in the society.

The Tools to Achieve Conflict Resolution... I suggest that managers, supervisors, and leaders explore the area of alliance or the win-win possibility of conflict. This method of problem solving allows both opposing parties to achieve goal realization and satisfaction. The win-win philosophy does not suggest weakness on either side. It is an assertive, non-aggressive method of managing conflicts that allows everyone involved to attain some satisfaction without giving up things they consider to be important.

In many of my business decisions I have used postponement as a way of handling issues while still remaining very confrontational. The principle of a Win/Win Approach enables each party or adversaries, to agree to disagree to set rules of engagement at the negotiating table.

The Win/Win Approach allows the bypass of personal differences open for optimism. Win/Win Approach creates a better working climate and more fulfilling relationships. Each party must be willing to lose some and gain some in order to reach a peaceful resolution without bottlenecking demands; by going back to address the **needs issues** and what would be the best benefit for either parties or partners. Win/Win is a strategy that is widely used by corporations and governments all over the world.

United States of America is one of the best democracies in the world when it comes to solving her domestic crisis; like the bombing of the Twin Towers on September eleven, in New York; during several hurricane disasters and in the midst of unpopular policy, they faced challenges, and remained united as Americans. Through their powerful three branches of government, each political party enters into hot guided debates, sometimes one may think that individual lawmakers may not see eye to eye once they leave the house chambers; the opposing senators/ representatives may have a meal together or sit next to each other on a plane travelling back to their home states.

In stark contrast, in third world nations an opposing law maker's life may be jeopardized outside the parliament grounds, if one enters into prickly opposition with a ruling government. However, with advancing multiparty systems such dangers have diminished in the recent years.

In summarizing the overall organizational atmosphere in the area of conflict, it is worth noting the effect that managing styles have had on different leaders. Some leaders have created an atmosphere that is non-supportive where subordinates have acted out of a fear of being fired, and/or a fear of approaching the leader with suggestions. A leader with the inability to see things differently has caused delayed development in many third world democracies, in manufacturing industries, and in government.

The success of any organization depends greatly on its ability to view conflict in a productive manner and educate management to utilize a variety of methods in conflict resolution. I found that the Win-Win Approach does not require more effort and on the long haul it brings the benefits of preserving relationships.

The Creative Response is about looking at the problem-issue directed to reachable goals. There is no scientific evidence that gives the utmost meaning why ethnic cleansing occurs between tribes in remote parts of the world. When it does happen it is usually brutal and inhuman. Creative response provides an opportunity of hope between two opposing parties.

Albert Einstein once said that, "Peace cannot be kept by force. It can only be won, through understanding. Our longing for understanding is Eternal." When there is war between tribes, or nations against nations, UN appropriates a peaceable resolution through its diplomatic core relationships. It is the only way man can live in peace in the outskirts of what has become the global community.

The tribes of Africa taught their incoming generation to obey and respect traditional beliefs and the culture of their ancestors. Let us examine why people believe what they believe compared to why people have faith. First, people believe because they were taught to believe; when people are taught to believe that a short person is dangerous and must be killed by a tall person that is wrong, it is murder.

A story is told about a Portuguese slave trader who wrote to the plantation owners of the southern states; the use of a black man was good for picking cotton in hot climates of the south. Whether the argument is true or not the end result was not morally right, to enslave another human being just by the color of his skin. November 4, 2008 American voters told the world by the action of their votes, they could elect a man of a black ancestry. Growing up in Athi River a city of about five thousand people of different tribes of Kenya I was told by Akamba elders that a Luo man was considered a "boy". The term "boy" is used in a derogative manner by Bantu tribes who customarily practice circumcision. As time changed, I came to realize that a Luo person was just as good as another person. Luo tribes practice their own circumcision by way of removing (6) six front teeth of the lower jaw.

The Chagga tribe of northern Kilimanjaro, Tanzania, believes that a man cannot be buried unless he is circumcised. Once a man is identified by the undertakers, customary law requires the man be circumcised the night before his burial. I have never understood why a dead person must be circumcised, unless for an autopsy. For many years the cut tribes of Kenya have undermined a Luo tribe in leadership in the top seat in the Republic of Kenya, simply, because of circumcision stigma. The circumcision is discussed in length in chapter six. David was not pleased when Goliath, an uncircumcised Philistine ridiculed the name of the Lord God.

Belief is not a growth of your own understanding; it is simply an ideology passed from generation to generation which is subject to change by the influence of foreign cultures. In scientific terms, belief requires proof or logic. Acculturation is realized when people immigrate from one culture to foreign cultures, they are forced to learn and adopt a new culture for their survival.

There are many people who claim to be Christians because of their belief. How can one claim the rights of a Christian when he does not live up to the teachings of the Christian faith? When belief cannot be lived? Second, Faith — starts from the time a person can differentiate right from wrong.

A person reacts to life's experiences; situations, events and through the annals of life. Faith arises from the horizon of our personal encounter with Jesus Christ. Many people go through life based on their beliefs and never experience the beauty of having faith in a living God. The following are additional tools that may be useful in reaching Conflict resolution. Ω

Recap

Recipe for Conflict Management Resolution
Win/Win Approach, Mapping the Conflict, Empathy, Appropriate Assertiveness, Co-operative Power, Managing Emotions, and Willingness to Resolve, Development of Options, Negotiation Skills, with a Third Party Mediation and Broadening Perspectives, The Creative Response

Discussions and Understanding of Leadership

The Ways of Knowing:

Have you ever considered: How you know; how you came to know; what you know?

1) Non-scientific ways of knowing [Plato] major player

  i) **Common sense** is knowledge usually taken for granted

  ii) **Authority** is a assurance uncritical acceptance of another's knowledge

  iii) **Intuition/Revelation** is the process of how immediately the mind can grasp the truth

  iv) **Experience** is based on trial and error

  v) **Deductive reasoning** comes from general to specific

2) Scientific method of knowing [Aristotle] is a major player
- i) **Objective** ability to see negative or positive
- ii) **Precision** is driven from precise measurement
- iii) **Experience** is based on trial and error
- iv) **Deductive reasoning** comes from general to specifics
- v) **Inductive reasoning** comes from specifics to general

Discussions on Theories of Leadership

1. The Great Man Theory on Leadership
   - a. Leadership is a matter of birth
   - b. Power is invested in a limited number of people
   - c. Birthright and destiny is what creates leaders
   - d. Only those of the right breed can lead
2. The Big Bang Theory
   - a. Great events made great leaders from ordinary persons
   - b. Leaders would rise to the occasion
   - c. The right person in the right place at the right time
3. The Characteristic Theory of Leadership
   - a. Personality – salesman vs. scholar
   - b. Physical – size and strength
   - c. Intellect – how smart are you?
4. The Bible Account
   God created the heavens and the earth
5. Leader:
   - a. Commitment – there is a person for every task
   - b. Conviction – is the will to persevere regardless of

circumstances
c. Competency – the skills to make it happen
d. Character – the quest for piety and high ethics

Discussion on Leadership
1. How did you become (illegitimate or legitimate) a leader?
2. What are the negative aspects of leadership you experienced?
3. What are the positive aspects of a leader that you experienced?
4. What is your definition of leadership?

Purpose Driven Mission
1. Foresight = what should be done
2. Ideals= fundamental principles of the uncompromising views
3. Mission = purpose to pursue the vision
4. Vital / Aim = focus to accomplish the mission
5. Goal = description of the target
6. Objectives = assessable goals
7. Action = effort to achieve an objective
8. Assessment = suitability of the vision

Ten Ways to Avoid Decision Making
1. We tried before
2. It is too drastic a change
3. Our place is different
4. Not enough funds
5. It is costly

6. A group should study it
7. We don't have time
8. Let's put it in writing
9. It cannot be done
10. It is an unattainable task

Five Practices of Leadership
1. Challenge the status quo
2. Inspire a shared vision
3. Enable others to act
4. Model the way
5. Support others

Practices and Commitments
1. Treat every job as an exciting activity
2. Send people to (seminars + training) for new ideas
3. Set up procedures for new learned ideas
4. Think about your past experience
5. Become a futurist, focus and plan a head
6. Deal with failure and success as learned experiences
7. Think about the needs of your people before yours
8. Make things happens by making informed decisions
9. When a window of opportunity closes, another window will open
10. Experiment, take risks and learn from the mistakes/successes
11. Visit with people one on one, you may learn something new

12. Provide autonomy with support and keep your people informed
13. Audit your actions consistent with shared Leadership values
14. Recognize people personally and in public
15. Find people who are doing things right and connect with them.

FOUR:
Leadership During
The New
Testament Time

"And he gave some, apostles; and some, prophets; and some, evangelists; and some, pastors; and some, teachers;" (Ephesians 4:11) AKJV

FOUR: *Leadership During the New Testament Time*

Leadership During the
New Testament Time

T he church of the New Testament was divided into specific leadership roles with qualifications listed for these
positions. Paul wrote during the era of many pagan religions. The worship of the pagan god, Mithras was very popular
amid the Roman soldiers during the Roman conquest in Persia.
The Christians of the day were confronted by Neo-Platonism; a
philosophical system amalgamated with mystical Judaism and
Christian ideals as source for all existence. Plotinus wrote, "The
soul lives in the material world." Therefore, the soul "ought to
be the master of the world." In essence, the "soul" who is part
human being proposes the belief that it continues to exist in a
material world. Man has always had the choice to abandon one's
principles in order to gain material wealth, success and power in
the world.

Paul was fully aware of the teachings and beliefs of his day. The
soul was considered a spiritual system of faith joined together
with the supernatural (soul) part of a human being that continues
to live long after the body ceases to function. Therefore, the soul
is sometimes regarded as subject to a future reward or punish-
ment to the people left behind. It was an accepted thought by
many cultures during the New Testament world; that the soul
was capable to take some life form that allows it to transcend
through time and space by returning back to earth. A belief that
is widely taken by occults world wide and many religions of

faith, during Paul's day, even today in the modern world.

To further explain, a ritual performed by Native American Sioux Indians, when an infant or child died, illustrates the reverence Indians had toward a human soul. After the shaving ceremony the child's hair was carefully wrapped and locked into buckskin and placed in a sacred location within a tepee. The souls of the dead ancestors were the center of the sacred hoop of the Sioux nation. It was their belief that a mother should do everything for the sake of her children by developing herself into her children, for children to become holy people and leaders of the future Sioux nation. In other words, Sioux Indians kept the souls of good people. In keeping their rite, the Spirit became one with the nation. Thus, the "soul" was able to return to the "place" where it was once born as human. This way, the good soul would not have to wander on earth as would be in case of the bad soul.

Similar to the many tribes of Africa, they too, believe that bad spirits return from their dead ancestors to snooty people. The majority of tribes of East Africa believe that no one dies without a reason; there are always forces that cause death.

Throughout the old Roman world, Greek believers rejected a religion that lacked ingredients of redemption. The teachings of Jesus Christ, was the new Truth with the messages of hope and forgiveness. The new Truth was received as a religion of salvation from sin with a promise of eternal life. The new believers had a vision of the ONE God, precisely, as it was manifested on the cross at Calvary in the facial expressions of our Master Teacher, Jesus Christ. Therefore, the Greeks and gentiles who had experienced the *knowledge* of the Spiritual Truth were called Christians.

The plan of urgency of the return of Jesus Christ was created in the order of the worship service by the first twelve disciples and the early Christians during the first and third centuries. The urgency was contributed from the message and teachings they had learned from their Master Teacher, Himself, as His own words said, He would return like a thief in the night. In other words a thief does not declare or announce the hour and the time when to strike.

During my nostalgia high school days of (1970s), I knew of a very prominent couple in my community who refused to send their child to school, refused to have a savings account and refused to establish a retirement home, because Jesus was coming very *soon.

John says, "…he who reads and … hear the words of the prophecy…heed the things which are written in it; for the time is near." Revelation 1:3 NASB This is the notion, that there is no need to lay foundation in a world that may pass away very quickly.

Jesus' departure point took place at Mount Olivet, where the disciples were astonished by the manner in which the Master was lifted up into the heavens. Thereafter, suddenly, there appeared two men saying, "…this same Jesus…taken up from you into heaven, shall so come in like manner…" Acts 1:11 AKJV the disciples' faith was that Jesus would return very soon. Thus, the teachings of the Rapture picture Christ returning in the clouds just as He was taken up into heaven.

To emphasize the urgency of the return of Jesus Christ, it is illustrated in the following episode. In Mexico, September 9, 2009 a religious fanatic hijacked a jetliner with 109 people on board from Cancun to Mexico City. The Bible-carrying hijacker used a juice can with lights attached to the can as a "bomb". The forty-four year old male hijacker claimed it was a divine revelation that led him to hijack the plane because the September date was 9-9-9, in reference to the satanic number 666 turned upside down.

Later that afternoon, when the hijacker was apprehended and questioned by the authorities, he said, he took control of the jetliner because Jesus Christ is coming soon. He further told the authorities, there were three other hijackers on board with him, namely "the Father, the Son and the Holy Ghost". In the end of the ordeal there was only one ridiculous human hijacker equipped with a juice can.

Paradoxically, during the wee-hours on September 9, 2009 Protasia, my wife, while on night duty, whispered to other nurses that she had hoped that no one would do anything spooky, or behave silly. It turned out during the day TV monitors were flashing with the news of the hijacked jetliner in Mexico; the mad man had threatened the lives of men and women in the course of their holiday vacation and business trips.

After the incident, I was not sure if Protasia and I would be affected psychologically because she was about to make a scheduled international trip to New Zealand, in the Pacific. Separated by more than 2000 years, every day we hear similar incidents and claims about the return of the Master Teacher, yet the first twelve disciples and the believing Christians believed Jesus was returning soon, meant in days, months, years or for centuries to come.

Paul took center stage as an exemplary leader of his day. He had lived a perilous life. He wrote to the Ephesians church knowing his missionary journey was near to its end. Paul saw the urgency to send a letter to the Ephesians believers who he had converted during his treacherous missionary journeys by outlining the qualifications and responsibilities of a leader's role.

Some leadership positions were specific to the local church with authority confirmed by the congregation. They were to fulfill the immediate needs of the growing churches across the New Testament territories and the world to come. Similarly, like the disciples who had earlier on gone into a conclave and agreed for the selection of seven men to take care of the neglected Greek Jewish widows who had returned back to the Jerusalem church to live their final years on earth. The tradition has remained in practice within the New Testament church to help the poor, the abused and neglected children.

James, the brother of Jesus was a leader of the church in Jerusalem. Other leadership positions were commissioned by the church in Jerusalem to serve elsewhere. Paul and Silas were sent by the Jerusalem church as **evangelists** to take the Gospel of Jesus Christ to city states in foreign lands.

Paul wrote to the Christian Church outlining the role of the gifted men and women in the church. Ephesians 4:11, when each person is gifted with the talent of Teaching. The Bible says, *"And he gave some, **apostles**; and some, **prophets**; and some, **evangelists**; and some, **pastors**; and some, **teachers**;"* (Ephesians 4:11) AKJV

In Ephesians 4: 12-13, Paul outlined the roles and responsibilities of these leadership positions. Some of them as listed below:

• To educate, care for and guide the church.

• To equip, build the church and bring unity.

• To strengthen the church through these ministries.

A. Apostles

Qualifications of an apostle: they must have

1. Seen Jesus Christ [Acts 1:21] and

2. Witnessed His resurrection.

They were the original twelve disciples (less Judas) plus additional followers added soon after the death of Jesus Christ. Luke and Paul introduce us to some of the new apostles. These disciples spread the teachings of Jesus Christ far and wide, but paid a heavy price, even with their lives. However, Paul affirms in one of his writings that for him death was gain (because he would then see the Lord).

- **Barnabas** - "But when the apostles, Barnabas and Paul, heard of it, they tore their robes and rushed out into the crowd, crying out." [Acts14:14] NASB

- **James,** the brother of Jesus, Galatians 1:19, "But I did not see any other of the apostles except James, the Lord's brother." And "then He appeared to James, then to all the apostles." [1 Corinthians 15:7] NASB

- **Paul and Silvanus (Silas)** and Timothy to the church of the Thessalonians in God the Father and the Lord Jesus Christ, Grace to you and peace," (1 Thessalonians 1:1) NASB

- **Andronicus & Junias-Paul** wrote, "Greet Andronicus and Junias, my kinsmen, and my fellow prisoners, who are outstanding among the apostles, who also were in Christ before me." Romans 16:7 NASB

- **Paul** - Paul himself claims his own right as an apostle. "Am I not free? Am I not an apostle? Have I not seen Jesus our Lord? Are you not my work in the Lord?" (1 Corinthians 9:1) NASB

B. Prophets

The prophets had no authority over the church but were highly respected men and women. Luke mentions prophets several times in the book of Acts. One ancient tradition says that prophets should not spend more than three days in one place.

If a prophet was in one place more than three days in succession, he was declared to be a FALSE prophet. However, this is just a tradition with no biblical backing. Prophets in the Old Testament had to have every one of their predictions come true or they were declared to be a false prophet.

These qualifications mentioned below are for New Testament prophets.

1. They, too, had to have had first-hand experience with the risen Christ.

2. They traveled extensively and received no direct financial

support from other brethren.

3. Their ministry was to go from city to city and regions warning men and women of the consequences that would follow without acceptance of Jesus Christ.

4. They received messages directly from the Holy Spirit.

Prophets/Prophetesses mentioned by Luke are:

• **Agabus** - Prophets are mentioned, "And in these days came prophets from Jerusalem unto Antioch. And there stood up one of them named Agabus, and signified by the Spirit that there should be great dearth throughout all the world: which came to pass in the days of Claudius Caesar." (Acts11:27-28) AKJV Luke mentions Agabus again in Acts of Apostles, "And as we were staying there for some days, a certain prophet named Agabus came down from Judea." (Acts 21:10) NASB

• **Prophets/Teachers** - "Now there were in the church that was at Antioch certain prophets and teachers; as Barnabas, and Simeon that was called Niger, and Lucius of Cyrene, and Manaen, which had been brought up with Herod the tetrarch, and Saul." (Acts 13:1) AKJV

• **Judas and Silas** - "And Judas and Silas, being prophets also themselves, exhorted the brethren with many words, and confirmed them." (Acts 15:32) AKJV

• **Philip's daughters** - "Now this man had four virgin daughters who were prophetesses." (Acts 21:9) NASB

We do not hear more about prophets, because the majority of them were of the first followers of Jesus to be put to death. As time passed on prophets seem to disappear in the writings of Paul and as the New Testament church grew and multiplied in numbers both in Palestine and Asia Minor.

C. Evangelists

Evangelists were the carriers of the message of Jesus Christ from city and states to regions of the world. The majority of evangelists had not seen Jesus, but all had experienced the power of His resurrection. They were the missionaries of the ancient times. Throughout the centuries evangelists have continued to spread the message of Jesus Christ. Paul, Barnabas and Mark were exemplary missionaries and evangelists who performed the office of evangelist/missionary with great passion and commitment. Paul wrote his second letter to Timothy, "But watch thou in all things, endure afflictions, do the work of an evangelist, make full proof of thy ministry." (2Timothy 4: 5) AKJV

- **Philip -** "And the next day we that were of Paul's company departed, and came unto Caesarea: and we entered into the house of Philip the evangelist, which was one of the seven; and abode with him." (Acts 21:8) AKJV

- **John Mark -** soon after parting with Paul, John Mark established a church in Alexandria, Egypt. Twenty (20) years later, Paul wrote from a Roman prison asking Timothy to bring John Mark along with him. Paul had now repaired his relationship with John Mark.

D. Pastors/Teachers

Pastors/Teachers had experienced the resurrection power of the risen Lord.

Paul paints a picture of the pastor/shepherd and teacher throughout the pages of the New Testament as men and women who guarded the oral and written Word. They led the flock and often died while protecting their faith. In this age of technology pastors/teachers should be able to spread the gospel further and faster. The Word of God is available in more languages of the world than ever before. Evangelistic tools are also available to reach parts of the world hitherto unreachable by means of radio and communications satellites.

It took Leadership and vision for many of the Christian TV networks to come out with a solution to reach mankind with the word of God in nations that would not allow missionaries. That is not to say there are no challenges facing these evangelistic organizations. That is what leaders are to do - preach and teach the Gospel of the truth with honor and integrity. Let the people we teach and help in our ministry be able to say, we have seen men and women who have experienced the resurrection power of the risen Lord.

The Election Process and Role of a Deacon

Deacon and elder are not the same. They are from different Greek words. "Elder" comes from a word meaning old, denoting believers who are older in the Lord and who should have maturity and wisdom over the teachings and the plan of salvation. They are the spiritual mentors and leaders; they may not be the servers, in the church. The Church as we know today is made of a group of men and women who meet at a specified place for worship in the name of Jesus Christ.

Over the centuries the body of Christ – the church congregation has suffered splits because of theological differences. The splits of many churches are nothing else other than personal differences of opinions and theological interpretation. Some personal interpretation does not pertain to the Word of God. A split in and of itself does not guarantee the problem solving. Any theological differences must be addressed by the believers themselves, rather than seeking theological solutions from the worldly public justice system. It is the preaching of the message of the Truth in the Word of God that will bind believers together.

The problems of splitting continues as with the Groups of Homosexual leadership who have taken the center stage in the theological debates, and perhaps will continue with new debates in the future as the society takes another cultural change. When groups disagree, they break away from one central fellowship and form a new group; they begin to meet under new assumed names: Community Bible Church, Bible Church, Tabernacles, or a name of a local town and so on. Sometimes the breakaway is healthy and sometimes the split adds new theological debates in the lives of believers.

Martin Luther, the founder of the Lutheran Church, nailed the famous 95 thesis of theological differences to the door of his mother church, because The Papal of The Roman Catholic Church refused a dialogue with Martin Luther; that led to the current different New Testament churches known as protestant churches located anywhere in the world. In this case the split was healthy. Today, the majority of those who breakaway become converts of new denominations and TV evangelists.

In addition, the TV evangelists have a new field of harvest cut out for them, from the sitting congregations in church buildings led to the internet and media church. The TV evangelist has the largest audience in the modern world. I was a party in the making of Baptist Convention of Kenya (BCOK) which was organized in the 1970s. It was a prosperous young body of Christ; Baptist Churches averaged high weekly baptisms. I returned back to East Africa after more than three decades away from my beloved country of my physical and spiritual birth. I was troubled to find BCOK had been dragged into the public court system by some of our brethren I had left behind as guardians of our few faithful. The organization was nearly to the threshold of collapse and extinction.

The collaborators were some of the brethren who wanted the power share in office of the organization. They were not really *called* to the task, actions reveal character and heart. They confused the world in which we live and preach the message of love and forgiveness. For example, the church burnings in Eldoret, Kenya; it saddens the whole world to know the very physical church buildings that are meant to provide protection of the human race to whom we preach and witness were used to destroy innocent lives of men, women and children. It is possible that even the perpetrators, rapists, thieves and the killers may be suffering emotional turmoil of living in the *guilt* in the present. What hope is there but in Christ's love and forgiveness? Otherwise, they may well themselves, burn in eternal physical and spiritual death.

One of the best times of my life was in Church Planting in rural Coast Province, along the Indian Ocean, the Islam territory. I was concerned to find some of our brethren who left the faith had been swallowed up by worldly winds of change. These ones had left the faith completely. But the seeds had also fallen onto the good soil. I visited some of the old Baptist Churches; they had multiplied into hundred folds with a new breed of believers and from all walks of life. Some of the Baptist Churches are among the fastest growing in large numbers in congregations just like the modern "Mall" Churches in the great state of Texas. Some Baptist congregations failed to grow, especially Baptist Churches located in rural, poor areas of the Republic.

> **Distribution of Spiritual Gifts**
> Interpretation, Martyrdom, Tongues, Intercession, Voluntary, Giving, Discernment, Knowledge, Wisdom, Administration,
> **Leadership,**
> Pastor, Hospitality, Teaching, Miracles, Exhortation, Celibacy, Service, Missionary, Prophecy, Helps, Faith, Healing, Mercy

Throughout the history of Southern Baptist Mission in East Africa, the mission had the best supply of the Sunday school materials. This is how I received the printed Word, and how I grew spiritually. When the Southern Baptist closed its printing and publication houses, the weekly Sunday school materials that had flowed to the Baptist Congregations of (then) more than 35,000 faithful, came to a standstill over night! Baptist congregations in rural areas struggled to survive, withered and were swallowed up by other groups of faith. Isaiah 40:8 NASB The few congregations that remained plunged victim to the new wave of change with foreign doctrines and without proper Biblical training have caused mayhem among the leaders of the BCOK.

Solomon Center For Leadership, just by its title declares its mission and purpose to play an integral role in the life of the congregations located throughout the Republic. SCL is equipped with Leadership Seminars with messages to train the: evangelists, teachers and pastors with sound Biblical training which will forge the new hope in leadership for the struggling rural church leadership. The Greek word for Deacon is **"diakonos,"** meaning "an attendant" and is translated as "minister" and "servant," as in a waiter at table, or in other menial duties. The existence of this office goes back to the first century church in Jerusalem and continued in other mushrooming churches.

The New Testament church uses the same word "deacon" to denote Christians who serve as servants for this particular office set exclusively for service of the church. Individuals holding the title of a deacon serve the same way as other Christians who are members of the said local church. The writings of Luke, Paul and Timothy provide us with the requirement and the purpose of the office of the deacon.

Luke wrote, "And in those days, when the number of the disciples was multiplied, there arose a murmuring of the Grecians against the Hebrews, because their widows were neglected in the daily ministration. Then the twelve called the multitude of the disciples unto them, and said, It is not reason that we should leave the word of God, and serve tables. Wherefore, brethren, look ye out among you seven men of honest report, full of the Holy Ghost and wisdom, whom we may appoint over this business.

A moral authority of a Leader is Honesty and Integrity

But we will give ourselves continually to prayer, and to the ministry of the word. And the saying pleased the whole multitude: and they chose Stephen, a man full of faith and of the Holy Ghost, and Philip, and Prochorus, and Nicanor, and Timon, and Parmenas, and Nicolas a proselyte of Antioch: Whom they set before the apostles: and when they had prayed, they laid their hands on them. And the word of God increased; and the number of the disciples multiplied in Jerusalem greatly; and a great company of the priests were obedient to the faith." (Acts 6:1-7) AKJV

The first three verses refer to (1) Jewish custom, in a synagogue there was a daily path from house to house collecting food and money to assist the poor widows. (2) There were two categories of Jews: Those who spoke Aramaic, the ancestral language, and Jews who spoke Greek.

The Greek speaking Jews were neglected, because as Jews, they had forgotten their original language, because they had been away from their home land for many generations; they had returned to Palestine because they had believed and received Jesus as Lord and Savior. The disciples did not want to get mixed up with the complaint; they chose to elect among themselves as stated in verses 5-7. From that day on the church has kept the tradition – assisting and helping the impoverished and the destitute. Stephen, one of the chosen was full of faith and the Holy Ghost, "And Stephen, full of faith and power, did great wonders and miracles among the people." (Acts 6:8) AKJV

Jews believed that they were the chosen people; they never envisioned themselves to bring gentiles, or Greek-speaking Jews to the same fellowship they enjoyed with God. The synagogues and the Temple (Jerusalem) served as spiritual worship and the only place sacrifices could be offered. Stephen no longer saw the need of the Temple since Christ had died and resurrected; he viewed the Law of Moses as a base to win the whole world for Jesus Christ. Stephen became the first deacon martyr. The rest of the verses 9-14 tell us Jewish leaders accused Stephen of blasphemy and stoned him to death.

In verse 15 Luke reports, "And all that sat in the council, looking steadfastly on him, saw his face as it had been the face of an angel." These verses form significant teachings of the life and ministry of Stephen, a price we are destined to pay as followers of the risen Lord. Now let us look for several other characteristics mentioned in the above passages.

Qualifications of a Deacon

(1) Honest report: The Greek word here means **"witness,"** a word used many times in the New Testament and means "to bear witness." A deacon's life must bear witness of his faith in Christ. His entire life must be completely yielded to the Holy Spirit. If people inside and outside the church do not say positive things about a person, his potential as deacon may be doubtful and not be elected to the office of deacon. A deacon's character must have been proven to the people. That is one reason a pastor of a New Testament church may not appoint deacons to that office. Paul wrote, "Now faith is the substance of things hoped for, the evidence of things not seen. For by it the elders obtained a good report." Hebrews 11:1-2 AKJV

(2) Full of the Holy Ghost: The word "full" is repeated many times in other scriptures. In Acts 6:8 Stephen was full of faith.

Luke 4:1 Jesus was full of the Holy Ghost, John 1:14 says the Word was full of grace and truth. Luke wrote about Barnabas, "For he was a good man, and full of the Holy Ghost, and of faith: and much people was added unto the Lord." (Acts 11:24)AKJV

(3) Full of wisdom: The word "wisdom" is used many times in the scripture. "Jesus increased in wisdom and stature and in favor with God and man." Luke 2:52 AKJV Paul calls Jesus "… the power of God, and the wisdom of God." James, the brother of our Lord, the author of the book of James states, "If any of you lack wisdom, let him ask of God, that giveth to all men liberally, and upbraideth not; and it shall be given him." James 1:5AKJV A deacon should show wisdom in his thinking, his words, and his actions. When men act and choose wisely in their own lives they will lead well. It is a privilege and responsibility of the followers of Christ to elect their own deacons.

(4) Full of faith: Men elected to the office of a deacon must be men full of faith. A deacon must completely trust in Christ and in Him alone for salvation; if they are, they will effectively care for the daily needs of the congregation. "And without faith it is impossible to please Him. For whoever would draw near to God must believe that he exists and that he rewards those who seek Him." Hebrews 11:6 RSV

A deacon is to serve the needs of the people. The Greek word for business is "chreia," translated twenty-five times as "need." It means that a person elected to the office of a deacon supplies the needs of the church body. The selection of a deacon should be one who is knowledgeable of the daily activities of the life of the church. 1 Timothy 3:8-13 gives additional requirements to serve as a deacon. Luke does not call the **selection** – of men as an election to the office of the deacon. He refers to them as the **election** of the **seven**. The men set the standards for those who would be elected in a New Testament church.

The disciples provided the guidelines for the election of the office of the deacons as the first elected deacons in the first church in Jerusalem. The office of deacon was good for the first church in Jerusalem. The office has continued to be vital to the church and will continue to play an integral part in the life of the church until the return of our Lord Jesus Christ.

Finally, any church that fails to follow the guidelines, principles and teachings of the Bible is subject to suffer doctrinal separation because Christ is not given His official seat as Head of the church. Second, the church will be open for scriptural criticism, a good feeding ground for the devil to plant seeds of hate and division.

How to Select a Leader

When a leadership position needs to be filled, an announcement should be made to everyone in the organization. There should be established guidelines for the selection process including qualifications for each office. It is advisable for brethren to go into a conclave of prayer, asking God to provide them with a qualified godly candidate for the office.

[14]"Simon, (whom he also named Peter,) and Andrew his brother, James and John, Philip and Bartholomew, [15] Matthew and Thomas, James the son of Alpheus, and Simon called Zelotes, [16] And Judas the brother of James, and Judas Iscariot, which also was the traitor." (Luke 6:14-16) AKJV

A moral authority of a Leader is Honesty and Integrity
www.muumandu.com

When churches continue to grow and multiply, qualified men and women will be needed to fill the ministry positions of teaching, counseling and baptizing the new believers into the family of God. The organization should:

- Establish a process of selection for a candidate.

- Select people to fill the positions in the family of God.

- Select people whose lives are in accordance with biblical truths.

- Select people who live a life of integrity.

Choose men and women who are best qualified for the position. For a secretarial position, select a person who can perform that assignment. For a treasury position, select a person who has experience in the field. Select men and women who are **willing** and able to perform the duties of the office. A recruitment process should be in place to draw a large pool of qualified applicants to fill one or more advertised positions. Many large corporations, non-government agencies and governments of the world have established offices of personnel or human resources (P/HR) to pre-qualify or (screen) applicants.

With the advent of the internet many businesses now advertise on the internet. This attracts millions of applicants depending on the nature of the position, if it is to fill an international position or domestic. However, internet advertising is still limited to industrialized nations. Top leadership positions should first be targeted to be filled from within the organization; to encourage promotion inside the organization. Such practice promotes the organization mission and objectives from being unchanged. Many denominations in most cases tend to hire from their own pool of believers to protect their mission goal as a denomination.

The Selection Process

"Wherefore, brethren, look ye out among you seven men of honest report, full of the Holy Ghost and wisdom, whom we may appoint over this business." (Acts 6:1-3) AKJV

First, individuals should never campaign for an office in the church, or any other church institution, by promising monetary or material rewards. The Lord cannot be bribed with coins of silver to fulfill personal ambition.

A leader should never compromise his leadership position for a bribe. Such compromising is cowardly and self-uplifting which results to the **"Goliath fall."** A leader must learn to use the magic words "NO" and "YES" when appropriate. For the sake of his/her credibility, integrity, respect and honor to God. This is the mark and the test of a leader, who should avoid making promises that cannot be delivered or fulfilled.

There is a biblical process for doing God's business. First prayer is the core of everything a leader needs. God is honored when men pray, whether it is for wisdom, or for the healing of a family member, friend or neighbor. When God's process is properly followed, the Good News will continue to spread near and far; the number of new disciples will increase rapidly. Indeed, the church should continue to multiply while fulfilling the Great Commission as recorded in the gospels. We are to remain faithful and responsible in witness, teaching and baptizing new men and women added into the family of God. The new members are trained and equipped with the Word of God as the body of Christ grows in mind, spirit and in body; to take ministry leadership positions in an appropriate time, when the older elder brethren advances in age and finally depart from this life.

Serving God with a Purpose

Moses established how Israel would be governed; King Solomon perfected it.

A. The reign of King Solomon (2Chronicles 1:1-9:31)
    1. King David (1Chronicle 28:8-20)
        1. Charges Solomon to be careful to follow the commands of the Lord [8]
        2. Gives Solomon the plans of the temple [11]
        3. Be strong, courageous and work [20]

B. Solomon firmly set his kingdom (1 Kings 1-3:46 and 1 Kings2:25- 46) RSV
Clean house: Benaiah carries out King Solomon's orders.
    1. Killed Adonijah, Solomon's older half-brother [25]
    2. Solomon sends Abiathar (priest) back to Anathoth [26]
    3. Killed Joab for the murder of innocent men [31-34]
    4. Killed Shimei after he fails to obey – Jerusalem [46]

C. Solomon in a dream (1Kings 3:4-5) RSV
    1. I am only a child [7]
    2. I don't know how to carry out my duties [7b]
    3. I am here with your people [8]
    4. I ask for discernment to know right from wrong [9]

D. God rewarded Solomon's wishes and more
1. He gave Solomon wisdom and discernment[12]
2. He gave Solomon wealth and honor[13]
3. He gave Solomon a life no equal with any other king[13b]

E. Solomon established his government
1. Chief priest: Azariah, son of Zadok house of Eli
2. Priests: Zadok and Abiathar
3. Secretaries: Elihoreph and Ahijah, sons of Shisha.
4. Recorder: Jehoshaphat, son of Ahiud
5. Commander in chief: Banaiha, son of Jehoida
6. Twelve Governors:

The names of the **twelve Governors** were symbolic of the twelve tribes of Israel.
1. Ben-Bur
2. Ben-Deker
3. Ben-Hesed
4. Ben-Abinadab – married Tapthath, daughter of King Solomon
5. Baana, son of Ahilud
6. Ben-Geber
7. Ahinadab, son of Iddo
8. Ahimaaz – married Basemath, daughter of King Solomon
9. Baana, son of Hushai
10. Jehoshaphat, son of Paruah
11. Shimei, son of Ela
12. Geber, son of Uri

FIVE:
Challenges in
Africa Leadership
A. Contemporary Governance
B. Early African States

The first four chapters portray the indispensable foundation of Leadership.

The purpose of Chapter Five identifies the origin, culture and tradition of the people of Kenya, as it relates to the effects of governing. A legislator's first responsibility and greatest duty of his life is to know the needs of his constituency well enough to have the ability to serve the people he represents. This is the mark of a leader, one who promotes happiness and the welfare of the citizen.

FIVE: *Challenges in Africa Leadership*

A. Contemporary Governance

Ⅰn earlier chapters we addressed and discussed different branches of leadership: The History of Administration, Managing Our Skills, Types of Leaders, Basic Human Wants and the Biblical Stance on Leadership. This chapter discusses leadership governances in the 21st Century and what it takes to become a servant-leader in our time.

In earlier chapters a leader is defined as one who has vision, mission, and persistence. A leader is one who guides, motivates, encourages and inspires men and women to do things they would not otherwise accomplish without the leader's drive and strength. Understanding this concept is fundamental and KEY to becoming an effective leader. Apparently the success of leading and directing of others is what every leader desires.

Throughout my business career I was called on to wear many different hats. I had diverse responsibilities of buying, selling, marketing, dealing in real estate, motivating and counseling. I often found myself at a crossroads of decision-making for many of my enterprises. When at the crossroads of my leadership, I made a personal policy to apply honesty and integrity. It always served me well. Robert E. Lee was a Commanding General of the Confederate Army, during the War Between the States, modern United States of America. Even though his war was a losing cause, he is highly admired for his character, intelligence, devotion to duty, and his unparalleled leadership ability. When Lee wrote letters to his son during the war, he counseled him that he should always do what is right. It is a prayer that I have prayed for my family, and the men and women around the world in leadership positions, that they might make good decisions.

Lee's strong character went well beyond the battlefield. I believe a leader should practice doing the right thing the first time; the practice will encourage those whom he/she leads to do likewise. When moral policies and procedures are implemented in an organization, honesty and integrity typically are evident within that organization.

Leaders are accountable to their employers, their subordinates, their clients and the communities they serve. Citizens of any nation have the right to speak out, write their complaints if their security is endangered and whenever their civil liberties are violated. A leader should develop the art of listening to employees, his client's complaints and the community at large.

Regardless of the academic preparation a leader may have, additional specialized training and skills may be required to manage certain institutions or organizations. For example, a government worker in state or Federal Government sometimes requires specialized training, knowledge and skills. Leaders in these assignments should constantly monitor their businesses, using unannounced visits to enforce the business laws, ethics, protect the environment, discourage against corruption, and the protection of human rights.

Leadership requires stamina, because many endeavors take place over a period of many months or even years. A leader with unacceptable moral standards and unethical business practices brings about corruption and discrimination at the work place.

Character and integrity should be the cornerstone of a leader's success. James McGregor defines leadership as "leaders acting – as well as caring, inspiring and persuading others to act – for certain shared goals that represent values, the wants and needs, the aspirations and expectations of themselves and the people they represent." ^{Burns}

A servant-leader's first responsibility is to think of the people he leads as the greatest duty of his life. A servant-leader promotes happiness and the welfare of his people. I would also suggest that a leader should be willing to learn from other successful leaders.

Capitalism is defined as social systems that exist in nations of the world that practice capitalism. America is considered one of the best practitioners of the capitalist ideals anywhere in the world. November 4, 2008 American people made an historical mark in the history of the world by electing the first African – American, a man with a Kenya ancestry through his biological father. I have always believed that all tribes of Africa, Americans, Europeans and the Orient are created equal by God, no one single tribe should ever feel more special or superior over another.

With the advent of Africa independence between 1960s and 1980s, Africa experienced hostile leadership changes through military coups! These dictators had landed on leadership by the power of the gun, "might make right." Wealth created by the colonial settlers vanished slowly like a thief in the night, once thriving and flourishing businesses came to a standstill. Quality of goods and services slowly began to die away as native Africa leaders took charge in leadership. A few leaders were exceptional.

Christian leadership in many established churches in Kenya: Presbyterian, Anglican, Methodist, Baptist and The Catholic Church should be commended. The church leadership prepared her young faithful by endowing their leaders to religious institutions of higher learning. This was by far the investment they did in setting up modern Kenya and the rest of Africa where those religious institutions operate. The majority of Kenya's leadership are alumni of the Church supported schools and colleges. In addition, just to mention a few, Para-church organizations: The Southern Baptist, Campus Crusade for Christ, International, The Navigators, and United Bible Societies of Africa had a part in leadership training for the majority of their evangelical church leaders.

Christians and Their Government: The Christian relationship with world governments has never been a particularly happy one. Christians in many places in the world have suffered persecution, torture and imprisonment from various worldly governments. Historically, the church has had to live in a survival mode. Believers have often been victimized by ungodly, worldly regimes, and based on what we see in God's Word, this situation will likely continue until the return of our Lord Jesus.

The church in many modern democracies like those in North America, Europe and some nations in Africa appears to enjoy limited freedoms of speech and worship. While there are no true Christian governments (if you exclude the Vatican), there are Christian leaders who lead some of these worldly governments.

On the other hand, Christians find it very difficult living in nations like the Soviet Union, China, and the Islamic nations of Sudan, Saudi Arabia, and Iran. These are just a few of the countries where believers have no freedom of speech or worship, especially in southern Sudan. In these nations, Christians have been beaten, shot, or slaughtered with machetes like wild animals. In the past, Christians were in relatively safe hands when a ruler of a state would turn to God's love and forgiveness.

In other times Christians have felt they needed to take the law into their own hands and have rebelled against the state. When this happened many were arrested and charged with treason. Those who managed to survive did so by turning to the underground church that hid them away in safe houses. In Romans 13:1-7, Paul saw the government as an **instrument** to be used for the expansion of the heavenly kingdom.

In his day the Roman government maintained order and peace among the smaller and often ruthless kingdoms. Missionaries like Paul were able to travel on mission trips under the protection of Roman rule. Paul himself was a Roman citizen and this was used to his advantage on more than one occasion. From this we can see that Christian leaders would be advised to take **all duties as citizens** of their country seriously.

When Ungodly Rulers Reign: Early one morning in 1885 in Uganda, a nation in East Africa, twenty-four Christian young men came to a tragic and untimely death. They were burned alive for refusing to denounce their faith in Christ and to stop following the teachings of Jesus. Brother Joseph Mukasa, aged 20, was the first Ugandan martyr. He refused the orders of the king to perform "an unusual sexual practice." Their leader was Charles Lwanga.

These men are now commemorated by the Catholic Martyrs Minor Basilica which was built on the site where they were murdered. Eighty-five years later [1970s], similar atrocities and acts of evil took place during the reign of the dictator, Idi Amin. He went on a killing rampage, murdering more than 500,000 men, women and children.

History of a Servant-Leader: The concept of a servant-leader first originated with Jesus Christ. Matthew and Mark provide the full account of a servant-leader. ^{Mark 10:37- 44} James and John were brothers and sons of Salome; in both gospel accounts the brothers indeed asked to be considered for positions in the kingdom of heaven.

Their family connection to Jesus would suggest their appointment would have been more easily considered if Jesus was running an earthly kingdom. Their behavior caused bitterness among the other ten disciples. It was a serious leadership issue, which would have demoralized the disciples. The Master outlined the standard requirements for both the kingdom of the world and the kingdom of heaven. First, the requirement for the kingdom of the world requires personal **power over others.**

Second, the requirement for the kingdom of heaven is about **serving others;** the notion that one's greatness must be reduced to serve others; the principle of an ordinary person. In my early teenage years, I was a member and troop leader of a local Boys Scout chapter. The Scout motto is "always to be prepared" to do my duty to God and my country. The Scout motto taught me first the spirit of service, and second, "to always be prepared" to serve. Service is the crown and jewel of a leader. Mr. Robert K. Greenleaf, (1904-1990) a former executive for AT&T, wrote the following essay titled *"Servant-Leader":*

"Servant-Leader is a servant first. It begins with natural feelings that one wants to serve, to serve first. Then conscious choice brings one to aspire to lead. He/she is sharply different from the person who is a leader first, **perhaps** because of the need to assure an unusual power drive or to acquire material **possessions.** For such it will be a later choice to serve after leadership is established. The leader-first and the servant-first are two extreme types: between them there are shadings and blends that are part of the infinite variety of human nature.

The difference manifests itself in the case taken by the servant-first to make that other people's highest priority needs are being served. The test, and difficulty to administer, is: do those served grow as persons; do they, while being served, become healthier, wiser, freer, more autonomous, more likely themselves to become servants? And, what is the effect on the least privileged in society; will they benefit, or at least, will they not be further deprived?" by Greenleaf.

In earlier chapters we discussed exemplary leaders like Dr. Martin Luther King Jr., who led many civil liberty marches in the United States against government laws that discriminated against an entire group of people – Afro Americans. Not only were their civil rights being violated, but also in many southern states they were treated like slaves with little or no respect and were shown no human dignity.

Dr. King was an individual who believed that violence was not a proper means to achieve peace. History remembers him as a strong leader who founded the Civil Rights Movement in the United States and started the action to get discrimination laws repealed. He was an example of a servant-leader who believed that the goal of a leader was not self fulfillment but service to others. Unfortunately, because of his courageous stand against injustice, he was murdered by a racial zealot.

The Purpose of Government: Governments of the world enact laws to maintain peace among the citizens and to defend against take over by hostile nations. Some governments do not allow their citizens to bear arms. To do so is a violation of the law of the land. The Davidians of Waco, Texas are an example of a religious group who decided to take the law into their own hands. They armed themselves with various weapons, including illegal automatic rifles designed for war, because they felt the government was plotting against them. Unfortunately, they all died in a tragic standoff when they refused to surrender to the authorities, opening fire on the government agents instead. However, in United States of America, citizens have the freedom to bear arms. Conversely, some weapons, such as assault weapons, are banned. Those are the kinds of weapons the Davidians had. Government authorities wanted to inspect their compound to make sure they had no illegal weapons. They did not intend to remove legal weapons. Charles Kingsley wrote, "The noblest of all forms of government is self-government, but it is the most difficult."

Christian author and pastor, John MacArthur, once said, "I know personally people who refuse to pay their taxes because they believe that their freedoms are being violated. The truth is the United States was born out of a violation of Romans 13:1-7 in the name of Christian freedom. That doesn't mean God won't overrule such violations and bring about good, which He did in this case, but that the end doesn't justify the means." When leaders fail to uphold Christian standards of morality in government and business, corruption often becomes the rule of the day. (MacArthur)

Most third world governments have become cash cows for the politicians, government officials and law enforcement personnel of those countries. Bribery and extortion are the common rule in these countries. In industrialized nations like the United States, they are not typically so blatant. Instead, they use unethical business practices to stuff their pockets. An example of this is the Enron Corporation.

Top leaders of this company misused their position to buy and sell company stock. They became very rich through unscrupulous financial moves. When the financial market fell, practically all workers in Enron lost everything they had in savings and retirement funds, but not the company leaders. They had timed it to sell their holdings before the fall, leaving themselves rich and the regular workers penniless. Even though these leaders were eventually found guilty and imprisoned for their actions, the workers were still left out in the cold. The money was gone and could not be recovered.

Since the departure of colonial masters, the leadership in many third world nations has deteriorated. Through poor management and shoddy leadership these nations have depleted three quarters of their natural resources. In many developing countries family members who have no training for the assignment fill leadership positions.

These nations typically suffer a leadership crisis. A high level of competence and training is required to be effective in these roles and family members usually do not possess such attributes. C. S. Lewis was right when he said, "The human soul lives forever while worldly governments are only temporal." Leaders should use all their available skills and abilities to bring honor and high moral standards to positions of leadership.

In North America some church leaders are deeply involved with politics to the point of labeling individuals by what political party they belong to. Many Christian sponsored groups support full time lobbyists in both state and federal political arenas. Those who lobby for Christians are serving in a critically important position. However, some church leaders go overboard and support political parties.

The need of good leadership extends well beyond administration buildings, government capitols, and places of worship. Leadership is both a calling and a vocation. For example, men and women who serve as teachers, high level officials, community leaders, and pastors rarely get properly compensated for their efforts.

Therefore, it is a calling – a calling for these leaders to do something that will bring about good for the people or communities they serve. But even though they may not receive proper compensation, many of these do receive wages so the work they do is also a vocation. Certainly anyone who has children knows how difficult a job it is to be the leader in the home. Since there is no monetary compensation for this effort, this is definitely a calling. Indeed, parents must show strong leadership in bringing up their children to be good citizens in both the world community and in God's church.

Jesus showed leadership skills even at the age of twelve when He "led" the teachers of the law to a better understanding of the scriptures. Surely in the latter years of His life, He was a dynamic leader and one admired by all except those who felt threatened by His teachings of love and forgiveness. He called twelve men to be His closest disciples. He taught them, trained them, and equipped them.

These men of twelve shared His goals and mission and eventually were responsible for the on-going message of the gospel of the Good News to the whole world. Since we live in a materialistic world we can benefit from the disciples' example. They were not paid for their leadership services.

Instead, they accepted whatever the people gave them – sometimes food, sometimes shelter, sometimes a little money. Corporate directors of today can be compared to the twelve disciples. From their position of leadership, these modern managers make policies in boardrooms around the globe. Their decisions affect millions of consumers, much like the spreading of the gospel has affected millions around the world in the spiritual arena.

What matters is not how much money one is paid as the chairman of a world-renowned corporation like General Motors or IBM. Nor does it matter how much power one has as the head of a local, state or national government. What matters is who he is and how he uses his leadership position as an opportunity for serving others within his area of influence. That is the basis of true servant-leadership.

I have faith in the Christian precepts taught in the Bible, precepts like the doctrine of original sin. This has taught me to expect man to fail, because it is his fleshly nature to do so. However, I also believe that the more man remains in the Word of God, the more he overcomes his fleshly nature and becomes an imitator of Christ. The end result is he can better execute his duties as a servant-leader. God is obviously the greatest Leader of all, and Jesus proved that to us in the way He lived His life and led others to faith in God. This is our highest calling as leaders – to follow their example.

The Freedom of Speech: In 1995, in a far away country of Nigeria, Ken Sacro-Wiwa was silenced forever by the Nigerian Leadership, when he exposed conspiracy corruption between a military led government and a multinational corporation that was scrounging public-community resources and plundering the environment for self enrichment. There are many reoccurring Sacro-Wiwa cases in several government leaderships of Africa. When voices like Ken are silenced, others just arise with time.

The continent, caught up in military coups, dictatorships, civil wars, ethnic cleansing and genocide of the 1970s and 1980s cannot be erased in the hearts and minds of Africans. But there is hope for good leadership in Africa. Once in despair, there is now a replacement of anticipation in good Leadership.

For the most part, in recent years African governments have kept their promise on timely general elections with an average degree of free and fair elections compared to the decades of the 1960s through the 1990s. Egypt allows a multiparty system of presidential elections compared to Zimbabwe where laws restrain freedom of speech in assembly and by association. All our eyes are on South Africa, considered by many to be the world's best democratic government. Yes, the purpose of a democratic government is the provision of the freedom of speech.

Workforce: Government has responsibility to allocate financial aid to small scale farmers, to raise poultry and produce. By doing so the government should promote interested farmers to grow seasonal cash crops such as oranges, mangoes and flowers for export to the daily markets of Europe and the Middle East. Because three quarters of landmass in Kenya and the rest of Africa are dominated by an agrarian lifestyle, this can be one of the best ways to promote employment for the nations of Africa.

On a larger scale, governments of Africa are held responsible to open lines of communications to the industries and manufactures located in the governments of the north who are in dire need for cheap labor. Customer services in these nations continue to be outsourced to many nations of the world where English is spoken as a second language. With the invention of internet technology, every opportunity should be explored to provide jobs. Entrepreneurs, investors and inventors residing in every nation of the world should be encouraged through Embassies for the consultation on trade opportunities.

In South Africa, miners take three to four elevators traveling down to middle earth. On the way down, geothermal heat measures up to 130 degrees Fahrenheit; miners are forced to impel chilled water to the walls of the interior earth to lessen the temperature. One would only hope that the tunnel remains intact! Well, many such similar tunnels have collapsed in years past. According to UN International Labor Organization, about 20 million workers are immigrants to South Africa. A miner in a South Africa goldmine averages $7,300 per annum, more wages than most countries of Africa can offer.

Christians on Politics and Governance: There is no doubt there are brethrens in Christian services around the world who have used the name of Christ to further their earthly lifestyle in the expense of mission boards and the church at large. The Philippians church had men whose lives were open to scandals; their daily lives were not in accordance to the teachings of the Gospel. They were gluttons, self centered and immoral. Paul considered them as enemies of the cross. And so, in today's church there are men and women (TV evangelists) who use the pulpit simply as a source of income, who have distorted the truth and violated the principles of Christian ethics.

The following are (3) three reasons among many why Christians must be involved in social issues, politics and governance. First, Christians have the privilege of a dual citizenship in heaven and on earth. It is the duty of Christians to obey laws and pay taxes to the government under jurisdiction of where they live and work. In North America everyone is required by the law to pay taxes by April 15th every year. One of the best things I like about paying taxes are the incentives a tax payer gets depending on the tax bracket one may be in.

There is a system for every tax payer to get a tax refund, whether a tax shelter for the wealthy or a child deduction for lower incomes. It is my Christian joy and duty, first to tithe and then to pay taxes to the institutions. These are some of the reasons why Christians should be involved in political institutions that form world governments, which in turn shape our ideological beliefs here on earth. The only way a Christian can work within the frame work of a political system is to influence laws before they are passed to protect the environment, and social issues that affect our society. (Philippians 3:17-21, Romans 13:1-7, Matthew 13:33, 22:15-22, I Timothy 2:1-4)

Second, Christians must use talents and specific gifts given by God as outlined in Paul's letter to the Corinthian church. It was my privilege to have gotten involved in Kenya general elections of December 27, 2007 regardless of the outcome of the election.

In a democratic election process, I put my talents and God given resources on the table for men and women of my constituency to have an opportunity to elect a Christian for Kenya national parliament. As a talented, multi-trained in secular business and Christian services, I gave democracy a chance, knowing that God is sovereign over all nations. He is the only one that bequeaths power over kings and rulers. The church is responsible for the needs of the poor, orphans, elderly and social services needed within the geographical area of the community. (Acts 2:45; 4:34, Daniel 4:17, Proverb 21:1)

Third, Christians are the salt of the earth and the light of the world. The message is clear where by Christians should be vigilant in the support of spiritual and social issues of the community. During my tour in Kenya I noticed that Christians were under attack, especially those living in poor rural Kenya, where government programs are the major source for basic living, like water, food and shelter.(Matthew 5:13-16) Whereby the Christians should have helped, but lacked the finances, Islam stepped in and helped the needy communities. It was flat out a missed opportunity. The following list was compiled from attending many leadership seminars and from my experiences over the course of many years.

Attributes of a Successful Leader

---

1. Initiates action and has the drive to make things happen.

2. Persuades others to use all available resources to achieve the desired results.

3. Develops trust with those he leads.

4. Communicates with those in positions of political power; helps sway those involved to enact laws that positively affect the people.

5. Has keen political insights and applies skills that result in building trust and lasting relationships with those in power.

6. Accepts moral responsibilities; his integrity and character are obvious to all.

7. Handles multiple projects concurrently and brings them to completion successfully.

8. Thinks logically and makes sound decisions.

9. Has excellent managerial and organizational skills.

10. Leadership requires moral responsibility.

Discussion and Understanding of Leadership; shaped by the following Philosophers.

The Great Philosophers of Our Time: This section provides additional reading material of the six great western philosophers who influenced and shaped human thought and reason. **Plato's** method of thinking is based on deductive reasoning. In his writings he idealizes the reality of *intuition* of a higher power when he portrays God as a Supreme Good, a God who is responsible for His action for producing the order and beauty found in the world. However, there is no evidence to suggest that Plato himself ever identified God as the creator of the universe creating something out of nothing. [Plato 426-346 B.C.]

Aristotle, a disciple of Plato, further identified both inductive and deductive methods of thinking. He used science as the basis of logic to examine the world. Aristotle argued that there is a bridge between knowing and developing one's own life, the notion that science and logic produce the end result. [384-322 B.C.] Unlike his master - teacher Plato, God was the Supreme Intelligence, the source of clarity and order in an eternally existing universe. Aristotle distinguished between two principles in the order of essence: a principle of truth and a principle of potentiality.

Saint Augustine, [396-430] the Bishop of Hippo introduced the Christian theology and ethics that have influenced our institutions until today. He argued on the separation of state and church. Influenced by the time of his day he believed on a just war in the life of a man. The Crusaders war and Jihad are examples of man's just wars. In modern societies nations go to war against each other to protest their best interest. In Saint Augustine's writings, "Confession and the City of God" he believed that a person could not acquire virtue without the grace of God.

Saint Thomas of Aquinas [1224-1274] combined the philosophies of Aristotle and Saint Augustine at the time when theologians were confronted by the development of science and technology. The world was in a changing state of adding technology to the agrarian society. He developed four (4) kinds of laws intended to shape moral ethics of a person. The laws are: Eternal law, Natural law, Human law and the Divine law. These laws deserve another chapter because they were not intended to be discussed in length.

David Hume [1711-1776] refused the validity of knowledge; he argued its origin is impossible to be comprehended. Instead, Hume offered his own theory of knowledge saying that one can derive moral sense from its usefulness. This is the notion, "if it feels good, do it." His philosophy was widely practiced and still is up to today. The system of thought is widely accepted by many people whether it is morally right or wrong.

Immanuel Kant [1724-1804] lived in the zenith of the world of the enlightenment. In his essays (Critique of Pure Reason) he argues, "Objective reality conforms to the structure of knowing mind," the idea that experience counts in the life of a person. Therefore, reason becomes the final authority for morality. Ω

B. Early African States
AFRICA

The Age of Exploration: The Classic Africa, seen through the eyes of early Traders and Explorers during the Age of Exploration. Herodotus, a Greek historian was the first to write about Africa in 500 B.C. He believed that beyond the Sahara there were human beings. Like his predecessor, Ptolemy, a Greek astronomer, attempted to unfold the mysteries of Africa by printed representation drawings of the geography of North Africa in the second century. Ptolemy school of thought on Africa dominated Europeans scholars and aristocracy about the unsolved mysteries of Africa beyond the Sahara. Nine centuries later, in the 11th Century Ibn Battuta an Arab historian writing for Arab Sultans travelled the interior of West Africa. Unable to unlock the mysteries of the Sahara, Battuta retraced his journey through North Africa to the shores of the city states of Dar es Salaam and Mombasa, on the Indian Ocean, East Africa. It was not until 15th Century Portuguese seamen discovered the tip of Southern Africa by sailing around the Cape of Good Hope headed northeastwards; they docked on the island of Mombasa in 1498. However, the Chinese and the Phoenicians traders had been on the Indian Ocean much earlier, limited to the East African Coast.

A reference is given to China military Leader, Cheng Ho, whose death in 1430s marked the end of China's mapping, maritime, and the trading post on the Coast of the Indian Ocean. Therefore, the long voyage by the Portuguese seamen had finally ended some of the century old mysteries of Africa. The seamen had connected the dots. Now available, a complete outlined map of Africa was sold on the streets of London. Nevertheless, there were the ultimate, unanswered mystery questions dating back to the Egyptian dynasties, the Greek aristocrats, and Arab Sultans for the search of the origin and the source of the Nile River.

A century later in 1600s, Europeans, mainly the British Empire, discovered interior Africa through missionaries, traders and explorers of the day. They mapped the interior with the sketches of native Africans; their trails became the borders of the tribal territories, which would become the modern countries of Africa.

The earliest Africa maps date 1562. However, there are three Africa maps without dates or authors. Perhaps a group of traders may have died in route to the interior Africa during the Age of Exploration. Deaths were common during this Age. The earliest mention of Africa is by a British poet, Jonathan Swift, who sites "Geographers in Afric-maps, with Savage-Pictures fill their gaps; And o'er unhabitable downs Place Elephants for want of towns." ON POETRY: A RHAPSODY, Dublin 1733. By late in 1800s, Africa was fully mapped out by the Royal Zoological Society, England. Africa maps became available to the travelers masses of the day. Classic Africa maps are available in the libraries of New York Public Library and the British Library.

Africa is seen by the Islamic leadership of the Middle East, a continent as the last frontier, as Alaska was to the United States. Rich with oil nations of the North Africa, West Africa and Southern West Africa, rich with uranium, gold and untapped natural resources, a potential bread basket of fresh produce to the frigid climates of Europe---it should be futuristic economic muscle that is yet to be tapped.

There has been a growing sentiment with urgency to have a United States of Africa, similar to European Community and United States of America. The idea is not new, but in recent years, there has been a great urgency of the creation of African states far more than ever before. Why? It is for the purpose to counteract American capitalism and her ideological influence to the African continent. During the last meeting of the heads of states, February 3, 2009 in Addis Ababa, Africa heads of states, elected Colonel Muammar Gaddafi of Libya, the new chairman of the organization of African states. Some heads of states signed on, but failed short of 33 out of 53 heads of states, from those who failed to attend. Perhaps, unavailable, to shy away from unwanted consensus. The Colonel, Gaddafi, was not too happy.

Africa with her diverse ideological differences, poses a threat to the nations of the west especially with the emerging Islamic influence, over the poor-weak leadership crisis in governments of developing young democracies in Africa. The reasons listed above pose a threat to Third World War of Terrorism. I believe the United Africa will come; if it does, there will be an ideological war, fought by the minds and hearts of the majority of African leaders, from the state capitals of Africa. It is a view that should be re-examined by the nations of the north. The last mystery of the Continent is WHICH, HOW, WHEN she LEARNS to govern her depleting natural resources. What ideology will govern her for the remainder of the 21st Century?

Africa saw the rise of the military coups as stated in the pages to come. The founders and framers of the African Federation of Africa like: Mwalimu Julius Nyerere, the first president of

Tanzania, Jomo Kenyatta, Kenya, Kaunda of Zambia and Nkuruma of Ghana lose their sanguinity. The rest of the Africa states remained in the colonial quarters until late 1990s. Third, Africa was not ripe for The Union of African Federation of Governments because she was struggling with: Illiteracy, Economy, Poverty, Tribal differences and the balance of power in governance.

Early History and Mysteries of Africa: There are some places where it is very difficult to travel in this world. One of them is the African Sahara located off the south coast of the Mediterranean Sea. The African Sahara is the world's largest hot desert, where temperatures swing from cool nights to hot days that often reach 100 degrees Fahrenheit and more. Africa is 20 percent of the world's total landmass, the second largest landmass on earth covering 11,700,000 square miles. The United States of America can fit inside Africa three times, excluding all the islands and Madagascar. In the ancient days African people typically moved without borders, (except for climate and terrain constraints) until the arrival of the colonizers in the late 1800s.

In 1885 Europeans divided the continent for easy rule and conquest. Germany left the Africa continent soon after the defeat by the British Empire during the Second World War. The African land is the birthplace of many species, the sustainer of their life, and the cradle of early human civilization. The people of Africa never stayed in one place; their trails transverse the land for centuries. Modern Africa has 2,058 languages, one third of the world's languages are spoken in Africa by more than 800 tribes, and a population of over 900 million,* 14 percent of the world of people living in 54 independent democratic nations. Africa's annual rate of growth in most urban areas is very staggering at

3.5 per year.

In 1970s, Kenya's population was at about 15 million people; by 2000 the population overwhelmingly doubled to 38 million plus. About 71-81 percent of Africa's population is under 25 years old. Why the young generation? The majority of African life expectancy averages between 38-55 years old. Sudan has the largest landmass within the Sahara, while the nation of Seychelles Island, located in the deep tropics of Africa, is the smallest in size. Africa has 54 nations; about less than half* of the total nations are considered democratic governments. [*Note: figures are subject to change.]

The Arabs traders were among the first foreigners to settle on Northern African soil, followed by the Portuguese, British, Belgian, French, and Germans. The traders brought religion, new languages, farm seedlings and European culture to Africa. Concerning the Sahara, Ibn Buttuta, Arab Muslim scholar wrote, "All who are overtaken by it perish, and I was told that when a man has fallen a victim to this wind and his friends attempt to wash his body [for burial] all his limbs fall apart. All along the road there are graves of persons who have succumbed there to this wind." But the Sahara has not always been like this. Africa was once covered with green forests, rivers, and wildlife common to those environments.

Scientists believe that during the ice age the Sahara began to waft southward. Rivers dried out leaving behind sand dunes, almost wiping out every living thing. But not quite - the Egyptian dynasties were left behind, perhaps as a living reminder of the beauty of the Sahara after the ice age. Through the centuries the Sahara has continued to move south, claiming one hundred miles of territory a year. The Sahara, once green belt lands, turned barren, pushing the Africa man southward as it advanced. For the sake of identity **Leadership** will refer to the man as the Africa man. The Dark Continent does not refer to the color of the people – it is the sighting of the unknown knowledge of the African people themselves and of their land.

There are two major historians who wrote about Africa. Herodotus, a classical Greek scholar, wrote for the Greek autocracies who were interested in what lay beyond the Sahara. Whatever knowledge he possessed about the African interior came from what he learned from the trading merchants of Cyrene and Carthage. Herodotus never visited the African cities he wrote about. However, he did travel to Egypt, southward to the cities of Elephatine and Moroe, just below the first Cataracts in the land of Automoli.

The second major African writer was Ibn Battuta (1333), a Muslim medieval historian, who traveled in great length recording the Arab Sultan dynasties of West Africa [interior] and the East African coast. During his travels along the Niger River, Battuta encountered one of the fiercest African animals – indeed, one of the fiercest animals on the earth. He asked his companion Abu Baker, "What kind of animals are these?" Abu replied, "They are hippopotami which have come out to pasture ashore." "Hippopotami are bulkier than horses, have manes and tails, and their heads are like horses' heads, but their feet like elephants' feet." Battuta had seen these hippopotami when he sailed down the Nile [Niger] from Tumbuktu to Gawgaw. They were swimming in the water and lifting their heads and spewing out water.

Battuta later sailed to the East African coast where he wrote,

"We stayed in Mogadishu three days, food being brought to us." After three days he sailed to the south spending one night in Mombasa, and then continued south to the city of Kilwa. It is here he found the majority of people called Zanj, which literally means black in color. They had tattoos on their foreheads. From the experience of travels in West Africa, Battuta restricted the majority of his journey to the African shoreline of the Indian Ocean.

And so, interior Africa, separated by the Sahara on the north, and strange and fierce wildlife on the East, isolated itself from foreign historians and scholars like Herodotus, Battuta and others. Part of the reason it was difficult to transverse the Sahara, was that during Herodotus' time, camels had not yet been recognized as a prime means of desert transportation. Even though the Greek historians were unable to unfold the mysteries of the Sahara, Herodotus was convinced that beyond the Sahara there were peoples to be found and native cultures to explore. The Africa man was not known until the writings of Herodotus, who made reference to the Africa man before 500 B.C. The Africa man was forced to move in various directions within the continent, in response to the changing tides of the Sahara.

In recent decades (science) paleontology and pre-history have discovered a series of artifacts whose data should not be ignored by the schools of science and theology. Paleoanthropologist identified some of the fossil species of the origin of the Africa man. The purpose of study *"Zinjanthhropus"* is the earliest known tool-making man on earth. [L.S.B. Leakey]

(1) **Mastodon -** large extinct shaggy mammal, (Mastodon is not a man – it's an elephant like animal)

(2) **Cro-Magnon** - early modern man

(3) **Paleo-Indian man** - earliest North American inhabitants from Asia by the Bering Land bridge through Alaska from Siberia

(4) **Neanderthal man** - Extinct human race believed to live in many parts of Europe, North Africa and western Asia during the early Stone Age

(5) **Mayan man** - occupied Central America, developed math, religion, writing, and built monumental architectures

(6) **Incas man** - occupied South America between 12-16th Centuries, particularly the Andean region in Peru

(7) **Phoenician man** - lived east of the Mediterranean Sea along the coastal lands of modern Lebanon, originally Syria. The language is now extinct

(8) **Autralopithepecine man** - A prehistory man found in the caves of Olduvai Gorge in East Africa

(9) **Zinjanthropus man** - found in the same Olduvai Gorge in the mid 1959 is the earliest known man with the ability to make tools

Homo sapiens: The study of human origin will continue to haunt the contemporary human beings, because we are living in a time of scientific discovery and a stage of knowing. Born in a rural village when doctors were considered a luxury; the majority of people in tropical Africa were born in the dark-hidden jungles and the open plains.

When they died they were buried back to the earth resting with their long gone ancestors. They had no time to worry about their origin apart from the stories passed on to them by the previous generation gone before them. I once asked my mother including other distant relatives, where she and her ancestors originated, she pointed to some direction and said, "That place," with a sense of direction and affirmation.

In early 1970s I toured Muumandu Hill. The hill served as a hiding place for the Akamba during many tribal wars with Maasai warriors. The hill has numerous caves with human and domestic animal foot prints suggesting that humans once lived and worshipped in a few select hallowed places. Many of the foot prints found in caves and on sedimentary rocks around the hill, have since disappeared with time due to poor ecological preservation with exception of one remaining ancestral worship *[Ithembo]* ground in Kavete.

There are many such hills around Machakos County which served the Akamba tribe in similar manner. I have never claimed credit to the discovery of the footprints until the writing of ***Leadership***. It is possible there are many analogous places with human and animal footprints in many tropical hills throughout East Africa.

Three quarters of a century ago a biologist, Ernst Mayr, took a shot at the field of paleoanthropologist. Like the majority of others have done, he studied the Peking man, Java man, and Homo erectus and the Neanderthal man. Mayr came to a conclusion that the field of the study of the origin of man has been crowded with limited studies and perhaps more studies should be devoted to the subject matter before any conclusion is drawn from a few scientific samples. For more than a century, the Leakey team is convinced that the origin of fossil Apes-like man lay beneath the heath in East Africa.

In many occasions when contacting interviews for **Leadership**, I got frustrated with my elderly relatives because their long family ancestral history ended to dead ends, due to lack of record keeping. No matter who and where I interviewed their stories mixed with legends were linked together for accuracy. Therefore, the human fossils collected in many parts of Africa are subject to change due to climate variations over the centuries. Not all African tribes buried their dead. The Maasai lay to rest their corpse by tying it onto a tree at night in hope that a wild animal, like a hyena would feed on the cadaver said one Maasai elder.

The Akamba tribe buried their dead about six feet below earth, unlike the Maasai counterpart. The Akamba carcasses were not buried in caves or left over night in fear that a corpse may be reclaimed by a witch doctor for the purpose of healing medicine. There are other African tribes who buried their corpse in ways that we have yet known, because there are cases of the carnivores tribes.

What happened after that, no one really knows. It is possible that other carnivorous animals could destroy the remains which would have been evidence in some millions of years past. I agree with Lieberman, a paleoanthropologist at the University of California who states, "People who look for fossils focus on the places with the highest potential." In this case the majority of fossils of human remains seem to be found on the African continent.

The Leakey team is not alone in the search's race for the origin of the fossil-species of humans. Nowadays, theory of evolution of mankind is back again on scientific debating tables. The intelligent design has occupied the schools of thought and reason among many theologians and the scientific fields around the world. The intelligent design has once more stirred another controversy, surrounding the origin of mankind. Scientific breakthrough is warming up the agnostics who will attempt to contrive the human brain with the subject matter.

The controversy over the origin of man has simply been debated since the dawn of the civilization. Who should man believe? The oral tradition passed on by the African elder to the incoming young generations? The **Lakota Hehlokecha Najin,** chief of the Oglala Sioux, native Indians, was receiving a sacred pipe with instructions from the holy **wakan** woman, she gave two instructions, One: "With this pipe during the winters to come, send your voices to **Wakan Tanka,** your Father and Grandfather. Second "With this sacred pipe you will walk upon the Earth; for the Earth is your Grandmother and Mother...?" The **Branhma-Nirguna,** Hindu, follower who considers the Great Spirit as the creator, preserver, and the destroyer of life? Or the archeological digs from century old caves?

Walking on Sacred Grounds of the Native American Indians comprise of many large and small tribes spreading across North America Continent. Like the tribes of Africa, Native American Indians left behind rich histories of culture, tradition and art printed in caves and rocks across United States. *Kiva* is a Comanche Indian word for a meeting place, such as the Pipestone

National Monument sacred grounds located in southwestern state of Minnesota. The Native American Indians handed down oral histories from father to son until the last remains, of a full blooded native Indian, across the North American territories. Their languages were not written. Thanks to the Federal Government for preserving the epic histories of the classic Native American Indian tribes. Similar to the many tribes of Africa oral communication was used as a means to pass down traditions and culture to the next incoming generation.

Pipestone sacred grounds were preserved as a National Monument in mid 1930s. Pipestone is considered by many early American settlers and historians as a sacred ground for the Oglala and Lakota Sioux Indians. There are numerous published records by historians of mid 1800s indicating that Pipestone of southwestern Minnesota was indeed a sacred ground to native Lakota Sioux Indians of the Plains.

The winter of 1948, after the end of WWII Joseph Epes Brown of Connecticut spent cold winter months with Black Elk, one of the last surviving Sioux Indian chiefs of his day. Black Elk, to his credit was a world traveler; he had travelled and took with him Indian dancers to dance before the kings of France and England. All of these years, he refused to be interviewed by white American settlers. But, knowing that his life would soon come to an end, Black Elk allowed to be interviewed by Mr. Brown of Connecticut who captured the attention of the great Sioux Indian Chief in person.

Mr. Brown's interview provides us with the last oral histories, traditions, culture and the last will and testament, about the epic story of the last classic Sioux Native American Indians.

Pipestone County is the home of the sacred grounds of Lakota, and Oglala Sioux Indians and other Indian clans of the Plains. It is here, that the great red pipe of the great Lakota Sioux Indians was made. The sacred grounds provided the Sioux Indians with a unique red stone buried beneath the earth which they used to make a sacred pipe. Legend has that both oral history of the white settlers and native Indians considered the red stone to be the blood of the fallen warriors, perhaps due to the many Indian wars fought between ancient Indian clans and after the arrival of early white settlers.

Walking around the sacred grounds of Pipestone National Monument is like being at the hallowed *[Ithembo]* grounds of the Akamba tribe and among such places found in the many tribes of East Africa. It carries a deep meaning and reverence to the people with African descent, because the native Indian worshiped ancestral spirits similar to the ancient natives of Africa, they too, worshiped ancestral spirits. Native Sioux Indians worshiped the Great Spirit and gave sacrifices to their ancestors similar to the tribes of Africa.

I witnessed one of the few remaining Native Indians, whom I found digging and chiseling the soft red rock that was once used by the American Indian clans of the old to make a pipe. The pipe was a sacred smoking Indian instrument used by ancient Native Indians in ceremonies of all kinds such as making peace agreements between clans.

There was a large quantity supply of unique red stone buried just beneath the top soil; one walks on the century old grayish rock withered due to hot sun rays of the ages that has toughened the surface rock firmer than the layers below. The immediate hard rock has no commercial value, except it provides the landscape beauty and sculpture of the grounds.

The grounds had beautiful scattered springs of water, which provide life support to the millions of flowers and plants of all types blanketing the sacred grounds suggesting the existence of human life. The Pipestone National Monument spread for more than 10 square miles in the Pipestone area, whose town and the county bears the name Pipestone.

Before I left Pipestone, one of my host families, Calvin Farmer gifted me a pipe similar to the century old Lakota Sioux Indian smoking pipe. Modern pipes are sold commercially within the city limits.

Far away in the Great Rift Valley of East Africa, a similar stone, grayish white in color is mined in large supply by the area tribes to make delicate carvings, gift items and tribal motif for commercial use. The Bantu tribes of this particular region used the stone for their traditional and ritual purposes for decades. During one of the many tours to East Africa, I was gifted with a large platter-bowl inscribed with words *Millennium Development Goals*. Each carving uniquely created by a different people, from different stone, from different culture, tradition and purpose, are now part of my home library.

Pipestone, Minnesota had something special compared to all other native Indian reservations, that I had earlier visited in the great southwest states of New Mexico, Oklahoma and my home state of Texas. It was quiet and peaceful with some resemblance of other tribal sacred grounds found in many parts of East Africa. Less than a quarter of a mile away stood a replica of an 1800 white settler fort built of stained cypress wood pickets. Only this time, the fort was a modern shopping mall for the purpose of selling Native American Indian motif gifts of pipestone mined within the area.

One traveling without a guide may miss an important sight within a given area. Pipestone was one of those sights. My host family was of Anglo American decent, whose family traces back to the Pilgrims of 1630s. Like most white settlers of the day, Howard Jerome Farmer made a parallel move westward from upstate New York, Canton, St. Lawrence County, in search for a better family home until he settled in Pipestone territory in 1883 when the city of Pipestone was just five years old.

Representative Howard Jerome and Kathryn Farmer are the parents of William Perley Farmer. William married Lois Lamon and bore eight children. Son, Calvin, and his three siblings, the surviving daughters of the legendary Mr. William Perley Farmer were kind enough to take me in and around the sacred Sioux Indian grounds. Honorable Howard Jerome Farmer, Pipestonian legislator and Representative of the Southwest District, State of Minnesota; used his leadership influence to have a Bill in Washington to establish the Pipestone National Monument.

It was an awakening experience to walk in the sacred path of the ancient great Sioux Indian homestead and to encounter what were the hallowed grounds that I had read about studying different Native American Indians during my years of grad schools in Texas. The Farmer daughters took me into the Pipestone County Museum where I found old antiques, donated over the years by individual families, including an antique left handed plow and a pump organ bought by selling eggs to Chicago, that were donated by Mr. Farmer and his wife Lois long before he died. Pump organs were still in use in churches and dance halls as late as 1970s, going back to early American life. Plows of this kind, pulled by oxen, are still in use in many parts of rural Africa.

I travelled westward for about five miles to the old family house, still in good repair, surrounded by nothing but farm land and a few scattered cows here and there. Upon approaching the old homestead, I noticed a two story wooden house that had majestically withstood the changes of time through the frigid winds of Minnesota's winters, surrounded with old antique Model A cars of the 1930s. Calvin said, "My father drove this Model A out of the factory in 1928." Lila said, "I used to climb this tree, and that one" pointing at the homestead tree, fresh and tall; I wondered if she could give it a try.

Still caught up in the pigment of the Model As and other cars of the early 1950s - 1970s, I decided it was about time to ask the young man, a grandchild of Mr. Farmer, the fate and future of the cars that lay frozen back in time around the farmhouse without an attendant. Yes, there were a good number of useable autos, no fewer than 50 hid around the bushy farmland. Very quickly, I tried to get a deal for one of the Model As of 1930s which appeared in good repair, and perhaps, with a couple thousand dollars, one could still put it on the road for a weekend drive. Unfortunately, the surviving Farmer sons would not dare sell, for fear of wrath of an elder; they had no choice but see the antique cars waste into decay in the old farm rather than to liquidate some of the useable autos.

Disappointed of the waste, I moved on to my next point of interest to an old frame single room school house, carefully preserved by the Pipestone County Museum. The building was purchased for one dollar, donated and moved from the original site located one mile across the open prairie from the Farmer homestead where the Model As were left frozen back in time, to town by Mr. Farmer in the early 1970s.

When Pipestone town grew, the independent school district was properly established for the community and eliminated the rural one room school houses. This single room school house still had its original desks and antique school items of the day. Mrs. Lois Bruns is the oldest of the eight Farmer children, named after her mother, Lois Farmer. Lois confirmed that all her siblings attended the single room school house as had her father and all five of his siblings, even being taught by one of his sisters. Lila, still remembers the community party line, "229J3 please," she had memorized in case of an emergency. It was such a nostalgic experience to witness the excitement displayed on the faces of the Farmer children. According to my custom, I shot a photograph as each struggled to fit into an old oak desk they once sat in during the golden days of boys and girls.

My last person to interview was one of the few remaining Santee Sioux Tribe of Native Indians permitted to chisel the soft red rock from the [state protected] sacred grounds in Pipestone. He confirmed that Pipestone was and will always be a sacred ground to the descendants of Native Lakota Sioux Indians. "It is here where ancestors worshipped and rituals were offered," said the Sioux Indian. No other persons are allowed to mine the red rock unless they are of the bloodline of the Native Indians. In keeping with the traditions and culture of the American Native Indians, the Feds will always keep the mining open to the last full blooded line of the American descendants, and then revert the sacred grounds back to the gods and spirits of the ancient Lakota Sioux Indians.

In centuries past Africa was considered a dark continent, incomplete in all fields of study; until the arrival of explorers, traders, and missionaries from the nations of the north who claimed to themselves the discoveries of rivers, lakes and mountains. Separately, Herodotus, a Greek historian who wrote 500 Before Christ believed that beyond the sand dunes laid human life. Africa's discovery of some of the most important fossils in the human history has suddenly put to rest the theory of the Dark Continent; it is rather interesting that Africa has become a haven of study of the human civilization known to man.

For Africa, the Stone Age was a period of climatic changes and a movement of Africa races in reference to Bantu, Nilotic and Cushitic in search for food, and safety until the tribes began to settle in a string of villages on hills and valleys away from the attacks of enemies. These changes appear to be connected with a wider range of tools found in early pre-history among African tribes. The grindstone was used for the preparation of dried millet, corn-maize and wild seeds for food by many tribes across Africa. The making of: spears, clubs, bows *[a weapon used to fire arrows, consisting of a curved flexible piece of wood and a taut string fastened to the two ends]* and arrows for hunting and self protection. A number of these tools are still used by some of the native Africans.

According to Dr. David Begun, Professor, Anthropologist, at The University of Toronto, Canada, traces the evolution of Homo sapiens fossils of humans and apes going back to 300,000 years ago. The following is the summary of his recent research on Homo sapiens. The main reason for his study on Homo sapiens was to understand the leading causes of the origin of Apes-like man and man fossils species found in East Africa. He argued that Apes-like man is closely related to human beings. The oldest ape fossils study dates 16-20 million years old before the modern Apes-like man.

About 17 million years ago, Africa was once connected with Eurasia and vice visa, before the opening of the modern Suez Canal in Egypt to the east of the Mediterranean world. It is possible, that Apes-like man crossed the narrow land between the continents to Europe and Asia. Dr. Begun suggests there were the Apes-like man ancestors from Africa in Eurasia. After the big explosion took place 16.5 million years later, fossils Apes-like man were dispersed to modern Turkey, Germany and Slovakia.

Because of the natural explosion, it was unlikely that Apes and human ancestry would be found in Eurasia that resembles Apes-like man and humans of tropical Africa. Another possible theory, the Apes fossils branched out before the blast to other European destinations, Spain and China. The third possible theory, some fossils Apes-like man spread into various branches in Eurasia and some fossils Apes-like man returned and remained in the African continent.

Dr. Begun refuses the argument stating that temperatures noted in southern Eurasia were registered as subtropical. The climate that would easily support fossils Apes-like man originated from tropical Africa. Therefore, the fossils Apes-like man greatly multiplied in large numbers at around 8 - 10 million years ago, Eurasia climate changed from tropical to cold climates around the Alps, and the Himalayas, causing yearly monsoon winds between East African coast and Indian peninsular.

Unable to locate sufficient food, some fossils Apes-like man died out, while some managed to return back to Africa through the same path they left. It is possible the short distance between North Africa and Eurasia, identifies the existence of the earliest Neanderthals located in the caves of Subalyuk, estimated 50,000 years ago; and the earliest anatomical human species estimated about 200,000 years old is believed to come from Africa.

There is not adequate scientific evidence to suggest what took place during the separation of fossils Homo erectus turning into Neanderthals man and the remains of the Homo erectus man in Asia during the millions of years since fossils Apes-like man left the tropical Africa. There are some who argue that fossil Homo sapiens of Africa returned to the continental Europe, exterminated the original fossils, the Neanderthals man, by propagating into the current man found all over the world. That theory is subject for another debate.

It is self edifying; with fulfillment as appropriate, to know that every time a new species evolved, it came out of Africa. Nevertheless, the author of **Leadership** does not prescribe to the theory. Africa has always had its own plants, animals, and humans who wandered endlessly in and around the continent with its share of harsh climate through the ages.

The scientific theories of the origin of human fossils bare different and individual interpretation. Various research methods contain a combination of the said fossils arguments drawing similarities in some fossils research. For those who continue to follow the discovery of the human fossils; for some the theory remains the difference between theoretical interpretations and the validity of the origin fossil research.

There is a wide gap of disagreement within the paleoanthropologist, sociologists and others within the schools of social sciences, with respect to multi-regionalism which often portrays as a racist theory that tends to claim a different human "race" that evolved with discrete superior intelligent design compared to some "race" [people of color] sometimes referred to by the pigment of their skin.

East Africa is one place with a lot of fossils of Apes-like man. The studies of the human origins deserve much more research before paleoanthropologists can jump to a scientific conclusion, at least not yet. The author of **Leadership** believes that the origin of the Africa man is really a theological inquiry – that is, that the origin of the Africa man can be found in the pages of the Bible. Besides, the man does not require a scientific proof of his origin.

The tropical climate of Africa played as an haven of century old human species and exotic wild life placed there by the creator in thick mountain forests, rivers, lakes, hills and the open plains of Africa, both for the current living things, fossils of human species, fauna and flora to share the beauty and the grandeur of the continent.

The Pygmies, Bushmen of the Kahari Desert and the Maasai tribe of East Africa have lived side by side with wildlife since the dawn of time. In sharp contrast, the human race has in the past exterminated the American Indian Buffalo during the great American expansion to the America West; this left American Buffalos extinct in the wild.

Conversely, there is not sufficient data to suggest the Africa man is a result of scientific evolutionary discovery. Historians and anthropologists have never agreed on the origin of the Africa man. The origin of Bantu, Nilotic and Cushitic are discussed in length under the definition of community tribe. The present day people of the continent are called Africans, a people who have wandered for centuries in Africa's harsh climate, usually without enough food, mingling with wildlife, and fighting many tribal wars for survival until they were colonized. The typical Africa person speaks several languages and has multiple sets of moral values, traditions, and cultures.

The colonial administrators grouped African tribes in the areas in which they lived. About three quarters of all Africans live on a ranchett (shamba) in rural villages and towns where they grow crops and raise livestock for their daily living. These lands are their ancestral heritage. When they die they are buried in these lands alongside their ancestors. For example, one of the customs of the Maasai people is to bless the grasslands on which they feed their herd by saying, "stay uninhabited." They believe God gave them cows to be the rightful land owners.

Bill Clinton, a Challenge to African Leadership: The New York Summit of 2000 opened a new chapter in the history of the nations of Africa. About 66 percent of the population of Africa is dependent on agriculture: Corn, Tea, Coffee, and other daily staple food. "Africa accounts for around 60-70 percent of the world poor, in spite of the fact that Africa represents about 10 percent of the world's population." (The Heritage Foundation 2009)

The average income for the majority of nations lives on less than $1.00 per day. Due to the increasing child mortality and the HIV/AIDS factor, in many parts of Africa the average life expectancy is 46 percent in sub-Sahara Africa. With these facts on Africa, Secretary Salim of the Organization of Africa Unity said in his opening remarks, "Africa lacks a strong constituency in the United States."

Bill Clinton, president of the United States at the time responded, "Africa **does** matter to the United States. Globalization is tearing down barriers between nations and people of the 21st Century." The former president further stated, "When it comes to Africa, America must choose to make a difference by being involved."

In Africa, about 38* governments out of the 54 governments are heavily indebted poor countries as classified by IMF-World Bank. Bill Clinton, saw it fit to bail out poor countries, but first, a plan had to be agreed upon and implemented by the leaders of the third world nations, then debt forgiveness by the rich nations of the north would follow. Since Clinton left office, he has continued to help third world countries and other parts of the world with program initiatives to better the world leadership and her economies. Former President Clinton outlined five steps that the United States must take to be involved:

1. Build an open world trading system, which will benefit Africa. The Congress of the United States must enact the bipartisan Africa Growth and Opportunity Act.

2. Provide debt relief to African nations who are committed to sound economic, democratic and humanistic policies. Struggling democratic governments should not have to choose between feeding and educating their children or paying interest on their debt.

3. Give better and stronger support to African education. Literacy for all Africa is crucial.

4. Fight the terrible diseases of Africa, especially AIDS but also tuberculosis and malaria. AIDS has become epidemic and will soon double the child mortality rate and reduce life expectancy by 20 years. In Africa there are companies that are hiring two employees for every job with the assumption that one of them will die. We need to support efforts that help prevent people from getting the HIV virus in the first place.

5. Build on the **leadership of Africans** to end the bloody conflicts of killing people, which also kills progress. Tens of thousands of young lives have been lost in the war between Ethiopia and Eritrea, the war in Sierra Leone, the famine and war in the Sudan, and, worst of all, the war in the Congo. In the Congo wars there are at least seven nations and countless armed groups pitted against each other.

One of the major goals of *Leadership* is to build on the (5) five mentioned steps on the framework of **Africa Leadership**. Africa states face a challenge to free her from the bondage of poverty, disease, water shortage, and depleting natural resources. Long-standing impediment—poor infrastructures, unreliable energy resources, political instability, corruption, lack of honesty and integrity in governance of Leadership has continued to prevent the establishment of rural electrification in every village of Africa. The political - Leadership dysfunction in most governments of Africa continue to create a large number of displaced people. In Kenya alone on December 27, 2007 over 1, 500 were killed and 350,000 people were politically displaced.

In Zimbabwe, almost all professional men and women have fled out of the country due to lack of democratic government. Diseases and cholera have become a way of easy death. In recent years, Africa is now able to connect itself with the outside world through cell phones. To date about 70% Africa is subscribed and connected to a cell phone. Merchants in rural areas are now capable to order their goods and services for a delivery from wholesaler companies located in long distances; compared to two decades ago, when it was hard to report a crime, or sickness located in rural hospitals.

Now that technology is widely being practiced in the majority of the third world, the basic needs for the majority of Africans will improve with time. Much of African wildlife have become endangered and are at great risk from drought and are losing their habitats due to deforestation. Game wardens can call in for additional help when threatened by an enemy or animal poachers.

Millennium Development Goals in Africa is a responsibility of each nation to implement Millennium Development Goals, (MDGs) in their annual fiscal budgets. Persons in leadership positions of these nations must be committed to prioritize in their national five years planning budgets to establish committees and action teams to work toward achieving the MDGs outlined below

   1. Eliminate extreme poverty and hunger

   2. Achieve universal primary and secondary education

3. Promote gender equality and the empowerment of women

4. Improve the child survival rate (lower the child mortality rate)

5. Reduce the maternal mortality rate by 75%

6. Combat HIV/AIDS, malaria and other diseases

7. Ensure environmental sustainability (primarily replanting trees)

8. Develop global partnerships for development

Leadership will not elaborate in detail on each of the MDGs goals. Elsewhere in pages to follow MDGs are addressed in detail by the African Religious Leaders and Bishops. It is encouraging that the leadership in Kenya created a department, Vision 2015/2030, to address the nation's long overdue development, which also promotes the achievement of the target MDGs. The Department is the country's blue print covering the years 2008-2030. The goal of Vision 2030 is to create an industrialized nation in the region, with middle class citizens who will compete successfully in the Global market space.

The next seven years are very critical to the governments of the third World including Kenya because at that time, the pledged "New York 2000" made by the governments of the north will reach its final mark to achieve the MDGs. However, Kenya has shown great promise in the establishment of Vision 2030 sanctioned within the country's Ministry of Planning. Austrian government cancelled Kenya debt October 2008.

The Global Call to Action against Poverty is in partnership with the UN Millennium Campaign. Various stakeholders include financial institutions and multi-international companies doing business in every third world countries will ensure that the MDGs are addressed, especially in protection of the environment and Global warming.

The Future of African Wildlife: The African wildlife is an industry whose income is a major source to many African governments. However, African wildlife is at risk of being wiped out unless strong measures are put in place to provide for accessible water to the animals and unless the illegal hunting and poaching is eliminated. *Leadership* acknowledges the great work of the governments of the north and many non-governmental institutions who spend millions of dollars and provide extensive manpower to provide protection for these majestic creatures.

When the author thinks back on his past, African animals often come to the forefront of his mind. Athi River plains once like a paradise for both human beings and wildlife that lived together in harmony, shared the environment. Zebra, giraffe, wildebeest, hyena, antelope, and lions roamed the open African range. It was impossible to take a stroll after dark, as one might never be seen again, becoming the meal for a hungry lion or some other African beast.

Forty years later I returned to the location of my nostalgic fishing expeditions, once a wildlife paradise. I was disappointed with disappearance of the wildlife species, because Athi River had doubled in population, had new small industries, and the additional Portland cement factory blew everywhere fine gray waste limestone powder twenty-four hours, seven days a week.

Humans who had taken over the riverbanks for domestic irrigation, interfered with the ecology of the river banks vegetation, fish, birds and crocodiles that once ruled in these waters died. Fortunately, the river does not dry up; because it originates about twenty kilometers from the Ngong Hill, flowing southward through the Nairobi National Park to the coastal region of Kenya. Elsewhere *Leadership* briefly discusses the author's fishing experiences.

Africa: in 2004 Michael Fay with a companion flew a Cessna 182 plane at less than one kilometer above the ground. The low-flying plane was equipped with digital cameras, shooting pictures every 20 seconds and capturing 100,000 high-resolution digital images of wildlife, communities and the African terrain. The Wildlife Conservation Society financed the project jointly with the National Geographic Society based in the USA. Africa Flight 182 lasted seven months and covered 60,000 miles (100,000 kilometers) from South to North Africa, photographing the Africa landmass and monitoring human activities relating to the wildlife and agricultural land use.

Africa Flight 182 revealed many new discoveries about African wildlife and people. Fay and his team found there are places on the African continent suffering by the exploitation of the ecosystems. For example, in Niger thousands of people are starving to death. In Tanzania thousands of hippos were seen huddled in shrinking pools of mud (once rivers), facing death due to draught. By contrast, in the large regions of Africa thousands of antelope still room free and millions of people live in stability on carefully nurtured soil and are implementing good land usage.

Good government policies are bringing the return of environmental stability. Fay stated, "In Zambia a great congregation of animals is one of the best indicators of a well-functioning ecosystem." African governments must not fail to address the conflicts of animals and humans in areas where human population is overstepping wildlife borders. For example, in the Nairobi National Park animals are at risk, because humans are taking over the northern and southern gates of the Kenya National Wildlife Park.

The departments of Industry and Wildlife must work together in the best interest of the wildlife and humans. The government should not allow industries to trespass the natural wildlife pasture land by allowing industry manufactures to pollute the northern-southern gates of the national park through dangerous chemical waste. It is an effort that will take concentrated collaboration of the citizens and government. The laws of the land must be enforced to protect the animal kingdom in sub-Sahara Africa. Fay says that some African leaders have figured out what they need to save their environment for the future of both humans and animals.

The Fall and the Rise of African Leadership: Africa ruled herself through tribal elders and Kingdoms. The scramble for Africa by the Europeans came with new schools of thought and governing: Democracy, Communism and Socialism ideologies were introduced to various parts of Africa. The new forms of governments were viewed by many Africans as foreign ideologies. The democratic dogma has its challenges with mixed feelings between modern government and former tribal leaders.

In recent decades, tribal intermarriages have broken down the tribal customs and cultural barriers of the past. Part of the transformation was due to the changing tides of modern society. The fall of African kingdoms brought about by colonial imperialism was a precursor to the end of the old ways of tribal leadership. The slave trade routes came in and out of Africa; they changed the course of Africa leadership forever. Millions of Africa tribes were uprooted from their ancestral lands by the colonial masters. They moved the tribes to new homeland reserves; others were sold around the world as slaves. Colonialism aided in the vast depletion of Africa's natural resources and disrupted old African forms of government. Walter Rodney was right, "The only thing that developed during the colonial period was the dependency and underdevelopment." The decades of 1957 – 1990s will be remembered as the fall of colonialism and the rise of African self-government through military coups and democratic forms of governments. It was an era when Africa regained and established leadership back from the colonials, who left brusquely due to constitutional pressures exerted by African leaders.

The African leaders were not trained how to manage and apply democratic principles necessary to run a government inclusive to all tribes. The tribe that was in the front lines of deposing the colonial government became automatically the tribe in charge in the country's leadership. Other tribes seeking a piece of the country's leadership did not welcome the new leadership arrangement. For example, in Kenya, the Kikuyu tribe through the Mau Mau uprising is widely claimed to be the tribe responsible for Kenya's Independence.

When a tribe rose to leadership, and failed to include other tribes in national leadership, often military intervention ignited from within, spread like a grassfire to other African nations. The military interventions became the only means to unseat civilian-ruled governments for most of the decades of the 1960s – 1990s. Then, in speedy succession, there were the governments in West Africa region: Nigeria (1966, twice in less than six months), Upper Volta (1966), Ghana (1966), Togo (1976), Sierra Leon (1967), Mali (1968) and Liberia (1968).

Central Africa was: Congo (1965), Central African Republic (1966), and Congo Brazzaville (1968). North Africa was Sudan (1958). East Africa big lakes were: Uganda, Rwanda, Burundi, Ethiopia, Eretria and Somalia. It appears that Kenya and Tanzania were the only East African nations that survived military coup d'état. However, there were attempts, a failed military coup in 1982 in Kenya and one military mutiny in the early days of Julius Nyerere of Tanzania. The rise of African leadership was the beginning of a new era of Africa leadership. Politicians powered financially by their former masters, Communist and Democratic government ideologies of the north, entered into international debt-perks to run the new regimes. The debts were incurred in order to continue to supply political war machines with money, some for domestic factories to manufacture goods for exports, and some of raw materials to governments of the north in exchange for imports to run their economy. In other words, African government leadership could not function without foreign expertise; the debt ratio grew, with the GNP surpassing per capita income. Why? What happened, the African governments received a blank "Visa Card" and billed their country's future debts which surpassed countries' GNP.

There was no consideration of fiscal restraint. Political leaders were in for the "Now Syndrome" never minding their future generation. In the meantime, African leaders were also receiving ideological carrots from: Communism, Socialism and Democratic nations of the north to lure them from their Elder/African Ideological leadership belief of governing to democratic elected governments.

The colonizers partnered with the African state governments, exploited their market share, and ransacked cash crops for loans payable in the future. The new African leaders were not experienced in balancing government expenditures with foreign democratic ideals. And so, when the cold war ended, it was a relief for the majority of African nations who had endured dictatorship rule under pressure from superpowers of the north. The World Bank officials said, "Africa was no longer an ideological strategic battleground." There is a new awakening in Africa leadership as there is a movement towards a multiparty system fueled by the democratic governments of the north.

The formation of the coalition government may become a new method of power-sharing to appease tribal leaders within African nations, leading to a "Can do" spirit of working cooperatively as leaders of one large African community. The majorities of the sub-Sahara governments are experiencing an increase of freedom of the press and even hold fair elections on a limited basis. The executive branch of government is realizing the challenge of democracy. When the legislative, judicial, and executive branches become independent functions of the government, African leadership will see a new day in Leadership. That is the goal of democracy in Africa.

The Troubled British Empire: King George V, grandfather of the current Queen of England, died in 1936. The next King in succession was his son, Edward VIII who abdicated his throne to his younger brother, George VI in December, 1936. The monarch had suffered a long time illness and leadership changes within a short time. Some changes were due to natural circumstances of sudden deaths and marriage outside the monarch tradition and custom. King George VI never dreamed he would be a King until his brother abdicated the throne to him. He is the father of Her Majesty Queen Elizabeth, of England.

And so, the decades of the thirties, forties and fifties were the great awakening for many nations in the world. The British Empire was crumbling at the height of the Great Depression. America's stock market crashed causing Black Monday in 1929. The British Empire leadership was at risk with her colonies. The years of 1946-1960s were the most difficult times in the history of the British Empire, especially in Africa. King George VI and British Prime Minister Churchill were under enormous pressure facing an enemy who lay across the English Channel, Adolf Hitler of Germany. Under these conditions it is obvious that British East Africa Colonial rule would remain in Kenya for the next 33 years. The purpose of colonies was to produce farm goods and raw materials to be sent to industries of Europe to produce finished products. The colonies were very important because they were a source of military man power, food supply and cheap labor. King George VI fell sick and died in 1952. The King's daughter, Princess Elizabeth was on vacation in Kenya. King George VI's death was a turning point for the British Empire's new Queen, Elizabeth and her colonies.

The Great British Empire continued to falter and crumble but not completely. The Empire had suffered more than 1,200 of indisputable organized uprisings, turmoil, mutinies, riots and guerrilla wars in the majority of her colonies — Kenya was not an exception. The Colonial office in Downing Street, London, could no longer contain the uprisings from the colonies. The empire had to give up control over the colonies, but continued to provide leadership and economic assistance. One wonders in amazement how such a great empire located on a little island achieved world dominance and leadership for hundreds of years. That is **leadership!**

Chapter Six observes select Presidents in East Africa, the founders of their country's political birth and their demarcating political ideologies that shaped the East African nations as seen today. In the heyday of the 1960s, the world was in disarray. I remember like it was yesterday when my friends and I boarded a morning train to Nairobi. The evening of December 12, 1963 was an historic day in the history of the peoples of Kenya; it was a birth of a new nation.

People everywhere, were full of excitement; fireworks covered the dark blue night skies, and spontaneously the British Union Jack was lowered down from the mast and the Kenya flag was raised up to its new home. In stark contrast, far away across the Atlantic Ocean, Americans were still mourning the death of President Kennedy, who was gunned down in Dallas, Texas while in office. The American Civil Rights movement was in its zenith, and America was at war in Vietnam.

Thus, African leaders through political pressure groups forced the British Colonial office in London to withdraw and surrender her colonies to the original rightful owners — the natives. For the most part, leaders in East Africa were direct negotiators of independence in their respectful countries. For example, in Kenya, young emerging political leaders extracted from several tribes, organized themselves into political parties and pressurized the British Colonial Administrators to pull out of Kenya.

The second historic moment of my life, I was in Dallas, my adopted city and state of Texas, when the American people elected the first African-American President and the leader of the free world. That was democracy at its best, the way it was meant to be.

The British Impact on World Borders: The African map of 1874 that was drawn by Henry Stanley whilst in search for David Livingstone had no national borders. Natives lived a nomadic lifestyle, and wandered freely with their domestic animals in search for food, water and grassland for their animals and a better life. For thousands of years they drifted without borders.

There are many reasons why it is difficult to pin down an exact place of the origin for the majority of African people. Anthropologists and sociologists confirm the movement of African tribes in clusters, groups based on language; with exception of the North Africa, along the river banks of the Nile River. There is an argument to be made, to some degree there are advantages and disadvantages of settlement and a nomadic lifestyle between the people of the Nile River and the sub-Sahara natives, each group worshiping God in their own ways.

British Colonial Administrators were the responsible surveyors for the mapping of modern Africa and the nations thereof. Because of the vast difference of the tribal distinctions in many parts of Africa, and especially the cultural and language barriers between tribes; the British Administrators found it easier to administrate each individual tribe within their sub grouping.

They provided administration by working with each tribal elder independently.

North Africa and Middle East: Far away from Africa and elsewhere the mapping territorial borders have caused wars between the nations. In recent decades, Iraq, under the leadership of the late President Sadam Hussein fought the first Kuwait war when he reclaimed Kuwait. The wars between the borders will always be fought in the Middle East.

The worship ground *[Ithembo]* mentioned in **Leadership** is contiguous to SCL facility in Muumandu Hill.

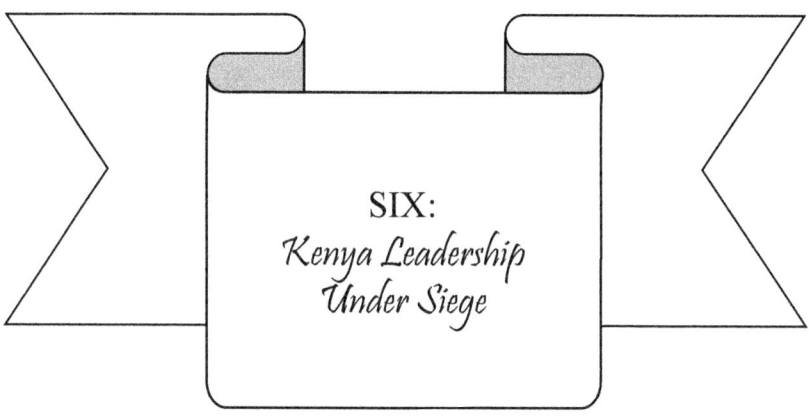

SIX:
*Kenya Leadership
Under Siege*

The first four chapters portray the indispensable foundation of Leadership. The purpose of Chapter Six is to show how the failed principles of democracy and leadership led to *the genesis of decades of the dark side of Leadership in Kenya.*

SIX: *Kenya Leadership Under Siege*

Discovering Kenya

What about the name Kenya? Caution, the name Kenyatta should never be confused with the name Kenya. The origin of the word Kenya is derived from two tribes: Kikuyu and Akamba tribes. The following story illustrates how the name Kenya came into being. From the journals of Dr. Johann Ludwig Krapf, the name Kenya has its origin from Akamba word "kiima ki-nyaa," for what is modernly known as Mt. Kenya. Dr. Krapf, while on a visit in rural Kitui sighted a snow-capped mountain without a western name. Asking for its name, the tracker, Chief Kivoi told him from his Akamba name and pronunciation as "kiima ki-nyaa." "Nyaa" is Akamba word for ostrich and "Kiima" is Akamba word for mountain. When the two words are pronounced together it translates as the "mountain of the ostrich" possibly named for its resemblance to its white long ended plumage of the bird ostrich.

Therefore, Dr. Krapf, reading lips of the translator and pronouncer wrote the word "ki-**nyaa**" which gave the present retranslation from a European evangelist corruption of the word "kenia" to the word Ke**nya**. Looking at the word Ki-nyaa, Dr. Krapf left out NYA, from the Akamba word "**Nya**a" and logged the corrupt word "kenia." Dr. Krapf pronounced the word Ki as Ke to write the word "kenia." Later, the name was corrected to reflect the original Akamba word "ki-nyaa" to the modern word Kenya. Kirinyaga is a Kikuyu word that translates to mean "that which has spots." The dwellers of the mountain call the mountain as "kirinyaga" because of the white spots (snow) seen on top. Consequently, their god is called "Mwenenyaga" translated as "the owner of the white spots as sitting on top of the mountain." Up to this day many of the mountaineer worshippers return to secret and hollowed places in the mountain in certain years for periodical worship to the god as Supreme Being. The mountain has its huge significance to the dwellers of the mountain and to those who associate with the term of covenants and other traditional interactions.

The Kenya tribes did not know the difference between "ki-nyaa" for ostrich, and "nyaga" for the white spots, the word is embedded in Kikuyu/Akamba languages. Even today the term "nyaga" reference to white spots is used by neither modern Kikuyu speakers nor the word "Nyaa" by Akamba. Other dwellers of the mountain beside the Kikuyu are: Embu, Meru, Tharaka and other sub-tribes Abere, could not properly pronounce the word Kirinyaga as per the Kikuyu, the owners of the word. In 1498 Portuguese traders and explorers arrived on the shores of Mombasa, East African coast. Little was known by western traders. A new discovery was added to the book of world knowledge. It was a turning point of Africa's mystery, a new era of discovery had commenced.

Three and a half centuries later, Dr. Krapf, a European missionary, driven from his Mission to the Gallas of Abyssinia, was commissioned to East Africa to determine if there was a "door" open for the introduction of Christianity. He found, as he imagined, such a place at Mombasa. There accordingly, he established himself, the Apostle of Christianity in East Africa, and the pioneer of the interior geographical exploration. (Charles Ndudas)

Thereafter, Krapf started for Akamba territory. His ambition was to open up a new region for the influence of Christianity. He traveled on regular established ivory trade routes for about 200 miles interior north, accompanied by a number of Swahili servants-load carriers and an Arab guide as a translator. Shortly after mid day December 3, 1849 Dr. Krapf and his company arrived at Maviani hill in Yatta plateau. There he was welcomed by Akamba leader, Kivoi, a man with power to levy taxes from the surrounding Akamba clans and foreigners who entered his territory.

Dr. Krapf wrote in his journal as having met Chief Kivoi. Naturally, such a man was recognized as a war chief by his clan due to frequent tribal wars. **Leadership** will refer such a man with influence, authority and ability to lead as Chief Kivoi. He was a leader who in turn may have ruled like the dictatorship of the ancient city and states of Rome. Akamba history never had an aristocracy, they never seemed to have developed permanent leaders or chiefs to guide their vass* Akamba tribe. Instead the tribe remained with the leadership of elders *'Atumia'* autonomous of each different clan within the Akamba tribe. The elders have continued to manage and guide the state of affairs up till today.

Dr. Krapf's report of his discovery of a snow-capped mountain which he had named Mt. Kenia was met with skepticism and outright ridicule by western scholars of the day. In those days, journals with drawings of sketches of animals, contours, and people written by explorers and missionaries were treated as affidavit and source of evidence by the sponsoring Mission Boards and the Royal Geographical Society.

On Dr. Krapf's second visit to Maviani hill in 1850, Chief Kivoi volunteered to guide Dr. Krapf travelling east-northward headed towards Mount Kenya. On the way the Dr. Krapf's caravan was attacked by the notorious Tharaka tribe who occasionally exchanged raids with the Akamba tribe. Unfortunately, Chief Kivoi, the Akamba war leader was killed in action. Dr. Krapf escaped for safety; he abandoned his journey to Mount Kenya and retreated back to his base camp in Mombasa. Dr. Krapf never returned to Kivoi's territory.

By 1920 the word "Kenya" had been widely used by the majority of natives, settlers, hunters, missionaries and the British East African Protectorate administrators. Therefore, the new colony was renamed the British East Africa Kenya Colony, the forerunner to the word Kenya for the Republic of Kenya. The British East Africa Colonial divided eight administrative provinces by slicing the country of Kenya like Zebra stripes from the Indian Ocean to southern Sudan. The geographical land mass distribution in East Africa worked out well in East Africa, but did not work out for the rest of Africa. The tribes and the clan issues of Kenya will linger in the minds of men and women for a few generations, although, during the last thirty years the young people of different tribes are breaking the old-tribal-cultural barriers through marriage, education and worship.

The meeting of Krapf and Chief Kivoi descendants surfaced for the first time in recorded history in a rural Presbyterian Church of Worthington town in southwestern part of the state of Minnesota. Dr. Johann Ludwig Krapf's epic story had seemed to disappear in the history journals of Africa. It was not until summer of 2008 while traveling on a speaking tour in the area towns, when a family friend and member of the Westminster Presbyterian Church of Worthington introduced me to Rev. Jim Krapf, her pastor. Since it was an election year in USA, we briefly exchanged a few words about the current political candidates of the day.

Several months later, Lila, a staffer with SHC, was a key note speaker at a women's Fall Gathering, at the same church with the same pastor, Rev. Jim Krapf. During the process of conversation with Rev. Jim, he confirmed his German heritage and his last name Krapf as a direct descendant of Dr. Ludwig Krapf, the first white man to report seeing a snow-covered peak near the equator, Mount Kenya.

One hundred and fifty-nine years later, separated by culture, being of a sound mind, a pastor, a missionary and Akamba by tribe, I realized that Jim and I had connected the dots of history with direct family linkage as descendants of the first Akamba chief Kivoi and Jim's great, great-grand Uncle, Dr. Krapf.

It was an experience of excitement and fulfillment, to know that our ancestors were part of the history of Kenya and my Akamba tribe. It had to be God's providence and timing for nothing happens without a reason. King Solomon wrote, "For everything there is a season and a time for every matter under heaven:" Ecclesiastes 3:1

Tribal cultural differences will eventually close the gap. Fifty years ago, it was taboo to marry from another tribe. Due to the changing socioeconomic tides in modern Kenyans; young people are seen going together for a date or to watch a Friday - Saturday weekend movie. Thirty plus years ago, when my wife and I got married, most of my friends were somehow sorry for us, we married from different tribes and different nations. In our time most people thought we were bizarre to fissure an old-cultural taboo. The good news, we have prevailed the cultural tides of change.

Religious teachings were an integral part of the mission process to close out traditional gaps. Christian worship spread Judeo-Christian teachings. Tribes began to accept and appreciate each other.

The sacred text of Judeo-Christianity teaches that all people are created equal; the notion that people of all colors and race regardless of the country of origin, people can work and live together as human beings. Cross-cultural barriers that have existed between African tribes against one another are now being held together by socioeconomic and political linkage; Christianity is by far the principal common denominator holding tribes together by the common beliefs and values the Bible teaches. This is happening in Kenya and in all parts of the western world.

Governing Kenya: Kenya is a nation located on the eastern shores of East Africa; most famous for wildlife safaris, Mount Kilimanjaro, Lake Victoria and as a holiday haven in Mombasa for Europeans. Hollywood picture makers, Safari hunters, poets, and the fabulous National Geographic Documentaries all lead to one common name, Safari. It is a splendid, gorgeous, dazzling and beautiful county where the old and new cultures are separated only by a few miles from the city limits. Just on the outskirts of Nairobi city limits, you are in Nairobi National Park with its majestic wild life, and century's old native cultures of the distant past.

The magnificent cities of Nairobi, Mombasa and Kisumu are located on a 600 miles stretch between the Kenya coastal region, and the lake basin region inside the Great Rift Valley that ends in Palestine. Over the years, Kenya, Tanzania and the rest of Africa have had award winning pictures: *Out of Africa,* filmed outside the city of Nairobi, *Return to Africa,* the *African Queen*, filmed in Tanganyika and others; not to mention the fabulous documentaries by National Geographical Society on the endangered animal species of Africa.

I was two months shy of thirteen years old on December 12, 1963 when Kenya became a Self Rule. The following year, December 12, 1964 Kenya became a Republic, under the leadership of Jomo Kenyatta. The event of December 12, 1963 marked a new beginning of my story from being a British subject to a new nation of Kenya. I was a young man filled with hope, new identity and optimism of a new nation. Later, in my adult life, I am saddened of the political climate of Kenya which has been mired with corruption, deceit, and tainted by a few selfish political bigwigs.

The city of **Nairobi** was built in 1889, as a base camp for **Kenya-Uganda Railway,** and is today the nation's financial district, government center and capital city of Kenya. The word Nairobi is taken from the Maasai word **Nyrobi** for "cool waters," located 5,500 feet above the sea level and 80 miles south of the Equator. Nairobi was built for 200,000 people, to date the city houses over 3 million people, using the same infrastructure! Kibera slum located within the inner-city of Nairobi, houses three quarters of a million people the largest slum in the world. There are other similar slums in other Kenya urban cities. Driven by natural catastrophes, hunger, squalor and open sewers, makes it difficult for a day's meal.

The Climate ranges from a cool 48 to high 90 degrees Fahrenheit, with heavy rains for the months of November to April. There are cool nights but no winters like in North America. It is an ideal climate for the European-American holiday makers escaping the frigid climates of Europe and the USA. Coffee, Tea, Flowers and Tourism are Kenya's foreign exchange earners. Tourism averages over one million visitors a year. But like most developing nations of the third world, Kenya struggles with high rates of poverty, diseases, infertility, and mortality.

Kenya has over forty-two tribes; each with their own language, customary law and culture. However, they are united by two official trade languages in scripted in the Kenya Constitution: Swahili and English. Swahili is a lingua franca language uniting the nations of: Tanzania, Uganda, Kenya and the lake region comprising of Rwanda, Burundi and northern Congo.

In recent decades Kiswahili has become the choice of other border states for the purpose of trade. East Africa is an important region; to the governments of the north, and is Key in Americans' foreign policy to fight the wars on terror, drug trafficking and the renewed century's old sea pirates on the Indian Ocean.

Kenya's Economic Muscle is larger than Uganda, Tanzania, Rwanda, and Burundi combined. 2007 was an important juncture in the history of the region Rwanda and Burundi were accepted to the East African Community to boost their economy. For example, a citizen from either nation can buy one auto insurance policy called (Comesa) for traveling within the five member states.

For the first time in recent years (from 2002-2009) Kenya was operating at 97% of her total GNP, borrowing 3%. Kenya government's own statistics indicate that during the years 2002-2007 there was a significant decrease in the nation's poverty level from 56% to 46%, a sharp contrast to the nation's high level of poverty in previous years dating back to Kenya's Independence in 1963; the poverty level had skyrocketed from 20% to 56%.

However, there are issues that must be addressed: the **unbearable** health conditions in post Kenya era under twenty-four years of Moi administration; the decline of national ethics, the nation's infrastructure and corruption orchestrated by elected members of the nation's Parliament in partnership with government administrators. The government is responsible to protect and guide the good will of the people.

Despite the progress noted in the previous section, Kenya faces serious challenges in the commitment to achieve Millennium Development Goals (MDGs) before the year 2015. Millions of Kenyans cannot access clean drinking water, basic food and shelter, a major element of the MDGs. In Kenya 1.5 million children are predicted to die of starvation during the year 2009 - due to the failed rains of 2008. In addition, the displacement of more than 650,000 in Rift Valley whose majority of IDP were farmers are without food and shelter.

UN statistics estimate that every 20 seconds a child dies in a third world country due to poor sanitary conditions and unsafe drinking water. Unsafe drinking water claims more than 1.5 million children per year. The UN report says 443 million children miss school every day because of illness related to sanitation and unsafe drinking water. In addition to the UN report, a report issued by the World Health Organization/UNICEF Joint Monitoring Program for Water Supply and Sanitation, indicates that 62% of people in developing nations of Africa have no access to basic sanitation. UN's WHO/UNICEF report (2006)

To improve unsafe drinking water and sanitation are two of the major goals targeted for countries like Kenya. July 7, 2007 was the halfway mark for achieving the MDGs. In Kenya organized NGOs under the leadership of **Evangelical Alliance of Kenya,** Bishops and religious leaders marched in the streets of Nairobi and other cities of Kenya, and made an outcry from a national stadium in Nairobi to the politicians and government of Hon. President, Mwai Kibaki to honor and put in place policy instruments to achieve MDGs by 2015.

I was one of a few registered political candidates; I participated and distributed tens of thousands of government MDGs in print to more than 60,000 voters in rural Machakos Town Constituency, for the months ahead of the Kenya general elections of December 27, 2007. My campaign team and I discovered that millions of printed MDGs materials were stored by the Ministry of National Planning without a clear method of distribution lines to the citizens.

During my campaign, at my own expense and time I volunteered and distributed MDGs booklets to the citizens, since then, I have remained committed to this cause. The MDGs must be achieved by 2015 and beyond. The words of the former U.S. President Kennedy, 'ask not what your country can do for you - ask what you can do for your country' revived my mission to help my countrymen. The political leaders in Kenya continue to worry about stuffing their pockets with the country's economic boom without minding the rest of the 80% of unemployed and starving people.

During the writing of **Leadership** coinciding with the World Water Day, U.N. Secretary General, Ki-moon, reminded the world that, "We are nowhere near on pace to achieve that goal." Madam Secretary of the U.S. State Department, Hillary Clinton, from her farewell speech to the U.S. Senate colleagues, referred to U.S. Africa policy with special emphasis on the horn of Africa. She said there are fragments of Islamic militants' movement that American foreign policy to Africa must be worried about and of the causes of the Africa MDGs. Madam Secretary was in line philosophically, a belief that Kenya has the potential to reach her MDGs given her economic growth and leadership stay on course. **Leadership** calls the leaders of the nations of the north to reaffirm their commitment to programs of global water solutions and other aspects of the MDGs past 2015 and beyond.

What Went Wrong? Historically, Kenya's general elections are a defining period for the nation's development agenda. Months before voting day, political machines succumbs the electorates with political pledges. Some pledges are usually campaign tactics for reasons to be elected in a public office. That is usually normal anywhere in other African democracies. The political-will created by the need to garner votes is transmitted into action before and after the general elections. In 2007 major public roads were built, civil service personnel salaries were increased, free high school education was pledged, and old state-operated corporations were revived to stimulate the economy and every perceivable agenda before the elections. The country experiences short term economic recovery. What was budgeted by the government to be fulfilled in the (5) five year term is usually left to be completed during the election year.

The Collapse of a One State Party: KANU in 1992 ushered in a group of small individual parties, but failed in 1997 to defeat the classic ruling KANU Party machine under the leadership of the former Presidents Kenyatta and Moi. Again in 2002 small political parties had learned their lesson. They joined together and defeated the classic KANU political machine. Party leaders Mwai Kibaki, Raila Odinga and others formed the first single coalition of parties called NARC and won the Kenya general elections of December 2002.

The long awaited change in Kenya political leadership had finally arrived. Kenya had been ruled under one single party since 1963. The lost hope and optimism I once held in Kenya politics appeared that I could cast a renewed hope and optimism in Kenya's political system. In less than 3 years of NARC leadership, internal wrangling between members within the coalition surfaced. Opposition wanted a new constitution which led to a referendum in 2005. It attempted to change the entire constitution of Kenya. But the change was rejected by the majority votes.

That was the beginning of the bitter opposition movement called Orange Democratic Movement. President Kibaki fired all the opposition ministers from the NARC government. According to the Kenya Constitution, no president can actually fire a member of parliament, except a member found in contempt of criminal charges against the law of the land. The opposition leaders remained in parliament for the life of August House known as the 9th Parliament. The gap widened in preparation for the Kenya general elections of December 27, 2007. ODM and PNU parties were formed and more than 245 briefcase political parties chose between ODM and PNU for their presidential candidate.

The Falsifying of the Elections: *Leadership* was written covering the span of years between August 2006 – February 2009 purported to capture the outcome of Kenya general elections on December 2007 and the post Government of Coalition. The statistics used throughout the text covers the period mentioned above unless otherwise noted.

No one would have ever imagined the tallying of the presidential elections would result into a disputed presidential election in Kenya. Soon after the Coalition Government was formed, a commission was appointed to investigate the office of the Electoral Commission of Kenya under the leadership of South African Judge Kriegler. Serious allegations of irregularities were reported on both sides of the political camps. In the closing hours of the elections ODM had swept successfully in many civic and parliamentary seats in Rift Valley Province and Kenya Coastal region.

On the morning of December 30th every Kenyan who had access to a TV station and radio station tuned in for ECK chairman, Kivuitu for a live announcement of the outcome of the presidential candidates. Kenyans living and working around the world, logged into their internet connections, CNN, and other public media with local affiliates in Kenya for the continuous live coverage. Every now and then one presidential candidate, Raila or Kibaki would take alternatively a lead going back and forth. Reporting went on smoothly, until one time a lead of one million votes for presidential opposition candidate Hon. Raila Amolo Odinga surpassed Hon. Kibaki and climbed into the lead. "All hell broke loose" during one of the series of the presidential announcement returns; when two different forms 16As with different figures were in question.

When ECK chairman, Kivuitu was randomly questioned in public by one of the ODM political candidates, the two gentlemen exchanged a few unwarranted words. Without cause, the chairman responded to his critiques in anger. The situation got out of balance. Unable to provide a satisfactory answer, and without a proper leadership on his own elections' guidelines, Kivuitu swiftly moved his command post into isolation to avoid further unwanted riot and other colossal damages. His security officers moved everybody from ECK national command post of elections, which was headquartered at Kenyatta Conference Center. During the exchange of words and tallying of votes, the live broadcast was abruptly terminated, which left the perception of the ODM presidential candidate in the lead with one million votes over Hon. Kibaki in their memory.

Before the sunset of December 30, Electoral Commission Chairman, Kivuitu accompanied by two of his commissioners convened themselves to an unknown room where they continued to broadcast live from where they had left off to the millions of Kenyans through a state funded Broadcasting Corporation without public interference. The votes continued to pour in at ECK Headquarters from all polling station corners in the Republic. Hon. Kibaki surpassed his opponents with a larger margin.

History of Kenya politics was about to be made. The chairman, Kivuitu, with his veto power, equipped with the famous form 16A filled with enough votes for the incumbent President Mwai Kibaki, the final tally win over his opponent Raila Odinga had arrived. Kibaki was finally announced as the official winner of the Kenya general elections of December 27, 2007. Hon. Kibaki was sworn under oath outside State House gardens as the 4th President of the Republic of Kenya. Soon after the swearing in was made public, the country was thrown into political bedlam. Kenya political machines had finally blossomed into the darkest side of a political leadership crisis the county had ever witnessed. The author of **Leadership** witnessed every turn of the events, before the tallying of the votes, and up to the post government of the Coalition Government of February 2008.

Who Was the Fall Guy? Did the ECK chairman run away from his leadership accountability? Could he have pointed a finger to the party leaders? Could Kivuitu and his commissioners have doctored the results? We shall never know what happened during the tallying of the disputed presidential election on that afternoon, just as well on what happened at the night of tallying votes for the candidates of Machakos Town Constituency. Think again, the events of December 2007 resulted to political turmoil which claimed more than the official record of lives of 1,500 people who died and more than 650 thousands of displaced Kenyans.

The creation of the ECK Section 41 of the Constitution of Kenya and section 42A of the said Constitution mandates the chair to three crucial job descriptions: (1) The book keeping of the national voter register (2) The maintenance of the voter register (3) To direct and supervise civic, parliamentary and presidential elections. In addition, The National Assembly and Presidential Elections Act, Cap 7, and its subsidiary mandate the chair to regulate and preside over the Presidential, Parliamentary and Civic Elections. It is the legal framework under the law of the land which enables the ECK to effectively conduct all local and general elections. The chair, historically, has always been a political appointee that enjoys a security of tenure with total independence from parliament. The legislature has set parameters for which to conduct all national elections, voting and tallying of the votes cast with authority to announce the outcome of the election to the citizens of Kenya.

Tallying Votes: Kenya's tallying of votes was not alone in the world of politics; similar to the year 2000 in a far away in the great state of Florida; the conferencing board was charged by the Supreme Court to recount all the hanging chads in which former Vice President Gore lost his presidential election to then George W. Bush. Democrats never forgot. The election of 2008 was their day in politics according to the general public approval. George ruled for two terms, surrounded by two wars on terror and the collapsed domestic economy.

When Bush left office January 20, 2009 he had the lowest job approving rate in decades. The governor of the great state of Illinois was accused of selling a Senate seat for cash and or goods and services. Next door, another great state, that of Minnesota had a similar problem of tallying votes for an incumbent Republican vs. a comedian Democrat. For the people of Minnesota, the Rule of Law took precedence. They waited seven months for the court system to determine the Senate winner. There was no bloodshed! In sharp contrast, ECK failed to wait the allotted 48 hours rule. Corruptions and cheating at the tallying polling stations of Kenya and other third world nations will continue to be realized in the years to come.

Polling: The official ECK records had 27,000 polling stations in the Republic. Each polling station was manned by a presiding officer with additional hired temporary seasonal poll clerks. Then there were also the returning officers, who like their supervisors, were aided with hired temporary seasonal poll clerks, who had their job cut out for them.

Presiding Officer: The tallying of the election vote process starts at each polling station. When all votes are cast at any polling station, the presiding officer makes three (3) containers, each for valid ballots votes, spoilt papers and summaries. All ballot boxes of votes are evident as hard copy to the register. In addition, the presiding officer prepares a statement of summaries of all the voting at the polling stations, which he/she must sign in the presence of all agents present. The containers, summaries, valid votes and spoilt votes are sealed off. All ballot boxes are transported with security police escort to the returning officer seated at the Constituency Headquarters.

Returning Officer: It is here the RO acknowledges the receipt of all the containers, valid ballots, and summaries from all the presiding officers from all the polling stations within the constituency. The tedious tallying process begins which may last anywhere between 10-25 hours of labor-intensive, nonstop, day and night counting of votes. It is here, the highest level of vote indiscretion is most vulnerable. The point persons from every political party are represented. It is here discreet corruptions were at work in the event for December 2007; voters voted along the party line. Sometimes, it was alleged by many voters, that the highest bidder with the majority of the corrupted ECK officials may have awarded non qualified candidacies.

Anonymous eye witnesses from a sample of hired poll-clerks interviewed confirmed suspicious deals. Leaders of political parties solicited their party and tribal loyalties to garner votes for them, especially those who had a presidential candidate, voted along the tribal lines. Just like in the race for President in the USA, African-American and Mexican-American and gender took precedence soon after Obama emerged as a clear choice between him and Senator Hillary Clinton. It was ironic, the ECK chairman refused donated computers by the USA which could have helped in the complex calculations of votes counting of the Kenya general elections and perhaps, could have eliminated the human errors that resulted to the rigging of the election.

A number of ROs testified under oath their lives were threatened by candidates if they refused to confirm or verify form 16A in favor of a particular candidate. The RO cannot change any spoilt or valid votes. However, the RO is privileged by the law, to announce locally at the constituency level the majority of the cast votes. The RO fills three (3) forms: 16, 16A and 17A in the presence of all the candidates. The three original forms are hard evidences of the register which are physically delivered to the ECK Headquarters in Nairobi.

Because of the logistics of the transportation of the ballot boxes to the National Headquarters in Nairobi, some may take anywhere from five hours to twelve hours depending on the location and distance of the said constituency. All ballot boxes are transported by road and or air. Rain always poses a challenge in the delivery process. Computers could have solved the transportation problem and the accuracy of the recorded votes.

When ECK receives all the ballot boxes including forms: 16, 16A and 17A for all candidates, ECK has 24 hours to receive a complaint. If a complaint is lodged by any candidate, ECK has

48 hours to recount the alleged votes and must resolve disputes of the complaint within 72 hours. After 72 hours elapses, the ECK by law must announce the winner of the election. A certificate known as [form 17] is issued to a parliamentary candidate and [form 18] is issued to the elected president, the results are gazetted into law. The chair opened up itself for censure on the validity of the elections.

Now, having said that, "Did the chairman, misuse his power to change an election? Did the chair fail to follow its own rules and regulations? Did Kivuitu, disobey the law, and unlawfully go ahead to announce the results of a disputed presidential election on the eve of December 30, 2007 without the said forms: 16, 16A and 17 from all the 210 constituencies? Did Kivuitu refuse to allow the 24 hours delay of complaints which is afforded to all candidates by law?" asks the author. His only excuse was he claimed that some returning officers went underground.

"How will the historians remember the momentous general elections that caused deaths to many Kenyans? Was the chairman coerced by the politicians, announcing premature election results? Will the historians argue, under the leadership of ECK Chairman Kivuitu, that he allowed the status quo to stay?" The public will never know if the chairman was forced by the political establishment to announce the presidential results too early, contrary to the law of the land. ODM and PNU party followers turned into a mob, shouting: "Rigging, Rigging." At this point everything went out of control. It was unstoppable and became a tsunami of people.

It appeared like a pre-arranged mob that was in the waiting, like a python ready to strike out at any moving human being, unattended properties and looting. **Leadership** obtained a copy of the Kriegler Commission Final Report which was made available free to the citizens. The following Executive Summary explains the findings which led to the dismantling of the historic ECK Commission in 2008 and how votes are tallied, transmitted, recorded, announced and even reviewed or audited. The integrity of the results process is a **sine qua non** of decent, free and fair elections. This is more so in the case of Kenya, because of the electoral system—first past the post, or so-called "winner takes all"—that is presently in place.

This report summarized the results of data and statistical analysis that was undertaken for 19 selected constituency results of Annex 6.A.

INDEPENDENT REVIEW COMMISSION (IREC)

REPORT on the Data analysis of the 2007 general elections results was based on sample constituencies and case studies.

FINAL REPORT

EXECUTIVE SUMMARY

Results are central in any given election. All preparations made before any elections, logistics and other forms systems put in place all come down to the actual voting that takes place, and how results from this voting from the 2007 general election. The analysis was undertaken as part of IREC's research process aimed at helping the Commission inquire into various aspects of the election, especially the presidential one. The report opens by outlining the approach used; criteria used to select constituen-

cies for analysis, methodology employed, limitations, findings and concludes with a set of general observations or recommendations. Stations—and which is the main basis of form 16—the document that by law is used to get the final election results. Finally, variance, discrepancies, and other anomalies were noted, including the implications thereof.

It must be understood that statistical analysis is limited in some respects in its ability to detect electoral malpractice or fraud. This is because some of these activities, such as stuffing of ballot boxes, may leave the statistics unchanged, hence making it hard to isolate these statistically.

Additionally, the data that is generated from the level of form 16A (i.e., polling station level) would say little in terms of electoral (mal)practices that may have taken place in activities preceding form 16A level. However, checking the accuracy of results tallies, entries and transmissions has yielded incredible findings, and possible areas of reform.

Our findings from the constituency analysis fall in different categories. We have discovered a litany of errors in terms of how results for candidates were added up at the polling station level and transferred to form 17A at the constituency level. There is a fair share of errors in computation, that is, addition of results at the constituency level in form 17A. Some of these erroneous results were transmitted to the form 16 and eventually to the national level, where they were, tragically, announced. Some of these wrong results (such as the case of Kirinyaga Central) resulted in one candidate who did not get the highest number of votes, declared winner. In others, especially for the presidential election, candidates' results were grossly under- or over-reported, as is the case of Masinga, Changamwe and so on. There are clear cases of omission, in terms of candidates' results not being filled properly, or omitted altogether, in the tally of results in form 17A. There are cases where presidential results announcements made have lower figures than those clearly stated in form 16.

Most of these errors and handicaps point to several system—and systemic—failures within the ECK and their planning, management and supervision of the results process in particular and elections in general. While a technical solution may lie in investing in a robust, appropriate technology-based system, the problem, and solution designed to solve it, goes beyond the use of technology or automation as the magic bullets to solving these problems.

At a matter of priority, the personnel or electoral officers and clerks hired to run the election must be well trained, effectively supervised, and putting in place system of on-site auditing of results before their announcement and/or transmission. Automating a flawed system, without streamlining its procedures and personnel first, would only make fraud and electoral malpractice harder to detect.

The future of flawless tallying of results lies in a right mix of appropriate technological solutions; integrity of electoral officers, and robust or fool-proof procedures. Here, a trade-off might have to be made between getting wrong, or un-checked results out fast enough, or taking time to tally and announce proper results.

The ECK should cease relying on experience in past elections *(implying age matters) at the expense of other competencies such as ability to used information technology, public administration and strong numeric skills. Whilst it's not being recommended that returning officers should be statisticians, there would be much value added in one being able to work with large volumes of information, perhaps under pressure. The same applies for clerical staff, or in particular, proof-readers and data auditors, that this report recommends as people who should be part of the elections clerical battalion*

The analysis and findings in this report are based on work done on 19 constituencies. There are other larger issues that are a matter of law and policy. How is it that ECK CANNOT review or correct results where it detects errors done on, say, form 16, by the returning officer, who are hired as temporary staff? This situation is a fundamental flaw and limits the checks-and-balance system of how results are received and their accuracy and authenticity guaranteed. In the final analysis, the integrity of results will depend as much on systems and structures, as on the goodwill and faith of electoral officers, the electoral management body and politicians." Kriegler Commission Page 5 of 56, September 2008. Ω

When Kivuitu resumed presidential tallying, the number of votes for the incumbent presidential candidate had surpassed the ODM leader by a large margin. Kenyans questioned the election results on the incumbent Kibaki. The fourth president of the Republic of Kenya had been sworn into office at State House gardens. This is contrary to the traditional changing of presidential transfer of power to the incoming new president at Uhuru Park in Nairobi. Historically, the grounds are the official ceremonial rostrum, where millions of Kenyans have in the past decades witnessed the changing of the presidential guard.

When the tradition was broken, peoples' hopes were also broken. It appeared in the eyes of the world that the incumbent president had rigged the election. The country was on the verge of a political collapse. If ODM had forced itself into Kenya leadership the country would have gone into a full-blown civil war. President Museveni of the Republic of Uganda [was the current seating chairman for East African Community], his government and United States of America were the first nations of the world to recognize the Kibaki government.

Leadership believes that the majority of Bush administration supported Kibaki presidency which led into a Government of Coalition, to avoid a political vacuum of leadership in the horn of Africa. A number of terrorists caught in Mombasa, the coast of East African nations had been transferred to GITMO, Cuba for military tribunal court. It would have been a failed American policy if Kibaki was not supported by America. Perhaps, it would have been atrocities similar to Rwanda and Burundi. Bush presidency was not about to let Kenya fall into tribal clashes.

European community of nations followed days later. By that time one half of the country had fallen in the act of ethnic killings, looting, rape, rioting and in deep political disarray. The situations were uncontrollable, people boarded buses, leaving the city headed to rural areas. Caught up in the drama, I remained in the city to witness the unfolding events. I changed into jeans, grabbed my camera, and went to town, as a freelance journalist. I began to take photographs of people running in all directions away from the city — within a few hours, the city of Nairobi was a ghost town.

I could not help but remember how similar it was during the failed coup of August 1982. In the same way, I endangered my life by going to the city center, as a freelance journalist, where I took scores of photographs of looted stores; streets were covered with dead bodies of Kenya Air Force soldiers along Forest Road and Third Parklands. My wife, Protasia, said, "Look at the sleeping soldiers." I replied, "These are dead soldiers."

It is safe to mention, regardless of the disruptions by the political party leaders, the reporting of votes from the provinces continued to pour results into the ECK command post. The credit is due to government administrators who moved swiftly and guarded the lives of tens of millions of people from killing each other; the steps the government took to block all live national television stations was for the best interest of the people and the national security. Why? The media had gone out of control and the national security of the nation was on the verge of collapse. Partly, it was to minimize riots, and to control the elections confusion in the country.

It was a crucial juncture. PNU, ODM and ECK panicked. The chairman appeared incapable to handle his critiques and the immediate crowd. It was a result of poor leadership skills; the chair had no business to engage in anger in a discussion with his critiques. ODM, largely in Rift Valley and Coast areas followers had nothing to lose. Like the Kibaki camp, they appeared to have had pre-meditated to cause trouble to the ECK Chairman and his Commissioners. It is purportedly said that Scores of anonymous ECK clerks ostensibly said that a number of Commissioners sided with certain political parties to have their candidates garner illegal votes. It is true Chairman Kivuitu was a preferred ECK chairman by all political parties. It is also true that the chair never anticipated a confrontation by his critiques. ECK poor leadership caused the public to prematurely assume a win for each of their presidential candidates. His poor leadership, in reality, caused the needless loss of lives, limbs, land and tens of thousands of displaced people. The buck stopped with the chairman.

The notion that Kibaki administration rigged the elections remains a political debate, one that will be judged by the historians. Due to the nature of the political climate at the time, PNU, ODM and ODM-Kenya leadership all were to blame for the outcome of the presidential elections in Kenya which resulted in the loss of tens of thousands of innocent people. I was there, as an eye witness, one who had contested for Machakos Town Constituency, only to find out later, I was rigged both at the division level and the constituency headquarters. I had vested interest and the right to know the outcome of the presidential elections.

After all, I had spent a few million of Kenya shillings into an election, my talents, and months of preparation for my campaign only to be cheated by the very system Electoral Commission and the people I sought to serve. There is an African saying, "When two elephants fight, the grass gets hurt." The elephants were ODM and PNU. The grasses were the citizens whose votes were manipulated; thousands displaced and tragically lost their lives in the process of an election. The world witnessed the unthinkable deaths on the eve of the announcement day and the first days of January 2008 where on the official record more than 1,200 innocent Kenyans died and more than 325, 000 displaced people. The fighting over the presidential results was squarely blamed on the illegitimate conduct of the Election Commission of Kenya. Some of the election commissioners were alleged to have rigged the election in favor of their party's civic, parliamentary and presidential candidates. It took a Kriegler Commission to prove that the election was irregularly conducted.

The Forms: Chairman Samuel Kivuitu admitted under oath during the Kriegler Commission inquest, the troubled agency made numerous errors at the polling stations during the transfer of votes to ECK Headquarters. The chairman made reference to form 16 which carried the final tally from the 210 constituencies for every candidate. The figures entered into form 16 by ECK clerks at all the polling stations were more than the official registry at ECK Headquarters, and more than inhabitants of the eligible voters in the constituencies. The agency failed its vested authority power to disqualify a candidate with suspected voter fraud. The disputed presidential elections resulted in the murder of 1,500 people, and more than 650,000 people were displaced with severe wounds.

Furthermore, ECK chairman had earlier refused donated computers from the United States of America, which could have helped computerize the national voter registry [called black book] which has always been recorded and updated by hand or manually. There is always a possibility of a human error. I strongly believe computers could have helped with complex figures computation, and the issue of duplications of the said forms 16 & 16A during Kenya general elections would not have risen. Records entered into the computer terminals anywhere in the nation would have reflected the true figures at the chairman desk. That is how banks communicate with other international banks and financial institutions around the world.

The chairman argued that the process would take too long to

train humans — to be ready for the general elections. Kriegler Commission confirmed and published its findings which faulted the ECK agency for poor handling of voter registration. Kriegler acknowledged that there were voter discrepancies throughout the country. The ECK chairman judgment call was amiss and very costly. For example, in Machakos Town Constituency, where I was a parliamentary contender, ODM-Kenya had the highest discrepancy with (29,093) voter irregularities in Machakos Town Constituency alone, followed by PNU (21,473) and ODM (8,577) voter irregularities.

Unless my memory is not correct, throughout my campaign in Machakos Town Constituency leading up to the final tallying night, I believe that it was not Kibaki who rigged, neither Raila who rigged the election. So who won? The Kriegler Commission was the official deciding factor and referee of the elections outcome. The Commission came to the conclusion that electoral commissioners in charge at the polling stations all the way to the national tallying headquarters indeed messed up the elections. Kenyans were left asking, "How did ECK Chairman Kivuitu come up with a clear winner of the presidential election?" Did he contradict himself when he said under oath he did not know who won the election?

Machakos Town Constituency had 15 candidates with a pool of more than 80,000 eligible voters. Deceit, riggings and unethical practices were observed and swept under the rug in the name of tribal euphoria throughout the nation. It was a much more highly contested seat compared to other districts in lower Eastern Province. Less than 65,000 eligible voters exercised their right to vote. The people of Machakos and Kalama Divisions were forced by their peers to vote along tribal lines — in addition, a majority of voters were paid an average of Kenya Shillings 100.00 per person (equal to $1.25).

The political leaders used a combination of atrocious techniques to further their political popularity; in areas where the tribe was not an issue. Again, in Machakos Town Constituency the use of money and theft of votes were used effectively. Furthermore, in Kalama Division my home territory, in its history is one of the hardest hit by poverty, compared to many parts of Ukambani territory.

Machakos Town Constituency is covered with numerous rolling hills with protected government forests which were set aside since the colonial days. The Kalama Division is the home of more than 35,000 registered voters who are without a police post. The Divisional headquarters in Kalama does not have vehicles to move around the division to restore peace whenever there are disturbances. Thieves and gangs from the neighboring Central Division tend to find refuge around the hills when running away from the law.

One day during one of my campaign trails, a woman was murdered from a domestic dispute, the killer was never found according to the authorities. Natives in this part of the constituency live in fear and anguish caused by unemployed gangs who come out from the poverty closets in search for their survival by feeding on political candidates.

Some gangs are usually on a pay roll by a few notorious political candidates. The buying and selling of votes was carried out by the cover of night. It is a major source of a day's income for a majority of voters. In Rift Valley and Coast Province, money, religious affiliation and threats were used to hire henchmen to garner votes for their civic, parliamentary and presidential candidates.

One anonymous religious leader said that during Moi administration *[during the one party system]* religious leaders and Bishops all over the nation were showered with millions of campaign money used to convince their congregations to endorse and vote for civic, parliamentary and presidential candidates into office.

In stark contrast, Kibaki campaign team abandoned the old tradition of giving money to the religious leaders and Bishops. The results were obvious; the church was divided and took sides with any political parties that recognized their presence at the polling stations. The church leaders directly solicited money from civic and parliamentary candidates for their church projects. For example, they needed money for additions to the church building. A majority of church leaders violated their trust, their congregations and the faith they preach. The church, the political leaders and the public at large were in it for themselves. As a political candidate, I too, had my share of political calamity. I was approached by a number of churches for campaign handouts.

I refused the order simply because a few churches had fallen in the trap of collecting money from political candidates, wooing them for their financial support, promising the candidates they would provide winning votes. For example, one Sunday I was invited as a guest speaker at a rural church only to find out that the congregation wanted my money in the name of the church to help their pastor buy insurance for his automobile.

I refused to offer assistance because of the motive behind the request. There were many such occasions I was faced with and had to make ethical decisions. I listened to my God given values, and refused to be a partaker of such unethical events. For the majority of the said churches were faithful, and in them God used my resources to invest in the lives of the needy children and widows through community churches.

The Kriegler Commission: The time of elections was unethical, vicious and evil for all parties responsible. It was too much to bear, when one imagines the killings were premeditated, and then followed the riggings. The ECK internal report states that in the sequences of announcements, all results were released in the order of presidential, parliamentary and civic elections.

The commission admitted some of the returning officers gave certificates to **LOSERS** and changed the names of the candidates to whom a certificate had been given. The commission violated its own rules and regulations mandated by the Act of Parliament. ODM/PNU supporters went to the streets prematurely crying foul play, "The election was rigged!" Lawless citizens torched buildings, businesses, churches, and schools.

The government appeared unable to control the mass protests in the Rift Valley area in particular. The city of Nairobi was left to a few of its tourists. It shut down at 4 PM daily, until the situation was calmed when the Peace Accord between the party leaders was signed. The Kriegler Commission enquiry found that it was impossible to know who won the presidential election in Kenya, based on the vote tabulation by the Electoral Commission of Kenya.

The system had so many irregularities, failed to follow its own rules, and the law of the land that regulate the commission. The Kriegler Commission warned the people of Kenya that if the ECK was not overhauled before the next general elections of December 2012 the horrors of 2007 elections would be worse. It was clear from the Kriegler report; ECK's dysfunction was responsible for the grisly killings, and unwarranted displacement of the tens of thousands of people. The nation bore deep wounds resulting in scars and confusion caused by the hurried results for the presidential elections.

Physical Wounds: The wounds were physical wounds. They are not going to go away any time soon; men, women, and children walked in villages, towns and cities with missing limbs and deformed bodies. To date, 2009 some of the children were admitted in a California hospital for surgery for their burns and disfigurement.

Economic Wounds: The wounds were economic wounds. Corporations lost tens of millions of shillings of investments when government properties were burned, and families were displaced from their farm lands. One year after the Coalition Government, the country is faced with a shortage of food crisis, poverty and starvation. One in every three Kenyans risks starvation following the failed rains in the country. Among the tens of millions, 1.5 million children under the school feeding program will die of malnutrition and poor medical conditions and the remaining population will be swept by the winds of HIV/AIDS. The Government was unable to plan properly during the entire year of 2008 due to the loss of infrastructure and destruction of farm property following the failed presidential elections.

Politicians from both sides of the aisle took months to negotiate self political positions in the newly formed Coalition Government. Farmers in Rift Valley, the country bread basket refused to return to their farms in fear for their lives. This is not the first time Kenya has suffered food shortages and starvation, the politicians have failed to employ longtime planning for the people of Kenya. The parliament is used by a few politicians as means to have power and oppress the poor voter though poor physical planning responsibilities.

For the last 45 years the agriculture ministry ought to have learned that every four years the country's rain fall cannot be dependable to deliver adequate food supply to the growing population of more than 38 million plus. Millennium Development Goals are the only recipe to save the country from poverty in Africa. But that is not enough; MDGs require planning, implementation and leadership.

The country of Kenya is blessed with a large underground natural cache underneath the earth scattered around the nation. Ukambani region lies between two great rivers, Tana and Athi, carrying billions of gallons of water through the Akamba land and to the Indian Ocean. And yet Akamba territory is one of the poorest regions compared to other provinces in the nation. The majority of the Akamba region has been neglected since its colonial days. Akamba political leaders appear to have not been able to plan for their troubled region due to lack of physical planning and leadership responsibilities for the men and women who elect them to parliament every five years. Historically, the majority of the Akamba political leaders had engulfed themselves with selfish wealth accumulation. On the final note about food shortages in Kenya, the future government should plan to harvest water during heavy rain seasons for use during dry seasons for irrigation schemes around the nation. Until Kenya undertakes measureable water harvest, the semi desert country will continue to face food shortages and economic downfall.

Psychological Wounds: There were psychological wounds; people obviously became depressed because of the loss of loved ones. There was a woman whose husband was attacked, pierced with arrows, cut on every part of his body, until his unexpected death, caused by slicing off his head like a roaster. She was simultaneously raped by four other men next to her husband's corpse. An elderly man unable to help watched seven members of his family hacked to death. His life was spared as he slipped away in the dark of the night. In Eldoret people went about throwing stones, forced children, women, and elderly into the church. They took mattresses and poured gasoline (petrol) on the mattresses, laying some on top of the church roof…, against the walls and at the doors, and windows and set fire to the mattresses. Elderly men, women and children trying to come outside the church were killed.

Political Wounds: Area politicians were responsible. Children died, some were made orphans by the criminal acts of the perpetrators. It is one thing to be orphaned because of natural disasters, but worse when other human beings premeditate murder. Will the rest of the Kenyans ever be able to trust leadership from those few individuals who perpetrated the killings of the innocent? Eleven months into the Coalition Government the Cabinet and Parliament agreed that the killers, perpetrators and financiers be brought to justice by a tribunal court.

December 15 was set as the deadline by the Commission of Inquiry into the Post-Election Violence, for the purpose to set a tribunal court to address the crimes against humanity. How do these murderers and killers live with themselves when Mzee Macharia knew at least 14 of the killers? The individuals, whoever they are, betrayed themselves first, and betrayed their own tribesmen. They were branded as killers and murderers in the expense of political power.

The Akiwumi Commission came to the conclusion: There were three underlying reasons for the clashes: (1) the "Ambitions by Kalenjins of recovering what they think, they lost when the Europeans forcibly acquired their ancestral land. (2) The desire to remove "foreigners," derogatorily referred to as "madoadoa" or "spots" from their midst. The reference was mainly towards the Kikuyu, Kisii, Luo and other communities who had found permanent residence in Rift Valley. (3) "Political and ethnic loyalty."

Kenya created deep rooted tribal elements in her national political machine. Any time during presidential elections, each of the 42 tribes of Kenya would like their tribal leader be the next president; while the majority of individual politicians, hungry for political power would do anything possible — corruption, buy votes and even kill to be elected. The notion that, "the end justifies the end means."

Elsewhere in **Leadership** I have noted the importance of each tribe in a democratic government like Kenya — each tribe has important traditions and culture that should be used to enrich and unite all tribes regardless of their differences of culture. Both Kriegler and Waki were first in many series of political transformations for a future Kenya, and that Kenya still has some basic issues to address as a nation. There is a hope and optimism in the

Waki and Kriegler Commissions.

Drawback: Earlier on, the Peace Accord had its drawbacks. The naming of the new government took some time, because the Coalition had not provided the president with a time table to form a cabinet. President Kibaki had selectively picked the key important ministries long before his principal partner and rival demanded a Coalition Government under the supervision of the former United Nations Secretary, Kofi Annan and Eminent persons from the Continent.

The Coalition was only good as long as both parties (PNU and ODM) remained devoted to the Alliance for the life of the 10th Parliament. First, if one party pulled out, the Coalition would cease, and become a moot note, what must follow would be a fresh general election. And or if the president of the state had decided to dissolve the parliament, a new election would have been enacted; unless the president had decided to rule the country by dictatorship. Second, in a Coalition Government there is no official opposition party in parliament, which left no checks or balances and accountability within the government.

Islamic Influence and Money: The Orange Democratic Movement Party enjoyed international support. Money was poured in to the ODM war chest like rainwater! It was a no brainer that once a Memorandum of Understanding (MoU) was signed between ODM and the Islamic leadership, it was like opening an oasis of money. Cash was everywhere. ODM candidates in line with Muslim-dominated areas especially in the Coast and North Eastern provinces went in for a sweep of most of the parliamentary and civic seats.

In contrast, PNU was the government in place. Monetary support for PNU candidates came from the bigwig career politicians in addition to each individual's war chest. Members of the PNU party had a problem of major power-struggles within the party. Desiring to hang on to their own individual dynasty, they were not willing to yield power to new politicians. The majority of incumbent PNU politicians were not re-elected.

Drug Trafficking: Mombasa (also known as Mvita), is the second largest city in Kenya, the only gate way to the country's interior and neighboring member states. The countries: Rwanda, Burundi and Uganda are landlocked member states dependent on the port of Mombasa for export and import of goods and services by rail and road. Mombasa is conveniently located on the shores of the Indian Ocean with easy access to the rest of the world.

Since the 7th Century Mombasa has been occupied by many Arabs-dynasties, including the Sultan of Omani, and European powers, Portugal and Great Britain. For centuries the town has undergone numerous battles between Arabs, Portuguese and The British Empire, a superpower that stopped the slave trade along the Indian Ocean.

Mombasa remained under the dominance of Arab culture during British colonial rule until today. Jomo Kenyatta, the first president of Kenya agreed in principle that Arabs could continue to practice their century old culture and religious rights as long as they did not interfere with the affairs of the interior. Since Kenya's independence, powerful politicians and corrupt government administrators have used the port as a safe haven for drug trafficking to the outside world.

The Kibaki administration is a close ally of the U.S. in the war against Islamic terrorism. This is in stark contrast to Odinga, an ally of Islamic extremists. On August 29, 2007 Odinga signed a MoU with Islamic leadership, pledging that he if were elected president, he would establish Sharia courts throughout the country, enact Islamic dress codes for women, ban alcohol and pork, indoctrinate schoolchildren in the tenets of Islam, and ban Christian missionary activities.

Mombasa and other east African ports located along the shores of the Indian Ocean are the fastest growing routes for cocaine going to Europe. In 1998 Kenya Police in Coast Province apprehended a truck full of drugs with an estimated street market value of 32 million dollars (Sh2 billion). The cargo was off-loaded from a vessel in high seas and taken to the shores. Later the cargo was intercepted by the Kenya police crime unit in route to an unknown destination.

A drug story filed by Patrick Mayoyo was published in Kenya (Daily Nation Newspaper) on March 22, 2008. It stated that Kenya Crime Police reported 5,401 drug cases for 2007 and 5,821cases for 2006 with a decline of 420 cases in 2007.

In the same report Mayoyo wrote, "A new drug baron with international and local connection has emerged at the coast; a link man with a wanted drug baron based in United Arab Emirates." Sheikh Huma Ngao, a director with Nacada, coincided with other international drug observers that Mombasa port is an easy target for drug traffickers because of the poor inspections of arrival and exit of merchandise. Government agencies should exercise extreme security control in cities like Mombasa, Malindi and Lamu where potential drug moguls may find sanctuary.

Daily Nation Newspaper reported the arrest of a drug baron at a joint at Nairobi West, a suburb of the city of Nairobi on the eve of December 24, 2008. The suspect was identified as Ken Ombina of a Nigerian origin. The irony of the story of the arrested man is that he is said to be well connected with high ranking security officers in the country.

The man was identified as using different names. He was reported to have been declared an illegal immigrant in Kenya by a former Immigration Minister back in 2007 whose deportation papers were still intact. The man went underground and missing until he was arrested by police at an entertainment joint. He had investigation that spanned over eight (8) years as the Nigerian man responsible for the majority of Kenya women arrested with drug and human trafficking in Europe and the Far East.

The Nigerian drug baron recruits include five Kenya Airport in-flight attendants arrested in London, Amsterdam, China and India with possession of a drug, cocaine. It was believed that Kenya Police detectives had in their possession sworn court affidavits for the arrest of such kinds of unwanted men in Kenya. But they have always made a safe exit without arrest and sometimes are believed to live undercover, cohabiting with local consumers in the country.

During many of the random arrests operation in December 2003 Kenya Police detectives found a list of names of high ranking Kenya Police officers at a Nairobi residence belonging to a notorious Cameroonian drug operative. The police impounded eight autos and found a list of names of high ranking Kenya Police Officers who were alleged to have been on the payroll for protective fees. The alleged man was never arrested, but conveniently, was reported to have fled to Dubai. The war on drug and human trafficking is a tall order to win in the majority of the third world nations where law enforcement participates in corruption.

More than 5,000 people surveyed between the months of February and July in 2008, lived and worked in the cities of: Mombasa, Nairobi, Nyeri, Nakuru, Eldoret, and Kisumu. 58 % surveyed said crime remained the same for 2003-2004 compared to 2007. The Coalition Government pledged to fight corruption as never before, only to be entangled with the scandal of the sale of a government property "Regency Hotel" to a Libyan company, the drugs embezzlement at the Ministry of Health and the notorious maize cartels.

The chief Corruption Czar was frustrated because the majority of the alleged corruption files belonged to bigwig boys of who's who in the politics taken to the Attorney General, have never been prosecuted for the crimes alleged. Consumer Insight Kenya, says corruption at the Kenya Police went down compared to the previous years: 2006 at 47%, 2007 down to 37%, and 2008 dropped down to 22%, a significant improvement since Kenya became a Republic. The following international agencies have their eyes focused on Mombasa drug trafficking to the rest of the world.

U.S. State Department's Bureau of International Narcotics and Law Enforcement Affairs and the International Narcotics Control agency. (2) U.N. International Narcotics Control Board. (3) National Agency for the Campaign against Drug Abuse (Nacada)

International agencies feared that the political campaigns leading to the December 27, 2007 elections--which results ignited unprecedented violence–created the perfect (storm) open door for the movement of drugs through the Mombasa port. It is imperative for African governments to form a trading block to stay competitive in global trade. The Organization of Africa Unity can play an important role in combating war against drought, corruption, drug trafficking, and the war on terror. Kenya has suffered massive terrorism attacks in its history: The Norfolk Hotel, Nairobi (1980), USA Embassy in Nairobi and Dar es Salaam, TZ (1998), and the Paradise Hotel, in Mombasa (2002) whereby millions of dollars in property damage and human life loss was devastating.

On and after December 27, 2007 I was traumatized, distressed, and in shock by the events that were happening around me. Having lived in the west, I was used to seeing a Hollywood actor die in one movie and get resurrected in another movie; a cowboy never dies! I had read in the news about the ethnic cleansing of Rwanda, and Kosovo, where my son served in the U.S. Army, and about the suicide bombers in hot spots around the world.

Who would have ever dreamed that such hideous killings would happen in the magnificent country of Kenya with its exotic animals, breathtaking landscapes, sociable people, sparkling white sands of Mombasa, desirable climate, the home of the grand, mighty mountains, the Great Rift Valley that extends to Palestine and the cradle of human civilization? This could not be happening to my country, I thought. I became a prisoner of my own imaginations. It was a classic example of power-greedy politicians whose leadership collapsed.

Contrasting Leadership Styles

The following table shows the difference between two leadership styles and the results we typically find in their subordinates.

The Boss – Servant Grid

Boss-Style Leader	Servant-Leader Style
Inspires fear in his followers	Inspires trust and enthusiasm
Says "Go" (do what I say)	Says "Let's go" (we are a team)
Says "I have the answers"	Says "We can solve this together"
Has no time for his followers	Takes time for his followers
Pass off blame for problems	Fixes the problem without assigning blame
Credits himself for accomplishments	Credits entire team for accomplishments

Definition of Community Tribe: Historians, sociologists and anthropologists often try to produce a definition of community or a group, in this case [a tribe qualifies for a community] whose boundaries are less fixed and thus can be compared with other communities. But such a fixed definition lacks in the African tribes who define their identity first, Akamba tribe, then Kenyan or first, a Luo, then Kenyan, in sharp contrast, a person from the great state of Texas is identified as an American over a Texan. Though native Texans are very proud of their state, they would rather be identified as Texans over being an American. They have slogans that read, "Do not mess with Texas, I was not born here, but I got here as fast as I could, Texas is like a whole other country."

Every summer, when our children were small, my wife and I drove hundreds of miles crisscrossing the majority of the great states of America. I would often get other motorists honking their horns when they spotted my Texas auto plates. In most cases the honking came from other Texas motorists driving the opposite direction or a Texan who had moved away from his home state for business — it was always the best thing to be recognized by your fellow statesman. This is an example of how many native Africans feel about their tribes. The identity of a tribe is a convoluted matter. The majority of people in Kenya would rather be identified with their tribe first, which provides social protection, land and identity of their well being.

Each tribe in Kenya has its own levels of conflicts, contradictions and complexity in their behavior toward another tribe. The Kenya tribes have always been at odds with each other for different reasons or other—ancestors left ill feelings about their neighbor tribes of the distant past which must be studied and analyzed for today's Kenya society and elsewhere in Africa.

The minority tribes in Kenya view that their world has been compromised by the majority tribes in power. For many years to date there are tribes in Kenya living a sub-standard life compared to the few tribes who have always had the upper hand in national government. It is hard to maintain a tribal balance between tribes when there is no equal economic distribution among tribes. This is one of the core problems of the ethnic killings during the disputed elections.

The majority of Kenyans' elite from populous tribes have learned how to use political power, greed, deception, corruption, the motto "take all when in power" without consideration of tomorrow. Such leaders are still confined in the web-cage ideologies of their tribe, (like a spider's web that traps its victim) over national hood. The notion that, there were tribes before there were nations of: Kenya, Tanzania, Nigeria or Malawi. The concept of national hood is a new concept to many African tribes, and their leaders.

The Distribution of Tribes of Africa is part of a continuing scientific study to form a better understanding of what the earth was like about four billion years ago and how life might have originated under these conditions unknown to modern man and especially the unknown mysteries of Africa. However, the Christian doctrine concerned with the nature, origin, and destiny of humankind has its foregone conclusion as recorded in the sacred text –The Holy Bible.

In 1969 Neil Armstrong, onboard Apollo 11 and his fellow astronaut brought back to earth samples of moon particles and expected to find some clues to some form of life outside the celestial spheres of the earth when a man made a giant step on the planet moon. This is clear evidence that man continues to search for the origin of mankind here on earth and in the outer space.

In recent years scientist researchers equipped with genetic data, collected out of Africa a disproportionately small amount of group samples that were taken from different groups of family tribes of African population. These groups of family of tribes stretch across the geographical landmass of Africa, separated by traditions and languages, are discussed in the following:

The current languages of Africa are classified in more than four major speaking groups of family of tribes covering three-quarters of the geographical area of Africa. **Niger-Kordofanian** also known as Bantu speaking group of tribes is the largest family groups of tribes in Africa covering more than half of Africa, stretching from West, Central, and Southern Africa to the Highlands and Plains of East Africa.

In West Africa, oral histories, additionally with the modern scientific DNA research, have enabled anthropologists to confirm the existence of the Yoruba, Asante, (Ashante) Brong and the Malinke (Mende) tribes of West Africa who because of merchandising gold and ivory formed powerful tribal chiefdoms and kingdoms more than 3,500 years ago.

The arrival of the western Europeans found these kingdoms already into their existing zenith reigns. The European explorers and traders ravaged the land, slaughtering the elephants for their tusks, killing the animal kingdom for ivory and skins, exploited the gold mines of the day for the treasures, selling them in the streets to the aristocrats of Europe.

The Europeans who came to Africa came from densely populated and limited city and state. The British colonies in Africa were there to stay; the Britons in particular in Kenya had no plan to leave. In sharp contrast, the French and German colonies exploited the natural riches of the African continent. The virgin lands of Africa were fertile for ranching for beef and milk, wildlife was in large supply for hunting ivory. It was "the land flowing with milk and honey." *Leadership* is in agreement with the policies set by World Wildlife Conservationists for the protection of wildlife kingdoms in Africa to remain in their sanctuaries and natural habitat.

The study took a period over ten years in collaboration with the institutions of higher learning in North America and Africa totaling 113 DNA samples of populations taken throughout Africa. The genetic study was comprised of one of the largest groups of international genetic researchers who revealed the African Genetic Evolutionary Story of the centuries. An existing 1,300 genetic markers data was re-analyzed, and then added to new additional genetic markers data collection totaling about four (4) million of genotype used to complete a ten year study.

A total of 4,000 people were used in the study together with 121 genetic samples of African populations collected from various regions of Africa; including four (4) African-American genetic samples population. Additional sixty (60) non-African genetic samples were also added to the grand study.

The genetic study of the history of Africans and African-Americans was an attempt to find conclusive answers to scientific research in reference to the origin of man, their response to pharmaceutical drugs and what might be the future genetic risk factors among African-Americans' diseases. The family groups of tribes are represented in four (4) different colors; tan is for Niger-Kordofanian, purple is for Afro-asiatic, red is for Nile-Saharan and green is for Khoesan.

A report published in Science Express Online, April 30, 2009 was the largest irrefutable scientific study ever of the Genetic Structure and History of Africans' and African-Americans' genetic diversity.

The distributions of 121 African populations of groups of tribes each with different languages are shown in a color- coded illustration to show distinct places of their inhabitance since ancient and modern Africa. www.sciencemag.org shows African tribes in different color separation. The star represents samples of Khoesan group of tribes collected from the "Centre d'Etude du Polymorphism."

Method of DNA data collection: The genetic structure and history of Africans and modern African-Americans' project originated from the University of Maryland at College Park, University of Pennsylvania and Vanderbilt University, all located in the United States of America. It is the opinion of *Leadership* that major institutions of higher learning and research from European nations who colonized the continent of Africa should have taken a center stage in the genetic study of the history of Africa; because they too, were the initial European inhabitants who received first-hand oral tradition and gave us written history of the native Africans.

The African institutions of higher learning and research are noted as following: The order does not represent seniority of significance in the Genetic Structure and History of African tribes. The DNA collection in East Africa came from a group of population in Arusha and Dodoma regions of Northern and Central Tanzania. Kenya DNA was collected from the regions of Rift Valley, Nyanza and Eastern Provinces of Kenya. Sudan DNA was collected from the region of Khartoum and Kasala Provinces of Sudan.

The study revealed that Africans originated from 14 different ancestral populations, which made it easier to correlate tribal cultures, traditions and their languages. A Bantu speaking tribe and non-Bantu speaking tribe can easily be identified by means of their origins. The genetic diversity of African populations provided a reliable case study closing the gap, as per archaeological results of the genetic sampling provided by the Leakey's discovery of Apes-like man fossils dating more than 200,000 years ago.

The ancient, undocumented slave trade before 1400s and the mass slave trade of 1800s onwards may have interrupted the ability to verify the original family trace-tree ancestral roots of Africans to the newfound lands of North America and Latin America.

In addition, the study overwhelmingly concluded that modern African-Americans may not be able to link themselves directly to a particular group of a single tribe, because of the wide range of mixed ancestral diversity from the entire region of Africa.

However, the discovery of DNA provides an aplomb data that may assist and ameliorate the African-American, African-European and African-Asiatic the ability to facilitate their ancestral trace-tree to one of the three or four major groups of families of tribes of Africa. For example, such as in (Niger-Kordofanian) Bantu speaking groups of tribes, Nilotic tribes, Afro-Asiatic and Khoesan tribes found in the modern West and East African regions.

During the genetic research, about 800 micro satellites were part of the panel identified as Marshfield pane of marker. Among these markers, Africa was under represented with only about six populations from Africa descents that were used. The study further suggests that 14 ancestral genetic clusters were identified using the genetic markers available.

African groups of tribes were easily identified because of their culture, traditions, language and geographical inhabitance. Tribes who have similar culture and language tend to jumble together for the reasons of security and trade. Regardless of what the study revealed, there was an exception to the rule.

In the Central African Region there is a group of family clans of a tribe known as the Pygmies, the dwellers of the Congo forest. For unknown centuries the tribe lost its original language, forced to speak Bantu languages for the basis of survival for trade and security. Similar cases are noted as referred to other small groups of tribes in East Africa. When genetic data was extracted from the tribe, research showed they were found to cluster together in the Congo forests.

The genetic study identified the Africans, African-Europeansand African-Americans living in North America. Their genetic histories are easily noticed because of the slave trade routes in 1400s and 1800s to all parts of the world. There is no doubt that African-Americans are genetically identified mainly to Bantu groups of tribes of West Africa. This is partly due to historical accounts and West African oral history and traditions, before 975 A.D.

Muslim Arab traders captured and sold Africans from North Africa and the East African coast to wealthy and royal families of Europe, Eurasia and Arab dynasties. Additional records indicate that the majority of Africans were located around the Dead Sea region. The immigration out of Africa has existed more than the current suggested 200,000 years or more. There are several records available in Arabic and other European languages indicating the slavery movement to Europe until The Great British Empire put to an end the mass slave trade of the Indian Ocean in the mid 1800s. The genetic study in Figure 1 (page 371) identifies the majority and origin of the Khoesan groups of tribes in East Africa as separate groups of tribes as in Bantu and Nilotic tribes. According to Maasai oral traditions, Khoesan does not make up a separate group of tribes. Rather the Khoesan group of tribes is part of a sub-clan of primitive Maasai of Kenya and Tanzania who are one of the Nilotic groups of tribes.

The Khoesan are best described as primitive clans of Maasai tribes of East Africa. However, in a similar case with the Pygmies of the Congo forest, it is possible that Khoesan may be a true group of tribes, who could have been forced to speak a Maasai language as a result of inter-marriage and survival when their tribal languages came to an end during the past millennium. Both oral tradition and the genetic study fail to give conclusive evidence that Khoesan is a truly separate tribe from the larger groups of tribes of Bantu and Nilotics.

What is common between Pygmies and Khoesan groups of tribes? The STRUCTURE observed that Pygmies and Khoesan may have shared similarity in their lost languages, due to their diminishing numbers in population. The Pygmies and Khoesan groups of families of tribes were swallowed by stronger and richer culture and tradition of a neighbor group of family of tribes such as the Bantu or Nilotics. Future genetic studies are necessary for the purpose of informative reconstruction of the lost proto-Pygmy and Khoesan languages, and their genetic effects on their geographical adaptation from a savannah climate to the tropical forests.

There is a possible connection to the Khoesan group of tribes.

Having said that, science may never be able to solve, provide clues or reconstruct the lost languages of the Pygmies and Khoesan group of tribes. In addition, future genetic studies may provide answers to why the Pygmies are short in physique compared to other groups of African tribes. However, there is no evidence to suggest that their height and physical construction are a result of genetic makeup.

The Khoesan also known as Dorobo and Okiek group of tribes comprises of smaller family clans related to the Maasai tribe, whose livelihood is sustained as bee gatherers. They are found in forests of Northern Tanzania and Kenya. The Maasai use a derogatory name, Dorobo as people who cannot keep cattle. The Maasai see themselves as superior over the Khoesan group of family clans. Dorobo and Okiek are origin to East Africa.

The study identified some genetic evidence in the south and southwest Africa Regions. The Khoesan group of tribes may be part of the Nilotic tribes who share a common ancestry gene dating to more than 35,000 years ago. The Science Express, The Genetics Structure of Gene study is part of a continuing science effort to prove that indeed East Africa is the cradle and the origin of human species that has spread to the entire world.

Afro-asiatic (Afroasitic) is grouped into four (4) groups of family of tribes who share a common ancestor: As mentioned elsewhere in **Leadership,** Afro-Asiatic consists of (a) Semitic (of Egypt), Mzab, of the Sahel group, the Berber speaking group of tribes of the Sahara and Beja and the Oromo tribes of East Africa. (b) Cushitic speaking groups originating from southern Ethiopia to Northern Kenya. (c) Southern Cushitic speaking groups from Kenya and Tanzania and (d) Chadic speaking groups from northern Cameroon who are close neighbors to the Nilo-Saharanian groups of tribes from southern Sudan and Chad.

Afro-Asiatic is third and smaller in population than Bantu and Nilotic. The majority groups of family of tribes bear the Muslim faith, scattered along the continental borders within the Sahel and the countries of Sudan, Chad and Ethiopia, Egypt, Somalia and North Africa-Arab speaking countries. Speaking about the Sahel itself is defined as a line. The word means "shore" in Arabic, which implies a continental margin divide, a grand beginning with a final end. The Sahel can be described as a stand alone country as it has no borders, stretching across Northern Africa roughly along the 13th parallel above the equator. It is a belt slicing and wrapping Africa from Senegal to the Red Sea, wider than the distance between the western and eastern coasts of the continental USA.

The STRUCTURE shows a consistent analysis of ancestry across African-American populations plus African oral traditions. The modern African-American samples of population were taken from the cities of Chicago, Baltimore, Pittsburgh and cities of North Carolina. The ancestry was consistent with the population sample matching the Bantu group of tribes of African Niger-Kordofanian.

The Genetics Structure of Gene study of the Science Express Online is part of a continuing scientific effort to prove that indeed East Africa is the cradle and the origin of human species that has spread to the entire modern world. Therefore, it is safe to say the study may never be conclusive. USA President, Barack Obama who has ties from African descent, announced major initiatives in the continuing study of African genetic history. He pledged 3

% of the USA GNP to research and development. Oral tradition along with DNA structure put to an end the lost histories of the myths and mysteries of the Dark Continent – Africa. There are still more mysteries of unknown Africa from rivers, forests, deserts and underworld of African caves.

The African Universities that provided and assisted in the actual field research are as follows: East Africa Region: COSTECH and NIMR, Dar es Salaam, Tanzania and KEMRI in Nairobi, Kenya. The Northern Africa Region: University of Khartoum, Sudan, Northern Africa. Western Africa Region: Regional Hospital, Sunyani, Ghana, Nigeria Institute for Research, Pharmacological and Development, Abuja, The University of Bamako, Faculty of Medicine, Pharmacy, Odonto-stomatology and Ethics Committee, Mali. Central Africa Region: Ministry of Health and National Committee of Ethics, Cameroon. Southern Africa Region: University of Stellenbosch, South Africa.

Nilo-Saharan also is known as the Nilotic in East Africa. They are the second largest group of family tribes in Kenya, whose relationship to the terrain bears the name, spread and migrated like the pollination of a bee, from Mali to the Dinker tribes across the Sahel to modern southern Sudan. Their presences in the East African region are known as the Nilotic tribes. The Nilotic adapted into new names with a new terrain: Nilotic-Plains, Nilotic-Highlands and Nilotic-Lake Basin of East Africa. It happened by no accident that among the Nilotic group of tribes is the Luo tribe, that bears the name of Obama Senior, born of rural Kogelo Village in Siaya District, the father of Barack Obama, the first African-American President of the United States of America, the leader of the free world. The name Obama is synonymous with the Luo tribe of Kenya, a name that represents the face of African-Americans of the USA. Most of all the African-Americans are poised to benefit with the highest expectations that the Obama presidency will have an effect on them and his African roots.

During Obama's first 100 days in office he said, "My father was from Kenya. The USA is under obligation to help Kenya on many issues, but Kenya must sort its corruption problems first." President Obama gave these remarks during his first European tour. Obama sent a clear message to the peoples of Kenya and to the rest of his African descent that his administration would not tolerate corruption and poor performance of the rule of law.

Historically, Moslems are known to band in group of thought and ideology. In every Kenya general elections Islam have sought a MoU with civic and parliamentary candidates for the purpose to represent their interests in the highest office of the land. The church in Kenya failed to provide political leadership during Kenya general elections, December 27, 2007 campaigns which resulted to disputed presidential elections. In United States of America, Rick Warren, pastor, Saddleback Church, provided a political leadership during American turning point in search for a president. He took an initiative to unite the Coalition Principals, during the tribal clashes in Kenya.

During the golden age of Europe, societies lived under their own culture, tradition and worship. Modern western societies have changed, they live in complex society, whereby a man lives and works in a survival mode. He must work to maintain a daily lifestyle, in the same factories, shops at the same grocery stores, attends the same institutions of learning and is governed by the laws of the land in which he lives. Societies of Africa live in their tribal lands and are governed by their century old culture, tradition and worship. However, influences from the western societies are encroaching African lifestyles.

Those who take the view that certain groups of faith must deny and separate themselves from the participation of local and national politics of the land send a message of "a don't care attitude", by allowing others whom may not share the same beliefs and ideology to make and pass laws of the land on their behalf. Christians cannot afford to use the phrase "separation of church and state" as an excuse to shy away from the participation of politics, simply because they want to separate themselves from the duties and the responsibilities of the society in which they live and cherish.

The MoU of 2002 with NARC Government was mild and signed in secrecy between the NARC politicians and when not honored by the NARC Government, it led to referendum of 2005. Muslims waited and waited for the next Kenya General Elections of 2007! When time was right Islamic leadership, National Muslim Leaders Forum (NAMLEF) entered into pack contract with each of the three presidential candidates in civics, parliamentary and especially the Hon. Raila Odinga, ODM presidential candidate.

The MoU 2007 was the most serious, dangerous and scandalous that almost put the country on the brink of civil war because of its contents. Since 911, Bush administration vowed to fight terror in every country he could smell, chase and smoke out Islamic terrorists. Kenya, Tanzania and American citizens were victims of Islamic terrorism through the U.S. Embassy bombings in Nairobi and Dar es Salaam in Tanzania. Due to Kenya's porous boundaries, the country had become a potential terroristic battleground for Islamic insurgents' hideouts (sleeper cells) and drug trafficking Gurus along the Mombasa-Lamu coast. Therefore, to have a president with Islamic preference, one who believes and endorses Islamic ideology, would have made it difficult to fight terrorism in the horn of Africa.

One of the key elements mentioned by MoU 2007 established Sheria law to be in the constitution of Kenya as the only true law sanctioned by the Holy Koran. Millions of Kenyans would certainly have revolted, because 80% of the population professes Christianity. This led to the ethnic clashes in December 2007. National Muslim Leaders Forum failed to recognize that Kenya was a solvent nation governed by a constitution that binds all tribes and religions with the freedom of worship.

The Borderless Territory – Kenya before 1800s: It is the reader to choose to agree with the archeologist's work of Mary and Louis Leakey in the Great Rift Valley, late in 1940s. The couple unearthed various species of human like fossils dating 20 million years ago during their life time career.

The Leakey's first known discovery was Miocene hominoid. The couple named the skull as *Proconsul Africanus* in 1948 suggesting a possible origin of the human race. The skull shaped like Apes-like-man was discovered on an African soil was believed to have common ancestors to the Africa man. The skull was estimated to have lived 14 million years ago with other Africa species.

The Leakey's famous discoveries are found in the caves at Olduvai Gorge in northern modern Tanzania in East Africa. This part of the world has numerous different types of fossils species which are yet to be discovered. The Leakey team has unearthed more than 100 forms of different extinct types of animal life forms at Olduvai Gorge. On a clear day July 17th, 1959 Mary herself, unearthed what would became the most important discovery fossil species in her career, the *"Zinjanthhropus boisei"* as known as *Australopithecus boisei.*

Mary Leakey's discovery added an important piece of history in the continuing study of the origin of man. In the 1960s the Leakey team made another discovery, the *Homo habilis* known as the "handy man," the creature with ability to make and use tools, was the earliest known tool-maker creature known to man; with this discovery Leakey was convinced that the fossil species was linked to the present African ancestors. In 1979 the Leakey team discovered a long trail of 89 human footprints dated to about 3.6 million years at Laetoli. Additional discoveries in recent decades surrounding Lake Turkana located in semi-desert of northern Kenya were the hominids; including Homo habilis and Homo erectus estimated to have lived around the area almost 1.6 million years ago.

Kenya Tribes: The present Kenya tribes are grouped into three different races; there is not sufficient current scientific data to suggest the arrival of the Kenyan's ancestors. The Bantu – speaking people are alleged to have begun arriving in the territory nearly 2,000 years Before Christ. The Bantu history and origin has attracted a worldwide debate among linguistics, sociologists, and anthropologists.

Current tribes in Kenya are in various sub-groups of major tribes which make it hard to know the exact number of the tribes in Kenya. People from other neighboring states cross into Kenya borders in search for a better life compared to other East African Nations unnoticed. Illegal immigrants have in many occasions crossed Kenya borders and claimed citizenship after staying in the country for a number of years since late 1959 leading to Kenya's Independence in 1963. A majority of added tribes moved as refugees during the 1980s and1990s from central African countries. Kenya has a very poor system in place to extract non-citizens, much less those who bribed their way into Kenya immigration apparatus between 1964 through the 1990s. Kenya's borders are not guarded like most nations of the north, especially along the Indian Ocean.

Oral histories from across natives of East and Central Africa suggest that their ancestors originated from Eastern Niger-Congo River and forests. The Bantu race embarked on a long treacherous [safari] journey from unspecified locations in Congo forest basins traveling north-eastwards crisscrossing dangerous rivers and lakes: Tanganyika, Kivu, Lake Albert, Lake Edward, western river Nile (Uganda), Lake Nyasa, (Victoria); guided by the mountain ranges of western Ruwenzori mountain range of southern Uganda and the great mountain of Kilimanjaro, present Tanzania, as a point of reference.

The Bantu history of origin remains a scientific nightmare, at this juncture, it is unknown. Summer of 2007 a scientific DNA research conducted by Linguistic and Cultural Diversity of Rome OMLL, suggests that Bantu speaking population originated from Eastern Niger-Congo River, and forests about 2,000 Before Christ. On the other hand Leakey's discovery of the earliest human species dating back to 600 B.C. is worth some consideration.

Leakey states the aquatic civilization of middle Africa around Oldvai Gorge, was filled with happy human living beings that lived on tilapia fish, edible plants, birds and wildlife. These civilizations once flourished during the splendor of Africa past millennium. The shores of Lake Turkana and Ormo River are almost desert because of the expansion of the Sahel Desert at 100 miles per year.

Bantu speaking tribes make up three quarters of the largest population in Kenya namely: **Central/Eastern Bantu**: Kikuyu, Akamba, Meru, Tharaka, and Mbere. **Western/Rift Valley Bantu:** Gusii (Kisii), Kuria, Luhya. **Coastal Bantu:** Mijikenda, Swahili, Pokomo, Segeju, Taita and Taveta, neighbor to the Bantu-Chagga tribe of Kilimanjaro.

The Nilotic – speaking tribes arrived about the same time with Bantu. Some suggest that Nilotic came from the northern Uganda/ southern Sudan border. Nilotic speaking people are the second in Kenya's population, namely: **The Plains Nilotic:** Maasai, Samburu, Teso, Turkana, Elmoro, and Njemps. **Highlands Nilotic:** Kalenjin, Marakwet, Tugen, Pokot, Elkony, Kipsigis. **Lake Basin: Nilotic:** Luo, the third largest tribe in Kenya with additional Luo speaking population around the city states of Uganda and Tanzania.

The Cushitic speaking tribes arrived between 500 Before Christ, B.C. and 600 after the Birth of Christ, A.D. The group of tribes mentioned is referenced in the Old and New Testament time. Their history is associated with ancient Egyptians culture under Alexandra the Great mixed with Arabian and Jewish ancestry. The majority of the Cushitic - speaking tribes came from Lake

Tana located in northern highlands of Ethiopia; also known as the source of the Blue Nile. For hundreds of centuries, the Blue Nile has gently flowed, a journey (safari) of 2,750 miles through the Sudan-Egyptian desert pouring its water into the Mediterranean Sea. In the region surrounding Lake Tana, there are ancient Coptic Monasteries that date back to ancient times, occupied by Ethiopian black monks with Jewish ancestry.

Eastern Cushitic: Rendile, Somali, Boran, Gabbra, Orma. **Southern Cushitic:** Boni-sanye, the majority live on the northeastern Kenya and southern Ethiopia borders. The tribes are nomadic people, travelling with their herds of cattle and camels across the northern-eastern Kenya, southern Ethiopia desert in search for an oasis of desert water for their animals. The Cushitic tribes make up a third of the Kenyan's population. Kenya census of 1989 and 1999 lists more than 42 tribes each with their spoken languages of: Bantu, Nilotic and Cushitic.

The Synopsis History of Zanzibar between 975 A.D. - 1963: from oral histories Bantu speaking groups roamed between shores and the interior Africa before 2,000 B.C. There is no evidence of oral histories available to suggest the presence of the Bantu speaking groups on the Islands of Pemba and Zanzibar. It is problematic to establish the presence of the Bantu speaking groups on the Islands of Pemba and Zanzibar earlier than the first century. The Bantus made hollowed tree trunk canoes purported to cross small bodies of water, small lakes and rivers located in the interior of Africa. The Bantus who lived near the Indian shores had not developed a vessel similar to Arabs made dhow to sail on larger bodies of waters like the Indian Ocean. Besides, the Zanzibar Island is located more than twenty five miles in deep open sea, away from the mainland.

On the other hand, we know the Africa man was used to life in the jungles, forests, deserts, plains and around the small lakes compared to the oceans like the Indian Ocean and Atlantic Ocean on the western African coast. In contrast, the Arabs travelled on dhows which were better and stronger on the open sea. Second, there were no archeological digs on any of the Pemba and Zanzibar islands before the arrival of the Arabs 975 A.D. in search for the signs of humans' species. Therefore, transportation logistics that would have enabled the Bantus to sail on sea to the islands before the arrival of the Arabs leans to doubt.

To be exact, there are available records from the Omani Arabs and Shirazi Persians merchants with narration, as when and how they arrived on to the African shores during the first century. The island of Zanzibar is 60 miles long by 20 miles wide. It was good for tropical cash crops; the inhabitants were well served by its location which shielded them from the outside enemies. The majority of Arab resident traders of the Indian coast arrived from different kingdoms of city and states of the Middle East. They occupied the coast in large numbers between the 7th and 10th Centuries. The East Africa coast provides integral information with valuable history about the culture of the traders of the day.

The island of Zanzibar was known worldwide for her sweet aroma of cloves, nutmeg, cinnamon, pepper and many other spices which brought the Sultans of Oman and the establishment of the iniquitous slave trade that changed the history of Africa and her people. One would be flabbergasted with the beauty of the plantations and of the freshness of spices. The world of the spices had its axis in the Island of Zanzibar. For centuries the Island of Zanzibar and her sister Islands of Pemba and others lured the traders and the merchants from the Middle East, Persians, Phoenicians, Assyrians, Arabs of Omani, Indians, Chinese, Portuguese, Dutch and English. The Arabs sailed the coast of Africa by the use of the Monsoon winds from Omani, Muscat and the Orient for the purpose to trade for ivory, spices and slaves.

The story of East Africa would not be complete without the mention of the histories of Zanzibar and Pemba. The islands in the later years were controlled by the British East Africa Kenya from Nairobi, Kenya. Shortly before Kenya Independence the Zanzibar leadership was warned by the British that all the remaining strip of land and the coast of Mombasa would remain under the control of the new Republic of Kenya.

Among all the Sultans who ever ruled the East African shores, are the Shirazis Persians, whose descendants came from southern (Persia) modern Iran and should be credited for the majority of the development of the golden culture and tradition of the Zanzibar paradise. There was a legend told by the descendants of Shirazi Persians, which states that one night in his sleep the Sultan Al-Hassan bin Ali, of Shirazi had a bad frightening dream; in his dream the Sultan saw a rat that had consumed the wooden foundation of his palace.

Sultan Ali was not alone; he lived during the medieval era, and it was not uncommon for rulers of his day to be over-powered by another emerging, stronger, militant leader within the kingdom. Sometimes takeover of leadership came from within through generals, brothers and other relatives, especially when leadership was inherited but not earned. Leadership takeover may have come from another neighboring kingdom, city and states purported to increase military strength and collect revenues from smaller kingdoms. A leader remained vigilant at all times.

He took the dream as a threat to his Kingdom. Having taken seriously his dream, he gathered his six sons and their followers and set off to the open sea in search of a better place. His dream was not by accident; at the same time Sultan Ali wanted to escape the local cleric's disputes on who would become the Caliph, the successor of the Prophet Mohammed. The Sultan Ali with his six sons, and their followers, each with their own dhows sailed out into the open sea for what would be their greatest, treacherous safari of their life time.

Soon after they sailed past the horn of Africa, the dhows were caught in strong, unpredicted Monsoon winds. The dhows in a caravan of six were certainly put into disarray, thrown into separate directions. There were not modern telephones by which family members could signal each other as the dhows disappeared into the endless harsh and grim storm of the sea. The family of six with their relatives landed on six different islands including Zanzibar in the East African coast about 975 A.D. The nightmare of the dream resurfaced, when the Sultan could no longer trace the disappearing dhows into the stormy winds of the sea. There are no available oral histories to suggest when and how long the Sultan and his family took to meet up again. However, records, confirm the Sultan Ali was the first family of royalty to establish a new Kingdom. It was one of the greatest Kingdoms in a new found land called the "Zenj-Empire" which translates as the country of the black people of the East African Coast. The Zenj-Empire lasted until 1502 during the Portuguese conquest.

The Shirazi Persians were more liberal and fewer in number.

They were the rulers, administrators, and the civilized. They entered into intermarriage between native Bantu speaking groups like Tumbatu, Hadimu and others of the day for the purpose to form new families. It is important to note that during the first interracial marriages between Bantu and Shirazi Persians the marriage only occurred between male Persians and Bantu women. Similarly, during the war between the white settlers and Native American Indians, such as the Comanche, the Navaho, and the Sioux Indians, when they stormed the white settlers' forts they killed all the men and the boys and took with them young girls for the purpose to repopulate.

Persians and Arabs enjoyed the luxury, beauty and riches of the coasts; they had Bantu women for their households and the men till the gardens and their spice plantations. This was the golden age of the coast. Persians were few in number and more aggressive, compared to their counterpart Arabs of Omani and Muscat, being fond of the Bantu women who worked in their households; out of unwed women children were born into the majority of the Persian households. Children born into these kinds of relationships had no father-figurehead. Without fault of their own, they bore derogatory names on their heads, and were considered outcasts and cursed by the communities they lived in. They were fugitives of life. Until such a time they populated the islands and began to marry among themselves, they ended up in the madarasses in the mosque. They were recruited and well suited as dhow workers in the open sea.

The new biracial people gave rise to a coastal community with distinctive features of beauty and a language that bears their name, waSwahili which means people. The word Swahili comes from the Arab word sawahil which means "coast" with a mixture of Bantu root words.

The Swahili or Kiswahili is the language. The proper name for the people is called waSwahili, one individual is known as mSwahili. The word uSwahilini refers to one's homeland. Today, the KiSwahili language is the largest single spoken language of Africa. Modern KiSwahili language has acquired many words on loan from English and vice versa. KiSwahili language has captured worldwide audiences during the last 6 decades including the movie makers of Europe and Hollywood, for example, "Simba Lion King".

The word "safari" is widely used in daily English tour business operations to mean an expedition or adventure. The word "safari" has a much deeper meaning as per the architectures of the KiSwahili language. When someone goes on a safari it means the journey is adventurous and very well dangerous, the journey in itself poses an eminent danger. Sailing on a dhow in 700s A.D. during stormy Monsoon winds meant one's life had no guarantee, even sailing on a modern ship along the horn of Africa; the pirates are ready to cash in!

Theodore Roosevelt was a legendary American professional hunter by his own right. He sailed across the Atlantic Ocean, Mediterranean Sea, Red sea and Indian Ocean, on safari hunting in Kenya at the turn of the century. Teddy and his son survived mosquitoes' bites and dangerous animals of the wild. Millions of American boys grew up reading about safari expeditions in the dark-continent; with that someday they too would go on safari expedition hunting in Africa. Teddy published his greatest work on "Africa Safari Trail 1910". At the end of his safari he took more than 1,100 trophy animals with him to the Smithsonian

Institute in Washington D.C.

Like Teddy when a professional hunter goes on a safari game hunt in Africa, it means the expedition is a process of hunting a game, while in the same process; the hunter is always being hunted by the very animals being hunted. Many safari outfitters recommend if you cannot shoot a 10 inch square in less than 20 yards, you are not ready for the safari. One must be able to shoot a target with accuracy between 200-250 yards! Unless you want to become the one being hunted! That is safari for you.

Detroit, Michigan is the capital city of the world's largest auto manufactures. GM took the word safari to market GM Minivan Safari which appealed to soccer moms, Friday night football fans and church convention attendees. All these activities required a GM Safari minivan for long journeys across the state lines.

The word "Mesa" is the word for table in Spanish and Swahili. If it were for the Swahili speakers the Table Mountain of South Africa would have been called "Mesa Mountain" which means a flat surface. "Rafiki" is a word for a friend and is last in my series of the Swahili words; it is the richest word in the language. There are many such words and phrases circulating in various languages of the world from the Swahili language.

There were two families of Zanzibar descendant groups: Omani and Muscat Arabs, one of the original groups were commercially involved in the lucrative slave trade, ivory and spices. They kept to themselves in marriage, because they still had a homeland to return to in order to find a bride. The Shirazis Persian group immersed themselves mainly in property ownership, landowner-ship and agriculture. They were the masters of the great plantations of spices of Zanzibar.

However, the Shirazis Persians group and Omani Arabs shared one common ideology; Islam was their religion. The earliest building is a mosque built in 1107; it is the oldest standing mosque in East Africa. Perhaps it could qualify for a Pilgrimage. There are other memorable places in Lamu where archeologists discovered a much older building dating back to 775 A.D. Another attraction is the original home of the famous Christian, Dr. David Livingstone. He kept an island home for a rest when he would return to the coast from his interior ministry. Indeed, Zanzibar had the earliest such evidence about the art and worship by a people of a distant past. Zanzibar is worth a visit to experience the history and birth of a culture whose people and language has changed the world.

Centuries later, during the reign of Sultan Seyyid Said of Zanzibar; the Sultan was under tremendous pressure from the British Empire to end slavery in his kingdom. The Sultan signed the Moresby Treaty of 1822, banning the slave trade in his kingdom. Twenty-three years later, the Sultan signed the second and final Hamerton Treaty of 1845. One of the clauses of the treaty requested the protection of the Sultan's subjects and her future descendents. The Hamerton Treaty made it illegal to buy, sale and own a human slave in all of East African Dominion. For the first time the coast of East Africa permanently became free from slavery. The British Empire banished slavery in Zanzibar, stopping the supply of slaves from the East African Coast to the rest of the European region and the rest of the world.

However, after the death of Seyyid Said, the new Sultans who followed were Sultan Barghash and Hamud Ibn Mohammed who continued to smuggle illegal humans for slave trade. The British Empire patrolling the Indian Ocean played a war of cat and mouse to catch the sea pirates with human cargos on board. Finally, Sultan Barghash on June 5, 1873, signed the treaty which made it illegal, and all the gates of the slave market were closed forever. The legal status to own a slave in Zanzibar was finally abolished in 1897. Kenya legal status of slave ownership was abolished in 1904.

Tanganyika (Tanzania) was under German Rule. The slavery status was not finally abolished until 1919 when the British took control over Tanganyika under the guidance of United Nations. The first USA Consulate in East Africa was established in Zanzibar in 1836; the same year Texas won her independence from the Dictator Santa Anna of Mexico. Four years later The British established their diplomatic relationship in 1840 and France thereafter. There is a direct correlation between Abraham Lincoln's emancipation of the slaves (January 1, 1863) and the British taking charge of the Atlantic Ocean, ceasing the source of the slavery coming from Africa.

In the final hours in preparation for British Colonial Office at Downing Street, London, to hand over all her colonies back to the natives, Zanzibar was on the list. A conference held in London in 1962 introduced a road map for self-government rule based on democratic ideals. The Zanzibarians were not about to change their ways of culture and tradition under new leadership, other than a Sultan. With the shifting Monsoon winds of change, the emerging new generation caused by intermarriages, culture and languages could no longer maintain a Sultan government.

People opposed to Sultanism had differences of opinions. They wanted a change, they agreed on legislative council of Zanzibar which formed two major political parties. Zanzibar National Party represented Omani and Muscat, the Zanzibarian Arabs, and Zanzibar and Pemba People's Party, (ZPPP) was an offshoot of the ZNP. Both were Arabs who shared one common ancestry and ideology. It was easier to agree on a democratic government without abandoning their ideology. All parties voted for a democratic government under the leadership of Mohammed Shamte Hamadi as chief Minister and President of Zanzibar. Modern Zanzibar is now part of the mainland government with a special arrangement in Tanzania government. Zanzibar maintains their own form of government separate from the mainland government of Tanzania. The president of Zanzibar automatically becomes vice president of the Republic of Tanzania.

What was Wrong with this Treaty? A brief history of the Memorandum of Understanding claimed by National Muslim Leaders Forum and as often used by presidential candidates every general elections year to get votes from Muslims. The MoU 2007 was the most serious, dangerous, savage, callous, torturous, and scandalous that almost put the country on the brink of civil war because of its contents.

During the heyday of Great Britain rule along the Indian Ocean no one knew that the reign would not last forever. In fact no earthly reign will ever last forever. The Romans are the best example of the superpower's demise. In 1895 there was an agreement between The Great Britain and the Sultan of Zanzibar, for the purchase of the ten mile coastal strip of Mombasa, from the Sultan of Zanzibar for $125,000,000 at $6,875,000 with $3,750 in 3% interest.

Muslims of Kenya are minority, and among the wealthiest Kenya citizens. They control the media outlets, insurance firms, multi-national and domestic business holdings through proxies, banking, and hospitals. During the 10th Parliament [2008-2012] 45% out of 220 Parliamentarians were of Islam religion, the majority of Muslim MPs contestants were in the Orange Democratic Movement Party under Hon. Raila. Muslims sat on the majority of important seats in the National Assembly, such as the Committee of Experts, Independent Boundaries Review Team and Immigration. Under the protection of the Constitution of Kenya, Muslim would want the top seat of a President in Kenya. Muslim would want to gain the control of Kenya as they controlled the coastal region in centuries past.

Overall, Islam, in recent decades has built mosques in every major city and town of Kenya because of the religious freedom allowed by the Kenya constitution. In addition, the Kenya constitution has provision for: civil rights, social-economic apparatus and the practices of one's cultural passage of rite. This includes traditional marriage and matrimonial property carried out by every tribe in Kenya.

It is safe to say that a majority of Kenyan tribes, including law abiding Muslims, are afraid of Islamic ideologies and practices that may not be acceptable by the rest of the industrialized nations of the north because of the war on drug trafficking and international "terrorism". The nations of the north, especially North America have zero tolerance on terroristic acts and may tend to profile majority of people with Islamic origin names and likeness. In 2008 39% of Kenya were opposed to the establishment of religious courts like Muslim (Sheria) law courts, Indus and Tribal courts that may still exist in Kenya. The number of those who oppose the Kadhi practices continues to grow. The Great Britain Colonial Office in Downing Street, London, struggled to maintain her colonies in East Africa and elsewhere in the world, only to lose them by allowing governments of self rule.

When Kenya and Tanganyika (modern Tanzania) received their independence from Great Britain, Tanganyika 1961, and Kenya 1963, became solvent nations by their constitutions. All previous treaties and diplomatic ties that Britain signed between the Sultan of Zanzibar became null and void. Furthermore, today Zanzibar no longer has a Sultan; she became a democratic nation and part of a solvent united government of Tanzania.

MoU 2007 revived an old century treaty. The treaty was between the British and the Sultan of Zanzibar. There was a stipulation clause in the treaty to provide Sultan's subjects and her future descendants with protection in perpetuity. One of the fallacies of this MoU was based on a false non-Islamic premise. The protection of Sultan subjects and his future generations can no longer be valid. The *Majimboism* creates ethnicity, tribal borders and the reference to one's faith and religion, if this premise were to come to pass; it would result into decimation to the peoples of Kenya.

The Diminishing Tribes of Kenya: The official count of the tribes of Kenya is staggering, and confusing to many natives of Kenya. I visited various parts of Kenya but did not find a truly exact count of the tribes of Kenya. One would assume that the Electoral Commission of Kenya website would list all the tribes including the languages spoken in Kenya for the purpose of conducting elections. I managed to locate the 1989 Kenya Census, reported in the Kenya Fact Book, [15th Edition, and

1997-1998]. We conducted various interviews from a cross section of the natives of Kenya. They too, did not know the true count and the languages of their countrymen. They did not seem to be bothered.

The majority of the people interviewed could only guess! The last group interviewed was the unexpected: the missionaries, native evangelists and tour operators. These were the frequent visitors to Kenya; tourists take great pleasure in site seeing Kenya's last earthly Eden for the wildlife sanctuaries of East Africa that has survived decades of animal poaching during the early 1970s, 1980s and 1990s.

The group's professional advantage point adds validity as they have gone around to the nation's cities, villages, rural-towns, lakes, remote rivers, deserts, countless islands and to the last caves still with people found living in government forested lands, and the grandiose shores of the Indian Ocean, in search for the last diminishing tribes of Kenya.

The interviews reflect some of these tribes are fewer than 500, if not less and are in danger of extinction before our very eyes. Many of them are nomads, poor and Stone Age type people living in deserted parts of the Republic of Kenya.

As long as there has been a man, there has been a tribe. A tribe, large or small, American Indians or African, is the oldest form of social organization on earth. A tribe is a collection of people living in an organized social group, who share common beliefs, traditions, values, and with a common understanding about an absolute on a supreme being, creator (God). A tribe is sovereign, and has genealogically structured clans within a larger group. A tribe prescribes to a common ancestor through ancestry lineage.

A tribe, small or large in population, is governed by a set of standards of norms, culture, and tradition that guide their survival and existence as a people. Some tribes are governed by a spiritual leader, King or Queen, or a war lord. For example, the Swazi tribe of southern Africa is ruled by a king or monarch. The Buganda tribe of Uganda was ruled by "Mutesa" a dynasty of Kings. Majority of the modern African tribes are tied to their kinship, language, culture and are economically and politically unified in order to hearten the interest of their tribe far and wide. A tribe, large or small in population, must negotiate with other tribes within the geographical areas to live in unity and peace. During the killing spree of 2007/2008 Kenya general elections, many smaller tribes remained faithful to their neighbor tribe, forced to vote for a candidate against their choice.

Therefore, a tribe may live in one geographical ancestry area; while other tribes are forced to live a nomadic lifestyle, because of the shortages of seasonal and annual rainfall for domestic gardens and pasture for their animals. However, due to technological breakthroughs, a single member of a tribe can live and work outside his community, yet remain loyal to his/her tribe. In recent decades, members of different tribes, family and friends across the globe are able to go into chat rooms and blogs and instantly communicate via internet services.

Third world nations including Kenya have the fastest communications on cell phone systems than the majority of the people living in industrialized societies. With a dial tone anyone can communicate with anybody in a far removed remote area of the world in a matter of seconds. Now, having said that, one should not be entangled in a definition, and lose focus and miss the identity and purpose of the tribe. In the tropics of Africa, tribes are here to stay at least for now in Kenya. Therefore, approaching tribal ethnic clashes, negotiators and peace brokers must understand each tribe's values and culture to develop and nurture peace and unity between tribes within a community of people living under one nation.

Having identified the tribes of Kenya, there are a few tribes who are at risk and on the verge of extinction. When a language ceases to be spoken by its original members, and their culture and tradition are acculturated into a larger group; the tribe ceases to exist, and becomes extinct. For example, the Suba/Basuba tribe, population 107,819 (census 1989) dwellers of the Islands of Rusinga and Mfangano were once a Bantu speaking tribe. They have been assimilated into a larger Nilotic Luo tribe, whose culture and traditions have overtaken the Basuba/Suba originally with a Bantu ancestry. Basuba/Suba Bantu is on the verge of extinction.

The Bantu Luhya tribe of western Kenya has consumed two or three sub-tribes into their influential tradition and culture: the Taichon, Marama, Bukus and, Maragoli sub tribes have been consumed into the larger Bantu speaking Luhya tribe. Because of the Luhya cultural influence over other subgroup tribes, the Luhya tribe ranks number two in the total population, behind the Kikuyu tribe.

The Sengwer, with an estimated population of 65,000 or less living in the majority of government lands of the Marakwet forest in Rift Valley, has historically suffered political discrimination. Their original lands were the first to be taken by the

white settlers. When Kenyatta administration took Kenya leadership, greedy politicians bought lands from the white settlers
and pushed the Sengwer tribe further into the government forest
without land to live on.

For more than forty-five years of self rule, the Sengwer people
have been tossed around by other tribes, encroaching into their
ancestral land rites. The Sengwer tribes and others have been
forced to live a substandard life without representation compared to the rest of the Kenya tribes. The tribe will take some
time to disappear completely because of the national political
landscape of their area. However, Sengwer tribe culture and traditions will eventually be lost and swallowed by the stronger
cultural influence.

The Yiabu tribe estimated 6,000 or less, and Watha or Sanye
tribes are located around Mount Kenya and the outskirts of
the great mountain. Both tribes are insignificant compared to
the larger tribes of Meru and Embu, Tharaka and Mbere. The
Watha/Sanye tribes will someday be assimilated between Meru
and Embu tribes depending on who will influence their ways of
life.

As the deforestation of the Mukodo forest continues to decrease
in many parts of Kenya, the Watha tribe will settle down in small
farming communities for unspecified amount of years before
they are lost into either tribe of the mountain. It is safe to suggest
that both Yiabu and Watha tribes are on the verge of extinction
as tribes of Kenya.

The Pokomo, Dahalo, Aweer, as known as Boni and Bajuni
tribes, are very small in number with Dahalo estimated 400,

Aweer estimated 4,000, compared to a larger Bajuni tribe of 10,000 people. The tribes will disappear into the Swahili people, the merchants and traders of the sea.

Due to the geographical location, Aweer, and Bujuni tribes constantly trade between the cities of Mogadisho, Kismayo and Lamu. The Pokomo live in small communities along the banks of the Tana River, fishing and hunting for beehives. Swahili merchants travel into the interior Tana River region in search for wild honey and crocodile skins which are sold in illegal markets in cities of Kismayo, Lamu and Mogadisho, for export to the Far East.

Rites and Traditions: Kenya Coast and her history: The Swahili origin — has archeological historical gaps available through structural ruins extending the coastline, over one thousand miles that pertain to the origin of the Swahili people. During the first century, an Arab written account published in Alexandria, a navigator's marine guide to the Indian Ocean, in Greek *"Periplus of the Erythraena Sea,"* sheds some light, about the origin of the Swahili-speaking people. The document *"Periplus"* lists trading posts between the Red Sea to the East African Coast. The Swahili speaking people were always literate; they imported paper and ink from the Middle East. They first used the Arabic alphabet and later changed into the Roman alphabet.

Additional information about the Swahili people can be revealed from the voluminous accounts of the Arabic and Portuguese administrators, religious leaders and traders of the day. Bantu-Cushitic pastoralists are the modern Orma (Oromo or Galla) Somali people. It is safe to suggest that the Swahili speaking group were amalgamated long before the first century, through interracial marriages between Bantu-speaking with Cushitic- people who had arrived earlier as mentioned under Bantu history. Inter-racial marriage arrangements were common with Arab traders, and the Phoenician traders who immigrated to the East African coast and Madagascar.

In the second century, an Arab writer, Al-Masudi identified some form of self-governing among the Swahili people of the coast. Swahili-Arab traders were the middlemen; they controlled the trading markets coming from the interior Bantu-Akamba people, who traded for ivory, crocodile, rhinoceros and lion skins. The Arab traders of the sea traded with Swahili traders for slaves, spices, pearls and gold which came from interior "Tanga-nyika" modern Tanzania for export markets of the Middle East, Europe and the Orient. There was no slave trade that ever occurred between East Africa and the West Indies except through Europe. The majority of slavery trade was carried to the rich families of the Arab world and during the Roman conquest. Around the 13th Century a Chinese document shows that Swahili- speaking people were exporting ivory, rhinoceros horns, and spices to Far East including India, city and states.

After many centuries the Swahili independence came to an end. Their communities were overpowered by the Sultans of Oman. Then came the Portuguese; their main intention was to acquire the trade spices, gold and to establish a Catholic Church over Islam. Portuguese were the first western power in the Indian Ocean between1498-1729. The Portuguese control was weak, corrupt and few in numbers which gave way to renewed Arab control under the Imam of Oman in the 1600s. In the mid-nineteenth century, The British Empire influence superseded that of the Arabs. Unlike their Arab predecessors, the British Empire took control of the coastal region as well as the interior; they encouraged European explorers to map the interior for expansion.

The Mijikenda tribes of the coast, made of nine different subtribes, are part of the Bantu race that moved south-eastward of Kilimanjaro toward the Indian Ocean, nearly 2,000-3,000 years ago; though there is no scientific proof to the arrival dates into the Kaya forests of the Coast. Their language and culture is similar to the Swahili people. The Mijikenda are very superstitious and practice witchcraft.

Medicine-Witch-Doctors: The medicine-witch-doctors are grouped into several classes: diviners, herbalists, magicians and fortune tellers. The practitioners are men and women whose roles can be very confusing depending on which part of the world you live in. These individuals tell their clients about the past and the present going into the future. **Fortune tellers** are found everywhere in the world including Africa. **Herbalists** are individual experts in the use of plant medicines, especially in Africa and the Far East. Herbal medicines are found in North America and European drug stores with manufacturer's labels originating in China and the Far East. The herbalist practitioners may not be included in the same grouping with witch-doctors or associated with magic.

Medicine-witch-doctors and **magicians** come in orders of evil and good: one that believes in the impersonal-spiritual forces of gods, spirits and ancestors. Magicians have a long list of definitions that can take a chapter on their own. Witchcraft was practiced during the medieval times throughout Europe, Rome, Africa and the times of Jesus Christ. In the book of Acts of the Apostles, the disciples were confronted by medicine men, who requested power from the disciples for wholesale. People of Christian faith when faced with magicians, have an assurance of the STRONGER will of God to whom they call upon. Magicians are found in every society of the world.

Witchcraft in Africa is realized in the form of superstition, a belief that has always dominated the African customary traditions and beliefs in spirits in their cosmos world. Mysterious illness, deaths and misfortunes are experiences linked to bad flying objects by the cover of night and the annoyance of the ancestors. The majority of African tribes believe that spirits may take the forms of animals and snakes, creatures most feared. This is a belief that many African tribes hold; that human souls are stolen at night by bad flying spirits who live and hide in some-darkened caves in the forests. The notion that, no one dies without a reason. The old nature is that the man must blame his behavior to a cause of someone else.

A medicine-witch-doctor, also known as a **divine** healer, is one who is feared, respected and believed that he has the keys to unlock the bad spirits out of a bewitched person(s). The MWD are not considered witches. Instead, they enjoy traditional privileges similar to a modern western medical doctor. They are bequeathed with traditional customary laws and spiritual guidance, as found in many societies of the world. These individuals are the most powerful personalities in the African society, whose powers are highly sought by politicians, for spiritual guidance in times of war, in sports, and local and national politics.

In addition, medicine men provide charms for a price for protection, good luck, council on marriage and the pursuit of happiness. These charms are worn as a pendulum around the neck, on fingers as rings, on forearms like a wrist watch, under garments around the body's waist to protect one's bungles of life and others are planted in front of the main entrance of a family estate. Charms are compared to antidepressant drugs prescribed by modern western psychiatry. I believe that medicine-witchdoctors will remain employed. Witchcraft will continue to be practiced as long as the African tribes are engulfed in fears of economic and leadership instability.

Then there are the perceived witches who are either men or women. They are believed to be controlled and possessed by the bad spirits, the source of illness and everything negative that happens to people. They are believed to move at night in search for medicine from all sorts of places including dug outs of human skeletons from burial grounds for the best act of bewitching a person or family. These witches are feared, because whatever they do is done in secrecy. Going out in the dark night to "haunted houses" and wearing scary costumes like on Halloween, is an example of North Americans' fascination with the world of witches.

Circumcision has remained a sensitive issue among African tribes. The Latin word (circumcisio) and Hebrew (peritome) describes the cutting and removal of a foreskin from a male organ /penis. Herodotus, Greek historian, made circumcision references to the Egyptians, Ethiopians and Colchians as the world's earliest people to practice circumcision. Josephus maintains that Phoenicians, Jews and Syrians of Palestine learned the practice from the Egyptians.

Circumcision has existed throughout the ages. But practitioners have not always provided a satisfactory rationale for the exercises. Undeniably, circumcision was practiced long before the Patriarchs reference to Abraham. The following are some of the unanswered questions. Was it an act in Bantu culture and tradition of initiation into manhood to marriageable age? Was the act connected to sacrificial worship? Was the act an offering to the deity of fertility in ancient Egypt? Was the act a sign of nobility and superiority in ancient times? Was the act a religious significance? Both Philo and Herodotus literatures concur that circumcision provided cleanliness, free from diseases, offspring and purity of a man's heart. The practice has more questions than answers.

For the Jews tradition the Bible has a clear proclamation that circumcision was given by God to Abraham, as "a sign of the covenant" Gen 17:11 between God and Abraham. From that time on circumcision has remained sacramental with meaning derived from its origin with Abraham and to Isaac whose children were circumcised on the eighth day according to the Law of Moses to this day. **Purification** after a birth of a child was a significant event in the Old Testament days among the Jews. Moses was instructed by God, "If a woman conceives and bears a male child… on the eighth day the flesh of his foreskin shall be circumcised" Leviticus 12:1-8 ESV Whereby, the Koran does not sanction the practice of circumcision as a religious ordinance. However, Arabs Islam are circumcised between seven and twelve years old; there is a reference to a Biblical time frame when Ishmael was circumcised. This is whom Islam links their descendants to Abraham. Gen 7:25 The reader must be reminded that Isaac and Ishmael were half-brothers, modern Arabs and Jews. Their descendants have observed circumcision tradition.

The Bantu tribes consider circumcision as an initiation of manhood to marriageable age for young men and women. It is one of the three traditional rites of passage a person must experience in life: birth, circumcision and marriage. The circumcision ceremonies are conducted in the early morning by the river side during the cold-rainy seasons of Africa.

In recent decades an increasing number of tribes consider having circumcision procedure be carried out by a medical doctor in the hospital. Girls' circumcision is on the downside because of the western influence through religious teachings. In recent decades among the Nilotic tribes whose tradition does not allow male circumcision, have considered to change their century old tradition, because an uncircumcised man has often had difficulty assuming a political leadership position where the majority tribes are circumcised. Raila, of the Luo tribe, and former presidential candidate in Kenya has often suffered tribal discrimination based on the clan belief.

"Researchers say circumcision reduces the risk of HIV infection among men. Health campaign workers are trying to encourage more men to be circumcised by offering free circumcision services. Elders from Kenya's Luo community in western Kenya have refused to endorse a plan to promote male circumcision, because it is against the community's culture. The elders are afraid that some men will think that being circumcised is an alternative to using condoms, which will put them at a higher risk of infection, our correspondent says. But the council has concluded those individuals who want to be circumcised are free to do so." [BBC' Muliro] At the dawn of the western influence and acculturation, female circumcision and witchcraft practices are slowly on the verge of elimination.

Many political leaders travel privately to the villages of the Kaya forests and camps of medicine men and women, in search for a magic charm for a political win over their opponents. I still remember many stories and legends told during my nostalgia days in high school in Mombasa. We were told about a famous medicine man called "Kabwere," the named medicine man was supreme over all other medicine men and women of the coast.

A story is told, that one day Kabwere was apprehended by the British Colonial Officers for practicing witchcraft without a license. In court the judge found the medicine man guilty as charged, he was fined and sentenced to thirty days in jail. The story goes on to say that when time to sleep came, the medicine man, due to his powers, always left at night without being noticed and returned to the cell early in the morning due to his supernatural powers.

The readers are cautioned that this is only a legend; this publication does not confirm or support the validity of the story. It is just one way to say there are bad spirits out there.

However, due to the increasing pressure of the winds of change through the Christian messages being preached daily by Christian groups in Kenya, superstition and witchcraft may have to take a back seat in the future.

In the early1970s, as fresh graduates from The Baptist Seminary, (today Mount Meru University) Arusha, Tanzania, under the leadership of the late, Tom McMillan, principal, four colleagues and I were sent to evangelize the Giryama-Mijikenda people, equipped with the message of love and forgiveness. Gyriama Evangelism Project was widely recorded in the mission records, as the best, successful mission project in the history of the Southern Baptist mission in East Africa. The project was an evangelistic model breakthrough, the how to, and when to, present the Word of God to a pagan. The Gyriama tribe believes in the practices of witch-craft and superstition as a way of life; and made it very hard to break a century old tradition and culture in a matter of a few months.

Like Paul, my four colleagues and I, toiled, risked our lives against dangerous, poisonous snakes of the wild coast, mosquitoes' bites and Islamic threats of the day. We followed the examples of the foot prints and teachings of Paul during his missionary journeys in many enchanted places of the old. Day and night we journeyed, singing nightly at campfires, sometimes meant to drive away the human fears of the lonely wilderness. These were some of the best years in Christian ministry.

It is with great honor and respect to mention my colleagues here and now: Solomon Kimuyu, Akamba tribe, group leader, Wilson Chico, Gyriama tribe, Joe Muchuki, Kikuyu tribe, and David Kombe, Gyriama tribe. We were the first ever such home missionary's team to present the Gospel of Truth to the Mijikenda-Giryama speaking tribe in the history of the church in Kenya. I still remember one of the best baptism service events I have ever had, where in one day I baptized 150 people! My arm remained sore for a couple of weeks.

The mission success appeared in Southern Baptist Mission Board meetings and captured the imaginations of the world evangelicals around the mission groups! An Anglican woman at an ecumenical women's Bible study, cried and exclaimed, how she and another Anglican had prayed for many years for such an outpouring of God's Spirit upon the Giryama people. She said, "God has chosen the Baptists to bring salvation to these people." (Scales, 1998) I will be forever thrilled to have been on a winning team.

Dr. Klem asked, "How could (4) four single fresh graduates without past experience change the Islamic influence in less than a year?" He wanted to know about the methodology used to convert the Giryama people to Christianity in such a short time. Dr. Klem was a Christian researcher with Daystar International Christian Institute, located in Nairobi, Kenya. Today it is a fully fledged four year university — Daystar University located in my home town, Athi River.

During the first seven months of evangelization, I discovered that one of the oldest established churches *[Anglican Church (Mission) of Kenya]* first established its mission station in the late 1800s along with the British Colonial power in Mombasa. The church launched a mission work at Rabai, and Kaloleni. The said church had never penetrated further into the interior Mijikenda-Gyriama tribe in fear of the old century Islamic influence. The Mijikenda-Giryama people had never been presented with the opportunity of the gospel of Jesus Christ. There are many Giryama stories I gathered over a period of time. Our message was simple and clear.

In many such interviews, I discovered that to them the True God was unreachable. It was best described to me in the following legend. An elderly Gyriama man told me that, "god-who is Supreme Being Creator" was long ago pushed away further into the sky when women were pounding and crushing corn into flour-powder to make their daily staple food.

The cylinder mortar-container called "Kinu" in Swahili, similarly, used by the Akamba tribe, is made of a hard wooden block, "Mvuli tree" hollowed out in the mid center.

Grains of corn or millet are poured inside the wooden cylinder mortar ready to be crushed into powder-flour form; with a smooth finished wooden pestle made of "Mvuli" wood called "mchi" in Swahili; it is about 2-3 feet long, used by women to put pressure into the *Kinu.* In the process of lifting up and down with human pressure, the process is best compared to a working four cylinder piston engine.

In another village an elderly woman told me that their god left long ago into the open sea, their god came once a year during the monsoon winds which bring good crops and with strange people who came and brought with them clothes and ornaments as a sign of good luck. Then they return with the monsoon winds to where they came from. Every two weeks we moved our tents from village to village. I managed to record some important oral histories of the past millennium about the interior Mijikenda-Gyriama people.

By the end of six months, over 100 Christian churches were started with more than 2,850 baptisms which revolutionized Christianity for the modern Kenya coastal region. Because of the distinct culture and tradition between Mijikenda and the Swahili people, assimilation with Swahili people will take some time.

MDGs Status in Kenya: Population: 38 Million. Languages: Swahili and English. Official government statistics indicate that over the last five years, the poverty levels have fallen in Kenya from 56% to 46%. This is in sharp contrast to the previous years where poverty increased from 20% at independence to 56% five years ago.

The improvements can be attributed in large part to improved government that has resulted in a turnaround in economic development. Economic Development has risen from near 0% to around 7% in the time frame from 2002 to 2007 – this of course is a significant upturn.

Despite the progress made, Kenya still faces serious challenges in the commitment to achieve the MDGs by Vision 2015/2030 and beyond. Many East Africans are without decent drinking water, proper housing, and proper health-care and a basic infrastructure. The nation of Kenya has one of the biggest slums in the world. Kibera slum has millions of people living without access to good drinking water, sanitary facilities, with poor access to schools and basic health care. Kenyan's MDG goal number two - free universal primary education-is a long way from being fulfilled in Kibera. Numerous schools in many parts of the country have aged, dilapidating buildings and classrooms without basic needs of desks and books. This is especially true in the large urban cities of Kenya.

Aging Asbestos Buildings: Special attention must be made to the aging colonial education buildings throughout Kenya. These are still roofed with asbestos, a product dangerous to human health. The chemical materials used in the making of the asbestos pose a significant danger to the men, women and children who daily learn or teach and perform administrative duties in these facilities.

In London, (February 15, 2007) a British woman, Debra Brewer, 47, filed a claim that she contracted cancer by hugging her father, who worked at the dockyard in Plymouth, England for five years in the 1960s. Her father died of asbestos related lung cancer in 2006. She sued the ministry of Defense for $146,000. Brewer's exposure to asbestos is believed to have occurred during her childhood when coming into close contact with her father, who typically came home coated with asbestos dust. From the time of exposure with asbestos, the lung cancer symptoms include respiratory problems and chest pain, stays in the human body for about three decades. Even a small amount of exposure to asbestos can have severe health consequences.

The prognosis for the people, who have contracted this cancer, is that death occurs in six months to one year. The medical community in Kenya has known for decades that asbestos causes cancer but has chosen to basically ignore the warning. It is about time for Kenya and other third world governments to take bold steps to protect children from healthcare related sickness. Most adults in Kenya have been exposed to asbestos during their lifetime. Most of these individuals who were exposed to asbestos will eventually become sick and many will die. Just look around for old colonial buildings.

For example: Athi River Baptist Church is among three or four churches built in early 1960s by SBC roofed with asbestos. This is the church I grew up attending Sunday services and during the week the church building was used as a grade school. That means, I was constantly breathing toxic air seven days a week! The members of the church were not aware until years later when I informed them about the dangers of the chemical found in asbestos.

To date the church is underway to recover the entire church with modern roofing. Asbestos roofs are found in many education and administration buildings, teacher colleges, and most low-income housing in all cities of Kenya. Practically all factories that were built during the colonial rule have asbestos roofs. It is interesting to find that all predominately white housing areas were roofed with tiles, not asbestos. In North America, the Federal government has taken steps to educate her citizens to file for medical subsidy for the families affected by asbestos.

Lead paint is dangerous to human beings. Houses and buildings should be stripped and re-painted every two to three years to protect from lead paint dust. The Kenyan Parliament should pass a law requiring all government housing, public institutions and places of business to put in place a program to replace these dangerous chemicals. However, with the continuing of the current government Vision 2015/2030, the citizens of Kenya have an opportunity to shape and build a better learning environment by demanding improvements.

For the first time since the creation of a Coalition Government, the president of Kenya in February 2008 said, "Over the last four and a half years, my administration spent 750 million shillings on co-curricular activities, including sports, music and drama, which gave the rise of primary enrollment from 5.9 million to 8 million children."

The president fulfilled his campaign promise; in 2008 fiscal year the government embarked on the provision of Free - tuition Secondary Education with the aim of ensuring as many primary children as possible attend free-tuition secondary schools. The head of state added that, "With free secondary education, we expect to increase the transition rate from 46.4 percent of 2002 to over 70 percent." The president was in harmony with the implementation of the MDGs by 2015/2030. As Kenya struggles toward achievement of the MDGs, it is quite evident that a different approach in fighting poverty must be followed; otherwise the situation will only get worse.

The Religious Leaders and Bishops: The Religious Leaders and Bishops called for a shift from charity to justice during a religious meeting the summer of 2007. The religious leaders meeting did not predict: that Kenya general elections of December 2007 would result in a Coalition Government, more than 1,500 people killed and more than 350,000 displaced. After the disputed presidential election, the call of the Religious Leaders and Bishops would depend on the unity of the tenth parliament for the period of 2008-2012. "The mid-term reflections on the Millennium Development Goals are so near yet so far," said the Religious Leaders and Bishops.

The leaders met in August 2007 at International Hotel, Nairobi, where they filed a declaration to the incumbent president, politicians, government administrators and the people of Kenya. By all means the religious leaders appeared united under one national course, yet, already deception was at work among the Religious Leaders and Bishops. When the country entered into general elections, some groups of citizens, mainly in Rift Valley and other nearby districts, full of rage, under the cover of night, pillaged, murdered, burned houses, churches, businesses and government property.

These catastrophes captured the attention of the entire world.

The logical rationalization was the belief that the then incumbent government stole the election. It is worth mentioning that one among groups of faith who stood that morning appealing their "call for a shift from Charity to Justice," National Muslim Leaders Forum (NAMLEF), in secrecy had signed the Memorandum of Understanding (MoU) between then Hon. Raila Amolo Odinga, representing the Orange Democratic Movement (ODM) and NAMLEF August 29, 2007.

The MoU was made available to the public via Kenya National Newspapers and other media outlets. The two parties involved denied the authenticity of the document. However, after sweeping the majority of the parliamentary and civic seats, they recanted. Once the parties concerned with MoU were in parliament they accepted what they first denied! What a teaching! And what a leadership!

The divided Christians versus Radical United Muslims (NAMFLEP) allowed Muslims in Kenya to unite together as a religion of faith, committed their resources (money) and votes to support one presidential candidate of their choice. The 80% of Christians in Kenya were divided along tribal lines; they let down their guard and assumed their politicians would prevail against a few radical Muslims.

For the order of Muslim embraces the practice of the theocratic form of government, the notion that religion and politics are one in the same worldwide. Therefore, radical Muslims, a wing within the Islam wanted a presidential candidate who would meet their social and religious needs. Islam in Kenya felt like they were short changed by other religious groups in power. The Constitution of the Republic of Kenya allows for the freedom of worship, the right to worship God of their choice including ancestral worship.

Islam religion embraces a government ruled by religious authority with the Koran as the holy text, providing direction to her citizens and the state. That is why Islam uses "Sheria Law" a court system of a Supreme law and divine law (Sheria law), which punishes those who fail to abide with the teachings of Islam. The primary purpose of a regime in a theocracy is to easily implement and enforce state and divine laws. That is why some radical groups of Muslims wanted the authority to control certain areas of the country with Sheria law.

[Theocracy: comes from two Greek words "rule by the deity" a form of government regime in which God or a deity is recognized as the supreme civil ruler. Islam governments are political regimes which claim an earthly representation through their religious leaders "imams" and other important titles within their hierarchical order within Islamic religion.]

Humans through the ages have in one way or another claimed gods and spirits, to be their legitimate invisible ruler. Archeologists continue to uncover ancient civilizations like the Hebrew societies, Tiberians and the Egyptians whose kingships were guided by gods and spirits.

Early North American civilizations like Mayans and American Indians are some of the notable North American communities who practiced theocracy in their culture, before their culture was destroyed by European immigration by mid 1600s. They were escaping feudalism and European aristocracy. Most generally, early Christians like John Calvin is credited to the influence of the government of his day to work within the frame work of theocracy.

In addition, the creation of Papal seat in Vatican City, Rome. In the decades past, Christians in North America managed to influence elected officials to run a worldly government while maintaining the separation of church and state.

Spring of 2008 I released the article "Leadership Crisis in Kenya" to western media. Within hours I received a call from a Kenyan-American, a resident of the great state of Maryland in response to my article. The gentleman shared with me of his early childhood experience between the ages of (15-19) when he would go to a nearby Mosque for food, in hope that he would qualify for Islam scholarship.

Most parents in rural Kenya depend on seasonal rainfall to grow cash crops. When the rains fail, it means for that year and the year following, the majority of children go without incidentals; because most parents cannot afford food, water for their animals, and clean drinking water, much less tuition for their children. Case in point the year 2008-2009 is considered the worst year in Kenya famine, because of the displacement of farmers during the Kenya tribal clashes November 2006 - January 2008.

It is a no brainer; children and youth are attracted to Islamic hospitality kitchen and doctrines for the purpose to draw young men into Madarassas. Once an innocent young-man joins Madarassas, one receives doctrine and teaching based on Koran sacred scriptures of the Islamic faith. Hunger and poverty forces dangerous acts in the life of person: Esau lost his birth right to his brother, Jacob.

Studies have shown that children must have sufficient nutrition-
al meals three times a day to have attention in class. Children of
poor neighborhoods, inner cities, and those living in the slums of
Africa cannot perform well in school, which results to poor and
unproductive citizens of any nation. Our Lord Jesus Christ over-
came Satan's temptation in the wilderness. He conquered hunger
by rebuking Satan, saying, "A man shall not live by bread alone
but the Word of God." It is the responsibility of the governments
of the world to feed, protect, and to fight enemies who threaten
peace and stability along international borders. Luke 4:4 AKJV

The end of January 2008, I was driving on Nairobi-Mombasa
Road, (similar to North America Interstate highways) an eight
(8) hour drive of 305 miles to Kenya coastal area. Somewhere
along the way I stopped for gas; I asked the gas attendant for a
restaurant. The gentleman told me if I drive for one more hour,
I will be served with a free meal! I asked, "Who serves the hot
lunch along the Mombasa - Nairobi Road?" He said, "I don't
know." He added, "The restaurant was built about 20 years ago
for the motorist and travelers." Mombasa-Nairobi Road passes
through Tsavo National Park, one of the largest wildlife parks
in the nation. Anyone driving on Mombasa-Nairobi Road, especially in late evenings, knows it can be deadly because of the elephant herd, deer, zebras and other wildlife crisscrossing Mombasa-Nairobi Road and wandering along the road day or night.

Tsavo National Park became widely known for the Man-Eaters
of Tsavo. It is in this park when a British Colonel Patterson was
hired to search for and kill the Man-Eaters of Tsavo at the turn of
the 20th Century. Another important personality is Teddy Roos-

evelt, an American president who boarded a locomotive train in Mombasa traveling northward crossing the Tsavo National Park into Kenya interior in search for the best hunting grounds. He would later camp in Konza, the Kapiti Plains located north of (the modern Amboseli National Park) for hunting his finest safari (journey) expedition.

And so, I decided to drive on for one hour; sure enough there was a gigantic Mosque with a large restaurant building within the Mosque grounds marked with the words, meals for all motorists and travelers. I was not sure if the restaurant was open during certain times of the year, or it was targeting political campaign workers, since it was an election year. No way would I eat in a Mosque, I said to myself. Furthermore, I had tens of hundreds of MoUs in boxes stacked in the backseat of my car! If only someone knew what I had. I would not have come out alive! Then, the scriptures came alive to me, that I should not compromise my life for a lunch meal.

I continued with my safari to Mombasa, one of the oldest cities on the Indian Ocean, which dates back to around the 7th Century. Mvita or Mombasa is a city full of history, ruled by many dynasties: The Sultans, Portuguese and British, then, the Kenyans who are the rightful dwellers of the town. Early 1970s I attended Mombasa Baptist High School; it was managed and operated by Southern Baptist Missionaries. While a student of MBHS, God called me to full time Christian ministry. I moved to a neighbor state, Tanzania for theological studies. Kenya Muslims are the dwellers of the metropolitan city of Mombasa. Islam has done it all and perhaps even much better than her counterpart, the majority Christian congregations whose benevolence kitty is down low!

In contrast with Islam, who gets evangelist money from rich Islamic nations to support rural Mosques with a hospitality restaurant kitchen to feed the poor in many parts of Africa-----and now along major highways of Kenya, should be noted by Christian men and women living in enhanced societies around the world. Islam religion takes a slight lead in the recruitments of the youth--new converts compared to their Christian counterparts in nations of the world.

Theocracy Regimes: In sharp contrast, Christians in North America have long maintained the policy of the separation of church and state. The notion, Christians may not directly practice theocratic form of government like their counter part Islam, but Christians would want to control their government through elected delegates of their choice in all branches of government.

For example, in North America, Christians would rather use special interest groups to support a candidate for state and the Federal government located in Washington, D.C. American people including religious right, tend to use their democratic principles to voice their social issues, public policy, foreign policy and economic issues, while maintaining their core value of the freedom of worship and the separation of church and state.

America is a system of ideology that is mostly liked by many immigrants who arrive daily to the shores of the United States of America. Liberal Moslem who immigrate to North America tend to go through a process of change, some of the changes are in the Islamic values, in view of women, and life in general. Somehow, being a Moslem woman living in American society, her needs are met, recognized and appreciated. In addition, the majority of women who immigrate to USA regardless of their ethnic or religious affiliation or countries of origin are not willing to return back. It is a view based on many years of crisscrossing many small towns, cities and metropolitan cities of North America.

The chauvinistic male figure threatens the millions of women across many cultures around the world. The situation of women in America began to improve since the Civil Rights Bill movement of the early 1960s going back 90 years. It was the era of a woman, black or white, who was not allowed to vote or be voted into for public office. During the last one hundred years **Leadership** acknowledges the great strides in the governments of the world through the Empowerment of Women and especially American women who enjoy the protection of state and federal laws.

As we mark the mid-term on the MDGs, we wish to renew our unwavering support for the millennium declaration adopted in September 2000 by world leaders in which they committed themselves to "free all men, women and children from abject and dehumanizing conditions of extreme poverty." The role of the faith based community, religious leaders; NGOs must mobilize communities with their vast assets, spiritual, moral and social to achieve the MDGs broadly and effectively to bring CHANGE. More than 50 percent of all social services in health and education are provided for by the faith communities, significantly complementing and supplementing those governments' and other service providers. In some areas, particularly in armed conflict situations, faith communities are the only providers of basic services.

For the first time in (2000 New York) the history of mankind, African Leaders from the global community came together to outline quantifiable and measurable goals to half world poverty with deadlines. All this put together constituted the most effective ways to build sustainable peace at all levels locally, nationally and globally. *Leadership* advocates this action, its promise, to the world's human family wholeheartedly, standing on less than the half-way mark set to achieve these lofty goals encompassed in the MDGs. Kenya religious leaders of civil society reflected on the eight Millennium Goals:

Goal One: Eradicate Extreme Poverty and Hunger: All faith communities and their teachings focus on the injustices brought about by extreme poverty, and the obligation to act. The religious leaders noted the importance and the urgency of going back to their religious traditions in order to achieve this goal. One hundred forty-eight million children (148 million children) on the globe go without food, shelter, and clean water.

In addition, thirty-thousand children still die globally, as a result of poverty. At the halfway point of the MDGs, military spending quietly surpasses the one trillion U.S. dollars mark, an indictment to humanity for all of us. Raw data: Infant mortality rates in sub-Sahara Africa: 102* children from 1,000 children die in less than a year. (*Figures are subject to change.) Kenya has abundance of natural resources within her borders but fails to capture them because of her greedy politicians. She has big rivers and lakes for which water can be harvested annually, pumped to the deserts of: North-Eastern, Eastern, and Coast Provinces for large scale production of agriculture. Kenya must invest in her public health sector located in remote rural parts of the nation in order to curb out malaria and other easily transmitted diseases.

According to the United Nations Development Fund (UNDP)

most countries of the Sub-Saharan Africa will in fact not half the-extreme poverty by 2047 if going by the current trends. We remind all concerned, and ourselves, that halving the proportion of people in extreme poverty and hunger, is in fact a protection of their fundamental human rights-and therefore an act of justice-never to be oversimplified as that of charity. The religious leaders underscore that MDGs is an OBLIGATION for ALL as outlined in our sacred texts. Religious leaders take note that achievement or non-achievement of this particular goal will determine whether all the other goals will be achieved.

Goal Two: Achieve Universal Primary Education: Ensuring that all boys and girls get the best quality and relevant education is a central tenet of all religions. Education is the greatest hope for achieving long lasting peace and social justice, and a concrete means to achieve all the other MDGs. Religious leaders laud the efforts made by some governments in abolishing fees at the primary level, and even commend those that have gone a step further to make secondary education free. (This puts Kenya on the right tract to achieving MDGs). Raw data: Africa: 60% of 15 year olds are illiterate.

Goal Three: Promote Gender Equality and Empower Women: Achieving this goal is also contingent upon achieving goals four, five and six. The religious leaders applaud the steps already undertaken to eliminate gender disparity in primary and secondary education so far, asked all concerned to redouble efforts to achieve this goal by 2015.

Goal Four: Reduce Child Mortality: The leaders commend the tremendous strides in reducing child mortality rates thus far. But even with the quality of tremendous accomplishments in modern medical care, the people are still faced with the unacceptable situation in which every three seconds a child aged under-five dies from a treatable or preventable cause. The religious leaders considers child mortality to be the greatest injustice being made to our children, and therefore call for the urgent efforts to reduce and then end the loss of children's lives.

Goal Five: Improve Maternal Health: Reducing by three-quarters the maternal mortality ratio will not only ensure that the society and our families are healthy, but those of children born and unborn are taken care of. We laud the efforts and clear goals espoused in the MDGs.

Goal Six: Combat HIV/AIDS, Malaria and Other Diseases: We commend the efforts made so far to halt and reverse the spread of HIV/AIDS and the incidence of malaria and other major diseases. The efforts are however still not satisfactory, and we see no reason why deaths attributable to preventable causes such as malaria are still rampant in Africa. Africa leadership must come together to find a solution to combat HIV and malaria. Deadly mosquito bites are the number one killer of children in Africa's tropical climate, especially in the Lake Basin areas and coastal regions. The nations of East Africa big lakes have signed "COMESA" (discussed elsewhere in *Leadership*), which empowers the flow of citizens doing business within the region.

Goal Seven: Ensure Environmental Sustainability: Let us not forget that we are simply the custodians of the earth for future generations. We cannot afford the unabated destruction of mother earth at this rate, and still expect future generations to have quality living. We consider the earth as sacred, and therefore, must be cared for and respected. We will strive to, and are calling upon all partners to reverse the loss of environment resources. We wish to point out that reducing by half the proportion of people without sustainable access to safe drinking water by 2015, and to significantly improve lives of at least 100 million slum dwellers by 2020 will take more than words and promises.

Goal Eight: Develop a Global Partnership for Development: These partnerships must increase effective aid and sustainable debt relief, focus more on fair than free trade and good governance. Our faith has extensive experience establishing and working through partnerships that cut across borders. The MDGs offer an important opportunity to work with members from diverse faith traditions on issues of common humanity and of responsibility to care for one another.

We call upon all governments, bilateral and multilateral institutions to commit to good governance and transparency. We call the religious communities and the civil society to advocate for open and fair trading, putting in place open financial systems that are rule-based, fair, predictable and nondiscriminatory.

In North America, the average household disposes of ten pounds of apparel each year, due to the change of climate, sizes and simply the greed of the want of a new outfit. Major charitable organizations sell their surplus goods in bales to buyers for profit making business/entrepreneurs to sell to third world nations for less than what they would buy for new merchandise — clothes, shoes and etc.

In the past decades Africa imported over $60 million of used clothes from United States alone. The majorities of Africans are willing to shop at used market places for clothing because it is affordable – keeps them warm, is something new – less expensive and a shirt on their back. The merchandise is so popular that it has acquired a new name: In Tanzania — *Mitumba* is the word for used clothes. The city of Moshi is the largest Mitumba supply in East Africa region; located at the foot of Mt. Kilimanjaro in northern Tanzania. In West Africa, Liberia — *dokafleh* translates "try it on".

Globalization is now the way of the future and must not be ignored by Africa leadership. Multinational businesses and financial institutions financed through the arm of the World Bank are desperately looking for new ways of doing business with and investing in Africa. The cost of doing business in many nations of the north has sky rocketed. For example, the United States is exporting a significant portion of its labor costs to third world nations. Africa stands a better chance of doing business because of the knowledge of the English language inherited from the colonial masters. The implementation of cyber cable optics is a technological breakthrough for the African leadership of East and Central Africa. Once trade policies are in place, the gap between Africa and the industrial nations will be narrowed, and Africa can become competitive in the 21st Century and beyond.

The Concerns: African religious leaders were concerned that the heads of states would not honor and fulfill the Millennium Goals. By adopting the MDGs in 2000, heads of states and government recognized that in addition to their separate responsibilities to their own individual societies, they had a collective responsibility to uphold the principles of human dignity, justice and equality at the global level, and declared poverty alleviation as an overarching goal in need of international attention.

We welcome the steps by a number of governments in their efforts to realize the MDGs. We salute the efforts of many governments that strive to better the lives of their people. We appreciate that by setting up the MDGs, our governments and the international community affirmed that for the first time in the history of humanity, it was possible to achieve such goals using the resources, knowledge and technologies now available to humankind.

We however, register our deepest concerns about reports indicating that at the midway point between their adoption in 2000 and the 2015 target date for achieving the Millennium Development Goals, Sub-Sahara Africa is not on track to achieve any of the goals. We are concerned that there is still a huge gap between rhetoric and reality. We are concerned that the rhetoric and commitments have not been adequately translated into action. And we remain concerned that the MDGs campaign has not adequately reached the grassroots communities.

Call to Action: Religious leaders and faith communities in Africa can advocate for Africa governments with the development partners to work together to achieve the MDGs by 2015. Let us all bring the full weight of our moral convictions to bear on behalf of the poor and the voiceless, the invisible and the excluded. The suffering of one billion of our brothers, sisters, children, mothers and fathers when few are enjoying unprecedented levels of prosperity – is contrary to what we believe in. We affirm the eradication of poverty is not merely an ethical and moral imperative, but also political. There is a direct link between poverty and injustice. The present inequality gap between the haves and the have-nots is unsustainable.

And so today, we commit ourselves to join with tens of thousands of people around the world as part of a global movement to advocate for an end to the crises of poverty through achievement of the MDGs. We are here to answer to this call, to put our faith into action again. We will pray, reflect and act in collaboration with other faith communities in Kenya, Africa and around the globe.

Anticipated Outcome in Kenya: Now that Kenya has added the country's Vision 2030 to promote the MDGs, the member states and the international community will remain on the sidelines to watch if the first Government Coalition in the history of Kenya can deliver the agendas promised during the last campaigns. As stated elsewhere in **Leadership**, history has clearly shown the electoral process to be a definitive period for Kenya's political agenda. Only time will judge the passing of the long overdue "New" constitution of Kenya before the next general elections.

In the aftermath of the Kenyan general elections (December 27, 2007), over 650,000 men, women and children were driven out of their homes and businesses and from their land due to hatred and political distrust. The 'political-will' created by the need to garner votes was translated into action in the period immediately after the elections. Thereafter, the country fell into an economic downward spiral during which nothing was moving across the nation and tribes turned against each other as enemies within themselves. People were forced to flee from their lifetime investments down to poverty level in the name of ethnicity.

The concentrations of Internally Displaced People (IDP) of more than 350,000 men, women and children have added to the national budgetary imbalances. This number does not include those who fled to the neighboring member states of Uganda and Tanzania. During the writing of *Leadership* there were 235 camps of IDP throughout the nation without enough clean drinking water, sanitary facilities and food. The government had not mentioned the immediate logistics for temporary schools for the displaced children.

Whatever the reason may be, it appears that the majority of the (IDP) were Kenyans. They are from a few ethnic tribes who were forced against their will to flee from homes they had established for many years, only to become a causality of deep rooted hatred of the political machines. Now, these citizens have been forced to camp among the most inhabited ancestral lands.

Accord Reconciliation Act: The full execution of the Accord Reconciliation Act of February 2008 depends on two named principals and their stakeholders. The coalition was expected to remove ethnic sensations of hatred and political mistrust. The established government had a moral obligation and responsibility to resettle the IDPs without any further delay. Until the Accord is fully implemented, peace in the country will remain a commodity of the distant past. Kenyan's invisible tribal lines are at risk of being redrawn in the minds and hearts of people, which could result in setting the country back fifty years. *Leadership* remained optimistic that this will not happen.

Kenya is a signatory member state of the ratified Great Lakes Regional Protocol on IDP, which has clear instructions for the resettlement of IDP. The U.N. guidelines require IDP to be assisted with materials to start life afresh. The longer lawmakers drag on in executing these guidelines, the more IDP are prone to depression, left vulnerable to disease and crime, and are in danger to themselves and society. These guidelines are consistent with U.N. human rights violations.

However, there should be a bright future for Kenya because the President has established a department for "National Cohesion and Constitutional Affairs," charged with the task of developing programs for IDP and other neglected communities. This move is in agreement with the fulfillment of the MDGs by 2015/2030 and beyond. During the writing of *Leadership* there was disturbing news from the Kenya Red Cross that pregnant women who fled their homes to safety had their babies in these crowded camps, where stagnant water was the breeding ground of killer mosquitoes and diseases.

Bush Administration on East Africa: On another positive note, the Kenyan government received 3.3 billion shillings in aid to re-settle the IDP. The financial support from the Bush administration was widely accepted as a good humanitarian effort to the horn of Africa. In his final African tour of the East African region, Mr. Bush gave over 700 million dollars in aid to combat malaria and HIV in Tanzania, a country located south of Kenya. In the past the U.S. has received criticism for not aiding some of the troubled weak governments of Africa, which are vulnerable to human rights abuse, drug trafficking, and Islamic terrorism such as in Darfur. Bush did it.

In addition, during the eight years of President Bush administration, the majority of sub-Sahara Africa governments received help in training of their armies to be on the defensive when threatened by terroristic Islamic Jihad. The U.S. has continued to provide air strikes in defense to root out any verified targets along the international borders between Ethiopia and Somalia, as well as the porous Somalia border, and the open Indian Ocean. The coast of Somalia has had a failed democracy since 1960s -1970s during Kenya and Somalia the *shifuta* war.

In 2008 – 2009 a century old piracy resurfaced claiming millions of dollars in captured goods from several international vessels on the Indian Ocean, the largest and the oldest trading routes of cargo ships along the south-eastern African coast for hundreds of years.

Coalition Government: When the August house (the 10th Parliament) was seated, it became obvious that a majority of the lawmakers were largely in an advocacy program of self-establishment for what the government can do for them. Almost every lawmaker wanted a higher seat in the Coalition Government. To paraphrase the rhetoric made by President Ronald Reagan, big government gives you everything and big government takes everything you have.

A big government does not necessarily translate to efficiency. It is not about how big or small a government may be; it is about how to solve the problems of clean drinking water, rural electrification, healthcare, rural infrastructure, urban and rural education, corruption, and drug trafficking throughout the nation. That is one of the main purposes of government. There is a tendency of thinking among third world governments that every elected Member of Parliament should be made a government Minister, or Assistant Minister or some other high level portfolio.

For example, during the Moi administration, he created new Ministries that were not there during Jomo Kenyatta government; it turned out his political cronies drove the country into economic mayhem. As hard as it was for the next incoming President Kibaki, who within (5) five years his administration turned the country around into 6.2 economic boom, he did it. The Coalition Government of 2008 doubled the number of Ministers and Assistant Ministers, which left some in ODM, PNU and ODM-Kenya complaining. Some MPs of either party threatens to abandon their parties which got them elected to office. In other words, it is not about representation of citizen's needs in a national parliament but rather is it is about selfish political employment at the expense of citizens needs.

The developed nations of the north have a similar problem as occurs in third world nations, the difference, in practice, is the government administrators and political leaders are often accountable to citizens. Congressional personalities in USA are easily reprimanded by the system of checks and balances to where they are compelled by the voices of the citizens until one withdraws and or step-aside from their congressional position.

Another example took place in Chicago politics, a prominent Congressional Republican was forced out of the race due to a sex scandal; it was an easy win for the Democrat candidate who jumped in at the last minute and soared to win in an expected congressional seat in a densely populated white Republican district. That candidate went on to become the first African-American Senator, and the first African-American President, elected November 4, 2008 President Barack Obama, whose father was of Kenyan descent. Many would argue that the young, newly, elected Congressional Senator happened to be in the right place and the right time, when American people wanted change in Washington.

I would argue that Obama won because of the poor behavior of the incumbent Republican Senator whose lifestyle was refused by the voters of his district regardless of the color, or party in which he represented and against a Republican led government that had lost the war of domestic affairs at home. Americans were no longer interested in the War on Terror. They had lost millions of jobs in almost every major business sector. Congress overwhelmingly voted to bailout the housing market and financial institutions.

About three quarters of the population of the third world nations reside in rural areas, where there is widespread unemployment. The government must put in place workable schemes to invest in rural areas in order to rectify the income disparity, which will enhance the economic sector and the support of institutions to achieve the MDGs by 2015/2030 and beyond. The government services must be decentralized and made available where the majority of the people live. To achieve the MDGs and the Vision 2030, the lawmakers should end all controversial bickering that creates instability and divisions among tribal lines.

The lawmakers should remain focused on the matters of building national and political stability for every citizen. Africa states will best be served by the leaders committed to the causes of eradication of hunger, disease, human rights needs and Africa's ideological survival. Kenya has 210 constituencies, each with one parliamentary seat, several civic leaders, and municipal councilors where applicable. All seats are elected for a five-year term. At the end of the term candidates should be evaluated by their performance and how they handled the MDGs within their constituency.

Historically, the majority of lawmakers wait until the last year of elections to allocate resources to the people. This is an unacceptable practice that has put development behind and allowed loopholes for corruption and fraud among the committees that run constituency projects. Because of the urgency of the implementation of the MDGs and the country's Vision 2030, each parliamentary and civic leader should be evaluated on the basis of the development achieved within their constituency.

Citizens should never elect a candidate on the basis of a political party. Rather, candidates should exhibit character, honesty and integrity. During the Kenya general elections (December 2007) campaign teams witnessed many voting irregularities. Some candidates were left off the ballots due to political maneuvering, which caused mayhem between electorates of the political machines – the end result was a disputed presidential election, claims of widespread corruption, and even many deaths occurred months before and the December 27 elections, tribes within Rift Valley burned villages, churches and raped and killed innocent people.

The First Casualty: Before *Leadership* was released for publication, the Coalition Government formed February 2008 had suffered her first major causality of a scandalous corruption deal. The then Finance Minister alleged to have sold a public property widely known as Grand Regency Hotel in secrecy. It was hard to accept the allegations — that the Finance Minister acted alone (lone ranger) in the magnitude of transacting forty-five (45) million Kenya Shillings for the sale of public property. However, the Finance Minister was charged with the responsibility and accountability of the public kitty. In his capacity he had the ability: to say NO and YES to corrupt or shady transactions. The

Minister had full knowledge that somewhere along the long road his colleagues would prey on him like a hyena visiting on a wounded animal. Well, he managed to survive the ordeal but he never regained his old docket back. In the end President Kibaki assigned him with another Ministry.

The expected integrity and honesty is discussed elsewhere in *Leadership;* which states that integrity encapsulates significance of wholeness and perfection, when these conditions of integrity are not met, they yield to immoral values, dishonesty and insincerity in the life of a leader. Therefore, integrity implies intrinsic obedience that dictates the wisdom of right and wrong. The life of a leader must be consistent, and controlled by the sense of good judgment.

Leadership does not discuss in detail the background history of the Grand Regency Hotel scandal because it is a chronic illness of corruption that spans two administrations: Moi (1978-2002) and Kibaki (2002-2007). The NARC government (2002) came into power with a pledge to wipe-out and eradicate corruption including The Grand Regency Hotel ownership. In the spring of 2008, Kenya Anti-Corruption Commission and the Governor of the Central Bank of Kenya, both issued press statements in the recovery attempt of the said Grand Regency Hotel distancing Central Bank from corruption. The Grand Regency Hotel has remained a **classic corruption scandal** in the history of greed, and deceit by the leaders of a democratic nation like Kenya. Why? It is the breed of high corruption of public funds.

Here is raw data:

[The Kenya Anti-Corruption Commission filed suit on behalf

of the Central Bank of Kenya October 2003 for the recovery of the Grand Regency Hotel. The administration took almost five years to file the case. April 9th 2008, the Commission registered consent in HCCC No. 1111 of 2003 as per the provisions of Section 56 B 2 and 4 of the Anti-Corruption and Economic Crimes Act to the effect that Mr. Kamplesh M.D. Patti and M/S Uhuru Highway Development Ltd transferred ownership and all their rights and interests in the Grand Regency Hotel together with all improvements including fixtures thereto, moveable and immoveable assets to the Central Bank of Kenya. Upon registration of the above settlement on April 9th 2008 the Grand Regency Hotel vested in the Central Bank of Kenya (KACC, April 9, 2008)].

[Central Bank of Kenya filed the following: Since 1993 the Central Bank created a Legal Charge for Kshs.2.5Billion over the Grand Regency Hotel in an attempt to secure funds that had been illegally siphoned through Exchange Bank during the infamous Goldenberg saga. Through court orders and injunctions, the Central Bank has over the years been totally locked out of the control and management to the Hotel. This is the situation as matters stand at the moment (CBK, April 23, 2008)].

CBK reported on April 9th, 2008 the bank hired Ernst and Young Firm of good reputation as receivers managers for the Grand Regency Hotel. However, an article appeared on September 18th in Daily Nation, it was finally revealed that Libyan Arab Investment Company, a subsidiary of the Libyan State bought the hotel during President Kibaki's state visit in June 2007 that put the Grand Regency Hotel saga to rest.

Failed Leadership: Sadly, it is inconceivably distressing on the anniversary of March 2009 after the formation of the Coalition Government, the two principals, Kibaki and Odinga failed to marshal enough votes from their political foot soldiers to pass the most crucial Tribunal Bill 2009. It became obvious that the political leadership which existed when the National Accord was entrenched into Constitution and signed March 2008; had disappeared when the two principals no longer commanded the unanimous support of their political coalitions of August House. It was a landmark case that MPs took control and without leadership the Parliament was like a runaway train. At that rate, no one seemed to know the country's next political destination. The Coalition Government failed to control rampant corruption within its own ranks including donated food for poor citizens, oil and heavy illegal arms trade with the neighbor states.

It was no longer about governing but how to gang up for deep pockets from public coffers. It was clear evidence that those who bribed themselves through the electorate to Parliament were the major distracters who derailed and killed the passing of the Tribunal Court Bill 2009. It is reported that junior MPs were bribed for one million shillings per diem and more for the committee chairs to exterminate the bill.

Assistant Minister, Hon. Mwangi Kiunjui said, "Parliament has become a house of mafia; persons associated with past crime have secured committee chairmanship. Parliament cannot fight graft, when its' organs are steered by people facing court cases, under investigations, blacklisted by previous House committee. Political blackmailing by corrupt network ensures the two principals take no action against graft kingpins in their ranks for fear of losing tribal support. Forces associated with economic crimes of the past have ganged up to defeat the cause of Justice. This lot is not bribed; they have common interests to protect inside House Committees."

The refusal to pass the bill meant perpetrators, rapists and looters and the killers of the innocent men, women and children will never have their day in court; because it takes more than ten years for crimes of humanity to be tried at The Hague, World Court, Netherlands. The alleged and unknown names of a few MPs and their cronies calculated their options with a Kenya Tribunal Court; they were afraid they would not survive or get away with murder, and would not be allowed to return to public life. The 10th Parliament has lost credibility and ability to fight the war on drugs, terrorism and corruption. While at the moment the 10th Parliament was hiding under the blanket of ethnic chauvinistic muscling of each other as political parties in the preparation with a new alignment for the next political campaign.

Hon. Muite, a former Kikuyu MP said, "Most graft involves the Executive, which is heavily represented in Parliament by Ministers and Assistant Ministers. They are the gatekeepers of corruption opportunities. MP influence to debate by voting when corruption issues come up." Raila, who is the country Prime Minister, said local Tribunal is the best option for the prosecution of the perpetrators of the violence. "The Hague is like rain and nobody knows when it will fall." The Prime Minister added that those MPs who voted with government stood for the truth.

Meyer Berger wrote, "Vote for the man who promises least; he will be the least disappointing." Five years later another columnist wrote, "A political leader must keep looking over his shoulder all the time to see if the boys are still there. If they are not there, he is no longer a politician." (New York Times 1965) In the midst of the killing of the Tribunal Bill, President Kibaki, was busy creating more Administration District offices in Kenya, in accordance to fulfillment of the Millennium Goals. Kibaki is quite on track. A country without leadership is doomed.

The Place of Women in Society: The descendants of the children of Isaac, and their counterparts Arab cousins, the children of Ishmael, go back to their matriarchs, Sarah and Hagar, the wives of Abraham. These women held positions of dominance, head of their families, authority and respect over the communities where they lived.

It is safe to say that Jews and Arabs get their identity and their pride in their heritage fostered from their matriarchs down to their present women. Women are responsible to maintain the identity of their culture and families they represent up to this day.

However, there are assorted families of well to do across the tribes of Kenya, who sacrificially, took a stand against their custom and tradition to educate their daughters and sons to higher levels of learning. Historically, girls were denied school over boys. Today, only handfuls of women are politically involved in Kenya's growing population compared to the majority of men in Kenya's political system. Honorable: Charity Ngilu, Prof. Wangari Maathai, and Wangari Martha Karua are among the few women active in Kenya political leadership.

The first female personality was Charity Ngilu, a mother, wife, former Secretary and Akamba by tribe. Her physique stands tall with a domineering voice. Those who grew with Charity, conveyed her to be a character of strong will, "a go getter," one who is never afraid of intimidation and authority. When compared to her women counterparts, Charity was a political guru, nicknamed the "Iron Lady of Kenya Politics." The years 1992 – 2007 were her political rumble.

In 1997 she ran as the first female presidential candidate in the history of Kenya politics during one of the toughest KANU political machines; a plan that was deemed impractical from the very start. Akamba male political heavy weights were secretly dispersed to cool down her political presidential ambition. She refused. For this cause, she had a share of being reprimanded.

Auspiciously, her husband was still alive, who provided Charity a political safety net from Akamba cultural wrath. It is worth mentioning that unmarried or a woman whose husband has died, especially when she has not remarried, have a hard time in Kenya political careers. Through it all, Charity, established herself as a key opponent of KANU a state supported Party in 1992 through 1997.

Among many male political heavy weights, she was the woman responsible for the creation of the NARC party which swept opposition into power in 2002. KANU under the leadership of the former presidential candidate Uhuru Kenyatta collapsed and lost the presidential elections of 2002 to Kibaki. The concord of Raila to say the famous words "Kibaki Tosha" could not have been possible without the political calculation by Charity Ngilu and the late Hon. Wamalwa. Charity remained loyal to Kibaki administration for the entire term; she tried to persuade Kibaki enact political changes, by keeping corruption outside government. When that failed she pulled her NARC Party and joined forces with ODM. The two parties and other party affiliates swept the majority seats of the 10th Parliament. She retained a Ministerial docket in both Kibaki administration and the Coalition Government.

The Second female was Prof. Wangari Maathai, an established academician by her own right. She was larger than life, regardless of what Kenya political elite may think. She became the first woman environmental activist of the '70s to challenge Moi regime; about the depleting environmental, natural resources and human rights abuses in Kenya. Prof. Wangari was disdained and her views were rejected by KANU leadership. Together, with the sweeping new tides of winds of the multiparty system of 1992, she was elected MP for the first time in 2002 on the NARC ticket for South Tetu Constituency.

The Kibaki administration appointed Maathai, Assistant Minister in the Ministry of Environment and Natural Resources, the very Ministry she had championed as an activist in her previous years. Through it all, two years into her political career, she won worldwide recognition, the world's coveted Nobel Peace Prize Award.

Prof. Maathai lamented "It is either lack of appreciation to what one can contribute, or sometimes neglect. I also wonder because we are talking of highly educated people who know the value of the prize and the environmental campaigns, and who would like to win the prize themselves." *Leadership* expresses regret with disappointment about the way women are viewed by males; yet daughters are raised in the preparation to take up leadership position in the family and society.

A Voice Unstilled: Archbishop Ndingi Mwana 'a Nzeki, is a book by Emeritus Archbishop of Nairobi. The Archbishop narrates a time his aid smuggled Prof. Wangari Maathai to safety at the pinnacle of the Moi regime during one of the worst government crackdowns of human rights activists of 1990s. Wangari was secretly transported in a private car to Nakuru about 170 kilometers west of Nairobi. She was dressed in veil attire (buibui) worn by a *Muslim woman to avoid the exposure of her body in public.*

Wangari remained under cover at the Diocese facilities in Nakuru, until the day when she joined other foreign dignitaries to address the public at Nakuru Stadium. *Leadership* is in agreement with the clergy who took his rightful responsibility of leadership as a citizen to protect the life of one innocent human rights person in the cause of her duty to the society. The protection of Wangari from the ungodly government was a tokenism effort and practice that met the minimum requirement of the rule of law of human rights.

Case in point, the third Female, Martha Karua, was elected to Kenya Parliament in 1992. She was the first woman to hold the docket, Minister of Constitutional Affairs in Kenya, one of the most important ministries in a government. She and many other women have suffered harassment and abuse from their political colleague (male, chauvinistic) elites who have dominated Kenya politics. During the 2007 general elections, women for the first time in history registered in large numbers for political seats. They were provided escorts to protect them. Some had their clothes torn and the lives of their family members were threatened, because they sought political civic and parliament seats. During one of Martha Karua's many campaign trails, her male opponent harassed her in public when he asked the voters not to vote for her, because she had not been circumcised according to the Kikuyu customs and traditions. In her defense, she eloquently asked her voters to ask her male opponent whether or not his daughters were circumcised. Martha went ahead and won the election.

Martha Karua, attorney by profession, resigned from the government which became the **second causality** of the Coalition Government as a result of being shoved aside when the president appointed new judges without her participation. Of course the judges fell under her docket, the Ministry of Constitutional Affairs. Kibaki felt entitled to the services provided by Hon. Karua. She was a hard liner and supporter for new reforms and fought very hard for his re-election, presidential disputed election, and after the presidential fall out she was elected the leader of the PNU delegation to form the Coalition Government.

What is the problem? *Leadership* takes the position that it is centuries old culture, interwoven with beliefs that a woman remains under male dominance without any authority over men. In addition, jealousy, cowardliness, based on male chauvinism, mixed with wrath of cultural tribal customs, corkscrew with lack of respect for women. There are many good tribal cultures, customs and traditions that truss the fabric of our society. However, there are some traditions interwoven with religion, used purposely to impede the progress of girls and women in many third world societies. Each of the women described here, represent a fraction of the millions of professional women in Kenya who for one reason or another fail to get the respect, dignity and recognition they deserve as hard working members of the society.

In other established democracies of the north the role of women in politics has been growing at a faster rate compared to the nations of the third world. In Great Britain, Margaret Thatcher, was one of the strongest Prime Ministers England has ever had. Margaret was tough, principled, eloquent and a trouble shooter. She was a strong supporter of the Reagan Administration but disagreed in principle with Reagan, when she attacked the Falkland Islands. The campaign overwhelmingly succeeded and she put The British Empire into its rightful place as a world super power. That was a woman in Leadership!

Far across the Atlantic Ocean in America, the world witnessed Hillary's aggressive presidential campaign (2008). She nearly became the first woman president in the USA. She was not easy to get rid of with her famous 18 million voters in her presidential bid. Democrats' chauvinistic male Electoral College rejected her endeavor and shunted her away, some of whom were her husband's former political appointees, one of the longest defenders of the Clinton machinery. James Carville, Clinton partisan, accused Richardson, governor of New Mexico, as a "traitor" for betraying the "Clintons" just like Judas betrayed Jesus Christ, when he endorsed Barack Obama. Hillary became Secretary of State. Richardson the loser was never appointed in Obama's administration.

Centuries ago, Hammurabi, the law-giver and the King of Babylon was right when he established the code of ethic and law in regards to the protection of women in leadership. Hammurabi lived in one of the most advanced societies of the day and recognized the civil rights and the protection of women, and he had great admiration for the place of women in the society. Listed below are six mandates to protect the rights of women:

1. Protected the rights of women and their marriages
2. Protected women against rape
3. Women were accorded retributions to crime committed against them
4. Women slaves were given a fair treatment
5. The law regulated the behavior of sacred women who served in temples like modern Nuns
6. The Law laid down conditions

It is safe to say the Hammurabi law may have afforded Hebrew women freedom and prestige. The women referred to in the books of Genesis and Exodus are seen as independent, eloquent, strong willed and displayed leadership skills like Miriam (Moses' sister), Ruth, Esther, Priscilla and many others. Therefore, in today's society, women must be viewed as necessary and equal to their contribution to families and for the survival of our modern society. In the industrious societies, it takes two incomes to raise a family of three. Women are part of the fabric and beauty of every society.

Mau Mau? The history of Kenya cannot be told without mentioning the brutal killings between the Mau Mau and the Royal British Army. No one living has ever favored the Mau Mau movement. I was not old enough to be told the secrets of the Mau Mau. It was too dangerous of information for a young man like me to know. But with time, one Kikuyu elder from Muranga, who worked with my father, finally broke the story to me, on condition that I must never repeat the story to anyone else. He said that I was about the age that Mau Mau often used young boys for scouts. I have always wondered if he wanted me to be used as an informant, because I played with white children of my age on some weekends riding bicycles around Kenya Meat Commission.

The majority of men and women who served Mau Mau have since died. There is a remnant of foot soldiers found among the Kikuyus and the Akamba tribes. The Mau Mau rules of engagement were quite simple, when a person took the oath; it was a binding covenant between himself and Mau Mau. Otherwise, it was a matter of life or death.

No one told about the whereabouts of the secret Mau Mau movement. They traveled at night, slept during the day, and young boys tending goats, sheep and cows about my age were used to transfer food from the village to the Mau Mau hideouts.

Mau Mau dress code was rough. They wore heavy coats to keep them warm at night, their hair was always braided and they wore long beards. They fought guerrilla warfare similar to modern terrorists. Mau Mau suspects when caught were transported at night by security men purported to lose their sense of direction. After sentencing, the prisoners were imprisoned in remote areas of the country. Long term prison facilities were located conveniently inside the wildlife reserves, near lakes, and the remote arid desert of the country.

Lukenya hill is located about seventeen (17) kilometers east of the city of Nairobi and about five (5) kilometers outside Athi River town, my childhood town. Lukenya hill may not be widely known by native AthiRivians as a secret colonial government camp site used to torture those suspected with Mau Mau connections.

During my nostalgia days, we made several trips as Boy Scouts to Lukenya hill. One day we discovered the secret campsite in the early 1960s. The camp site was built under a large rock acting as a barrier; the rock itself had caves and crevices that naturally provided a safe haven for the torturers, and remained unnoticed to the public eye.

The campsite was surrounded with five feet deep dugout pits as a trench going around the parameter of the campsite, blanketed with coiled barbed wire then chicken wire enmeshed on top of sharp wooden sticks facing up below the pits. So if one were to try to escape they would fall onto the sharp pointed sticks under the chicken mesh. Men were succumbed to brutal physical torture. A few survived the horror story. Those who could not survive died; their corpses were left out for the hyenas to feast on. It was a horrible death, worse than the hanging of thieves during the Roman Empire. In my day, no one would dare mention about Mau Mau; people were afraid of the secrecy of the matter. The story about Mau Mau has never been told in voluminous print and dealt as a subject to the public. Perhaps this publication will encourage others to write and reveal more about the group. Otherwise, it will remain mystical and a legend story of the past in a matter of years. Due to the location of Lukenya hill, up to this day, I have always had a chill go through me driving along the Mombasa-Nairobi Road knowing I was near the site. The rock can be seen anywhere from Nairobi National Park. Eroded by the times and winds of change; the rock hides the secrecy of confessions of innocent men who died in torture during the dark years of the early 1950s.

And yet, standing on the topmost area of Lukenya hill, overlooking down below the Municipality City of Athi River, you will experience one of the best sunsets, south-west of Nairobi. It is breathtaking scenery of the sun as it slowly disappears over the horizon behind the magnificent metropolitan city lights of Nairobi.

It is widely argued by many Kenyans and especially the Kikuyu tribe, that Mau Mau is credited to have hastened Kenya's Independence. Another theory, England feared invasion of Soviet Communism through the use of Mau Mau guerilla in Kenya. The King's Royal Army was engaged in war with an enemy they could never see. It was similar to guerilla warfare like the American Vietnam War and Bush's War on Terrorism. The British fought a losing revolution for more than seven years leading up to Kenya's Independence in 1963.

It is one of the darkest hours in Kenya history regardless of whether you are Kikuyu, a white settler or Akamba tribe. Unfortunately, history repeated itself more than fifty years later on the anniversary of Mau Mau as the tribal killings took place across Rift Valley in the cover by night, similarly on the same agenda. December 27, 2007 was another dark hour for the innocent tens of thousands of men, women and children killed and over 650,000 people were displaced.

The majority of those people were Kikuyu. The Mau Mau mission was to kill white settlers. This time it was war against fellow tribes. The story must be told to benefit the future generations of the Republic of Kenya and the Kenyans in the Diaspora. These acts of atrocities should never happen again to the millions of innocent Kenyans or anywhere else in the free world.

The oath recipe varied between Akamba and the Kikuyu. It was also administered in levels of classes. The advanced level was meant for the soldiers, the men or women who carried out the actual attacks on white settlers. If a Mau Mau was ever caught by the government agents, he vowed never to tell on others. Torture was applied once a Mau Mau agent was caught by government security, some refused to break their oath covenant to save others.

The content recipe of the oath itself varied between the Akamba tribe and the Kikuyu; in this case the Mau Mau oath was based on the Kikuyu recipe given on two levels. Level one was "don't tell, don't ask". The advanced level was the pledge to kill anybody that came in the way between the Mau Mau agents, white settlers and government security agents. The customs of both tribes are that oath administration is only administered by a select council of elders in Kikuyu who are called "Kiama", and for the Akamba is called "Nzama". For both tribes no one disobeys an oath administered.

On the night the oath ceremony was administered, a he goat or a bull was slaughtered. Its meat was mixed with blood and human feces added together! And sometimes on a higher level the blind-gut-cecum was filled with blood. One at a time a person licked a heated sharp blade of a knife until everyone had taken. The only caveat to refuse to take the oath meant death. After the administration of the Mau Mau oath, one elder was elected by his peers as the main informant. The oath administration was repeated across the land until all Embu, Meru, and other people of the mountain received it. It moved across tribal lines to root out the white settlers of the illegally occupied native's lands.

The Royal British Army was dispersed to the mountain forest in search for Mau Mau fighters.

Mid night October 20th, 1952 Governor Evelyn Baring, the person in charge of the Kenya Colony declared the State of Emergency.

Jomo Kenyatta among other politicians was arrested on the morning of October 21st, 1952. British security had fire arms, and the Mau Mau fighters had the cover of night. It was hard to catch them. Mau Mau fighters became so dangerous that whenever they attacked villages of disloyal Kikuyu working for the white settlers they slaughtered men, women and children like domesticated animals for food. 1953 was the darkest hour for the Kikuyu people.

In the war between the Mau Mau fighters and the British security more than 300,000 innocent Kikuyu were killed, it was not about the war for independence, but it was a war between the white settlers who occupied the natives' Kenya Highlands and the natives. Those who managed to remain with their children could not attend school. By the following year of 1954 the Mau Mau fighters had suffered defeat by the thousands, many who gave up to the Royal Army securities were set free. Those who refused to give up were sentenced to death on site when caught.

Fears resurfaced in 1969, the same time history of mankind was made as Armstrong landed and walked on the moon! Tom Mboya, of a Luo tribe was assassinated in broad daylight in Nairobi, causing a state of unrest. Oath taking was introduced again to all young men who were of age. It was my first year in high school in Kirinyaga, Mount Kenya. The frightening announcement came through the school administrators that all young men were to be administered the oath in preparation for tribal war if it ever occurred.

Since I was deep into Kikuyu land, Baptist Missionaries acted quickly and transferred me to Mombasa Baptist High School, allowing me to escape the oath taking.

Did Sir Blundell Save Kenya from the Communist Rule in Kenya? (Secret Deal)

September 22th, 2008 fresh evidence was published by Kenya Sunday Nation confirming some alarming evidence on what took place behind the closed doors in the early 1960s between then Sir Michael Blundell, a white settler leader and the British Government in cementing a deal to make Kenyatta, the Prime Minister, and then later become the President of Kenya. Each time the land issues are mentioned within the realm of the fabric of the Kenya political system it shows how far the country's politicians have refused to settle the half a century old land problem.

How long will this land issue hang on the shoulders of the innocent Kenyans? The children of the old politicians who mostly have passed on and some are still ruling through their proxies. How conveniently, the Kenyans are reminded by the media of the terror of the disputed Presidential elections of December 27, 2007 that engulfed bloodshed. It is a reminder of the continuing dark side of leadership that voters should be reminded as to who they should vote for to represent them next time they cast their one single vote.

Sir Blundell set out running on the mission of making and crowning a King in Kenya at a time when the Colonial power was running out of options. 1960s was a time of change. Moscow was in an Arms race with England and America, China as always was on the sidelines watching the team players between Communism and Capitalism in a free world. There were three players in the game: there was Tom Mboya, young energetic, a trade Unionist and a polished young politician.

I remember like it was yesterday when Tom Mboya came to my home town Athi River located 16 miles south of Nairobi, to address mad striking workers of Kenya Meat Commission. KMC was the only meat manufacturing plant in East Africa; the factory exported meat to the European markets until the collapse of the political leadership in Kenya in the 1980s and 1990s, the age of corruption and bribery as earlier described. I saw with my naked eyes Mboya's four seat beetle lifted up in the air by the multitudes of workers, while he and his guest still seated inside the beetle! Boy, he was liked. Thanks to the American support.

Second choice, Jaramogi Odinga; the man was fabulous, great orator, he held a strong lead at his home base of Nyasa a Luo leader. There was no politician leader who would match his talents including Jomo Kenyatta. Again, I had the advantage of the front seat at Athi River town. Every contesting politician came to give their speech at KMC and Kenya Portland Cement. The two factories hired over 5,000 workers, KMC being the lead factory. The factories represented every tribe in Kenya including Tanzania and Uganda.

It was politics at its best when politicians stood on a platform and gave their manifesto, like how they conduct politics in free civilized nations of the north. There was no fighting or buying of votes as compared to elections after the 1970s. The trouble with this ticket was Jaramogi was loaded with Soviet ideology. That was troubling for the British Colony and America, the two super powers who had just defeated the Soviets during the WWII. It was the age of the cold war. The Soviets almost pulled the ticket lead in Kenya. The rest of us had no knowledge of the ideologies between the Union Jack, Americanism or the Soviets.

Third choice, Ronald Ngala, a man from Mombasa, the interior Kenya had the majority votes. Ngala would not have carried the day. Unfortunately, he died a mysterious death in a series of other prominent politician deaths, like his counterpart, Mboya. Their deaths are described in another section of **Leadership**.

Mr. Pio Gama Pinto, another causality of the new independence, was murdered for threatening to report to the parliament about the cover up of the eight million UK pounds that had been given for compensation for the families of the freedom fighters who lost their lives.

Then came Jomo Kenyatta, he was nowhere on the list of the King making. Sir Blundell best described Jomo Kenyatta as "the wild card of the native politics in the colony." Bingo. For Blundell, the search for the next King of the Colonial Kenya had ended. Let us recap; Kenyatta was jailed for the charges of the notorious outlawed Mau Mau outfit. This is the scenario, if Sir Blundell did not hurry up in his King making, Jaramogi was the only possible candidate for the King of the Colonial Kenya, but given the chance Moscow would take control of Kenya through Jaramogi, the poor cat seated at the valley of hard labor in the outskirts of the northern semi desert of Kenya/Ethiopian border was the best possible choice Sir Blundell had.

It is reported that Sir Blundell took his final assessment to the colonial governor who immediately asked permission from London Foreign Colonial Office for Sir Blundell to present an offer to Kenyatta. Permission granted. Sir Blundell flew to Lowdar, where Kenyatta was serving his seven year term. Kenyatta and Blundell struck a deal "but only if he could personally give assurance that he had abandoned the extremist anti-white views he held before his imprisonment." The governor MacDonald authorized the release of Jomo Kenyatta to freedom early, to assume the duties of Prime Minister of the new Kenya.

Consequently, the Colonial office in London declared Independence immaturely to East African nations in succession as follows: Julius Kambarage Burito Nyerere, (1961) first President of The Republic of Tanganyika, Milton Obote, (1962) First President of the Republic of Uganda and Jomo Kenyatta, (1963) Prime Minister, of the Republic of Kenya and 1964 the first President of Kenya. Other African nations continued to fight for their Independence throughout the sixties into the 1990s.

Theodore on African Safari Trails: He is a part of the tribute to select presidents of East Africa. Theodore Roosevelt is an important figure in the history of Kenya and the continent of Africa, as a former president of the United States of America. Theodore Roosevelt was born in 1858 in New York into an upper middle class family. Teddy loved the outdoors, adventure, hunting, and horseback riding on the open plains of the wild American west. He travelled extensively as a soldier during the American-Spanish War. At the prime of his young adult life, Teddy suffered the loss of his first wife, Alice Lee Roosevelt; unfortunately she died in 1884, the same day as his mother's death. Due to the immediate state of affairs, he moved to his family ranch in the Badlands of South Dakota Territory for two years. He worked hard on the land driving cattle, hunting big game and even caught an outlaw. The ranch exercise helped him heal and recover from some of his depression.

The Family: Two years later, during one of his international trips, Teddy met and married Edith Carow during a visit to London in December, 1886, with whom they were blessed to have six children. Even as President, he loved to play with his children outside on the White House lawn, wrestling and making pillow fights. Sometimes it would be exhausting to the point the President would be forced to change his attire before attending to important guests for a family dinner. He was able to balance being a family man, husband and the duties of being President. His wife, Edith described him best when she called him "her seventh child."

Teddy learned to enjoy life's moments since the loss of his first wife and his mother. He managed to preserve his family values, who he was, his dignity, presidential duties and the love for his country throughout his life. Later in life, with the company of his son, Kermit, he travelled the world in search of big game for trophies. He made one of the longest journeys ever made anywhere, even though he made the trip to explore the great rivers of South America, which nearly cost his life. Certainly, the African safari made to undeveloped colonial Africa was by far the most challenging, compared to any other hunting trips he may have made outside North America. No other American president has ever made such a long and treacherous safari on foot, horseback and canoe like Roosevelt.

His presidency: Teddy closed the end of the century and the beginning of another, the gap between the 19th Century and the 20th Century into a new era. He set a new vision with optimism in the history about American life. When elected to the presidency, he was a man with a New Deal for America. He became the youngest president at 42 years of age in the history of American politics. His youthfulness worked well to his advantage compared to his counterpart career politician's log cabin presidents of his day.

His view on the presidency was that a president is like a "steward of the people," the notion that a president should do whatever he can for the benefit of the people without breaking the law of the land or the Constitution. "I did not usurp power," he said. Theodore brought excitement and power to the office of the president. He led Congress and the American people toward progressive economic reforms with a strong foreign policy; at the turn of the 20th Century he managed to steer the nation to actively be involved in world politics.

He realized the need to shorten the trade routes between the Atlantic and the Pacific Oceans was inevitable. Theodore championed the construction of the Panama Canal. He used the Monroe Doctrine *coined by President James Monroe in 1817-1825 where Monroe warned Spain and England to "Keep their hands off from North and South America"* which gave America the sole right to have permanent military bases in the Caribbean and Latin America. It was a great move to have in American Foreign Policy the sole right to have bases in America's backdoor in Latin America. It was a very important juncture in the history of America, because in less than five (5) years in 1914 nations of the world were at WWI with each other.

A moral authority of a Leader is Honesty and Integrity
www.muumandu.com

As President of USA, Theodore held very strong convictions on how government should govern regardless of good and bad times. During his presidency, he won the Nobel Peace Prize for the mediation of Russo-Japanese War; for sending the "Great White Fleet" around the world on a goodwill tour mission. Back at home at the domestic arena Theodore was a strong advocate on conservation---added more national forest in the great wild-west, and reserved thousands of acres of land for the public use. It is the love for outdoor adventure that forced him to convince America to preserve these lands for future hunting and recreation.

Therefore, as President and Commander in Chief, he brought with him leadership from the grassroots of New York, honor and experience he earned as Police Chief, Assistant Secretary of the Navy, NY Governor and as Lieutenant Colonel of the Rough Riders Regiment during the Spanish-American War where he led a victory charge at the battle of San Juan. Theodore Roosevelt brought integrity and honesty to his fellow countrymen through his diverse local, state and national leadership experiences. Theodore put a lid on the monopoly from the big company establishments: oil, coal, steel and railways. He was afraid the companies would grow too big and powerful, they could control the government.

Early spring of 1909, Theodore Roosevelt, a two term president, sponsored by the Smithsonian Institute, accompanied by his son, Kermit, sailed on an African hunting safari to Kenya. His mission was to collect specimens for the Smithsonian Institution. Upon arriving in Mombasa the president spent a few days in Mombasa gathering Swahili guides and porters totaling an army of 250 man-powers. It is here he met one of the survivors from the famous epic story of the Man-Eaters of Tsavo. With fresh first hand information from one of the survivors, it provided a realistic look at the safari ahead. The following day in April of 1910 was an important day in the history of the Akamba people of Muumandu Hill.

Theodore Roosevelt arrived at Konza railway station shortly after mid-day on a locomotive train from Mombasa. The officer in the caboose gesticulated the train to a halt. He gazed on the open range of the Kapiti (Wapiti) Plains covered with endless herds of wildlife: lions, rhinoceros, elephants, buffalo herds and killer biting-mosquitoes. These are the meanest and most dangerous of the animal kingdom. Their callousness has claimed tens of thousands of lives of great hunters, missionaries, explorers, and native hunters through the centuries, including a famous British game hunter who was commissioned to search for and kill the famous Man-Eaters of Tsavo. The president came into fruition that he had arrived at Kenya's best hunting ground.

From his safari journal (diary) Roosevelt describes two tribes as though it was only one tribe; the dark-skinned people who were warlike, cattle-owning nomads. First, he spoke of the Maasai people who live among the wild animal kingdom; they are no harm to wildlife. The Maasai believed that the Supreme creator made them as the rightful owners of the domesticated cattle in the world. The notion that, a Maasai warrior has the right and duty to repatriate cattle found grazing in the care of other tribes; a belief that caused many tribal wars between Maasai and her neighboring tribes. Second, the Akamba tribe, a people of the hills, who lived in strings of villages fudging on hills of (Mua hills, Iveti hills, Kiima Kimwe and Kalama hills) spreading north to south of Muumandu Hill.

Muumandu Hill faces the open range of the Kapiti Plains. And so, Muumandu Hill served as a hiding place for the Akamba tribe during many tribal wars with Maasai warriors. The Hill has numerous caves with human and domestic animal foot prints suggesting that humans once lived and worshiped in a few select hallowed places. A few spread out foot prints found in caves and on sedimentary rocks in streams around the hill have since disappeared with times of change and poor ecological preservation with exception of one remaining ancestral worship (Ithembo) ground. On a clear day one can see the grandiose snow cap of Mount Kilimanjaro, with its gorgeous scenery of the sunset. A modern passenger train powered with a diesel engine rolls on its belly for the night, meandering through Kapiti Plains and the famous Man-Eaters of Tsavo National Park, toward Kenya's coastal region. Dinner is served to waiting passengers entertained by a few gazelles and zebras running here and there. And if one cares to wait a few more minutes the magnificent city lights of Nairobi can be seen spreading from north to south fringing the Ngong Hill. From this vantage point, the president saw a mountain whose snow cap was dazzling under the equatorial sun. The mountain is no other than Mt. Kilimanjaro, mushrooming 19,000 feet above the earth, about 160 Kilometers south.

The president asked the (then) British East Africa Colony to build water towers on Muumandu Hill and other surrounding hills in Machakos for the natives to draw clean drinking water for themselves and irrigation for their animals. Nothing was done at that time, not during the Colonial rule, and not even after Kenya received her Independence. The administrators were not interested in helping or equipping the Akamba people except to exploit them. The author is committed to fulfill a dream that was never realized, with the help of our western donors will assist to put to rest the forgotten story. Somewhere in these mysterious hills water tower tanks, health clinics and the Solomon Center For Leadership will someday be built.

Teddy opened the gateway to Africa to his fellow Americans at a time when the average American had no knowledge of the adventures of Africa. They lived an isolated life away from the rest of the world. Up to this day tens of thousands of Americas travel to Africa in search of the foot prints of other great Americans who have gone before them. East Africa has become a pilgrimage for Europeans and North Americans with an average of one million tourists per year.

A tally of the total animal collection between Teddy and his son Kermit killed 1,100 specimens, 500 big game, 512 wildebeests, 17 lions, 11 elephants and 20 rhinoceros. It was the dream of every American boy to be like Teddy, who represented the "macho" man, a soldier, a politician, a hunter of African wild game, a cowboy and a writer of thirty-five books. To the elite, he provided the literary reading of: *The African Game Trail, American Problems,* the *New Nationalism,* and *African and European Addresses.*

No doubt, Hemingway like most Americans was an admirer of Teddy's travels and adventures. His early childhood interest in writing was most likely influenced by Teddy's writings, travels and adventures. Hemingway journeyed to East Africa and fell in love with the beauty of a breathtaking snow cap of Kilimanjaro. Hemingway's best piece of literary art is *The Snows of Kilimanjaro.* The president, full of charisma and energy tracked through the north eastern corridor of the Belgian Congo forest, and western Uganda, back to the Nile River, headed north to Khartoum, canoeing the Nile River through Sudan and Egypt.

After a yearlong safari hunt, there was no mention of anyone in the crew ever suffering mosquitoes' bites, nor injured during the entire expedition. However, Roosevelt got sick while on a canoe along the Nile River heading to Khartoum, he refused to accept a mosquito's bite during the entire time of his hunting safari. He chose not to shed a blemish on the continent of Africa. He argued that he could have been bitten during many of his political campaigns in the Rockies of North America. He nursed himself with a bottle of a brandy and continued through Egypt to London, just in time to attend King Edward VII's funeral, the grandfather of Her Majesty Queen Elizabeth. From London he journeyed to Norway to accept the Nobel Peace Prize for taking part in ending the Russo-Japanese War. He returned to New York, June 1910. He never returned to Africa. Final Remarks: Roosevelt returned back to the national political spotlight in 1912, his popularity had wore-out during his first terms as president. He ran on a Progressive Party ticket. He lost flat out to a Democratic candidate. One day while on a campaign trail in Milwaukee, he for the second time almost lost his life to a fanatical man, who shot him in the chest. He survived the ordeal. He looked back at this adventurous life and said, "No man has had a happier life than I have led; a happier life in every way." It is a clear indication that he had finally accepted the death of his first wife and the death of his dear mother, on the same day.

Teddy never returned to politics, neither to international travel. As former president he opened doors of opportunities for many Americans: mission boards, artists, Hollywood, journalists, more safari hunters and mountain climbers and other expeditions as a future potential player in the world. And so it has come to pass that the continent is now a member of the world cartel in exporting oil, fresh vegetables to Europe, and a woman's best friend, the "diamond." Teddy's life was full of travel adventures, he wrote scores of books and a number of articles to his credit. Teddy belongs up there among his predecessors along with Thomas Jefferson, John Adams and John Quincy Adams. Just before he died, Teddy said, "Life and death are parts of the same great adventure." Roosevelt is best known as the man who invented modern America. He died an honorable man on January 6, 1919 at the end of the First World War at age 61.

There are many great literature works that have been written about the first presidents of East Africa. The author of *Leadership* presents his personal findings, observations and views from having lived under the rule and leadership of the first presidents. *Leadership* presents personal interviews of relatives, close friends, former personal presidential acquaintances, men and women who worked for these presidents and from a child of one of the presidents. Both presidents were greatly admired by their respectful countries. I was born, raised in Kenya, educated, married and matured in Tanzania. Now, after more than three decades of pursuing higher education, working and living in Texas, my leadership and world view have come to an exemplary plateau.

Julius Nyerere, First President of Tanzania: The author of *Leadership* has selected to pay tribute to Presidents: Julius Nyerere and Jomo Kenyatta. These men were responsible for the founding democracies in East Africa their leadership was based on different ideologies and philosophies. Julius Nyerere as earlier stated, "He adopted a **combination** of a socialist model of governing from the Far East with an African Socialist mythology system of **culture** that has existed for many years at a larger scale in the form of a national government for the people."

In stark contrast, his counterpart Jomo Kenyatta leaned to the west and practiced a capitalist model of governing. However, Kenyatta would later embark on **amalgamation** of Democratic principles both Elder and Warrior leadership styles, a system that has existed long before the arrival of the foreigners. Call it Socialism, Communism and Capitalism; the imported system of ideologies failed horrendously, each system of belief produced human and economic catastrophe to the East African nations. However, the leadership in East Africa and elsewhere in the continent continues to struggle to re-discover their abandoned old tribal ways of leadership, a dogma based on the strength of character of African tribal leader(ship).

Kenyatta's Legacy: For the majority of Kenya tribes whose children were born before and after the 1800s, it would be impossible to establish a date of birth. However, there were other methods of knowing one's date of birth. Each tribe had a method in place to name a new born: for example, during the harvest season, famine, rain seasons, at night/day or on a journey (safari). It was not until the arrival of European civilizations when primary schools were introduced. Those who took advantage of the new civilization managed to register a date and time of their new born. European sending mission boards opened schools and hospitals for the natives. It is possible that Kamau's parents may not have known to read and write.

Kenyatta's birth date remains a conjecture among historians given the time and the condition of his upbringing. Available oral communications suggest that Kamau's biological father died when Kamau was at an early age. Therefore, the author takes a conservative date to suggest that Jomo Kenyatta may have been born in 1889 at Ng'enda village in Gatundu Division of Kiambu

District. I suppose, as a matter of public interest, his immediate family will someday publish the life and history of Jomo Kenyatta. He was dearly respected and admired by the majority of Kenyans.

When *Kamau's* biological father died, according to the Gikuyu customary law, his mother was inherited by his uncle "Ngengi." Wambui and Ngengi together had a son called James Muigai, who became Kamau's half brother. But for reasons not available to the public, Wambui left Ngengi's house to return back to her parents. Kamau also left his Uncle Ngengi's home for Muthiga to live with his grandfather, Kingu Magana. After graduation from primary school in 1912, Johnstone Kamau was an apprentice carpenter at Thogoto Mission station, under engineer, John Cook. When Kamau reached to maturity, he was baptized [1914] John Peter, a name he would later change to Johnstone Kamau. There are no clear reasons why Kamau went through name changes especially after he acquired a baptism name from a religious institution that cared for him, educated him and put him through school as an orphan child. His grandfather was a fortuneteller and a medicine man of his day.

We shall never know if Kamau's grandfather, Magana influenced him to abandon his western names Peter and Johnstone. Maybe he was under pressure from his Kikuyu elders whose opinions on the British Colonials were viewed as enemies by the native Kikuyu for having taken their ancestral land by force. It is possible in his day; it was hard for a young Kikuyu like Kamau to proudly maintain a western name given the political situation of the day. He completely abandoned his western names and never assumed his biological father's name Muigai. His father's name should have meant something to a young boy like Kamau since his father was no longer there. However, at least his half brother James was named Muigai by his biological father Ngengi. It was rare in those days for women to remarry especially if they had sons. There are no available records if Kamau's mother, Wambui remarried and moved on with her life and acquired a new family name. Wambui died at her parent's home.

Perhaps due to the rising political tension between white colonial settlers and the native Kikuyu and conceivably advice from his grandfather, may have influenced Kenyatta to rebel from all Christian names by distancing himself from the white colonial rule. In fact, his baptism name, Peter, he named his two sons of different mothers!

Rumor has it Kenyatta seldom identified himself with native established Kikuyu worshipers. Kenyatta admired native dancers: Kikuyu, and the famous Akamba dancers. In sharp contrast, his predecessor, former President Moi was a regular fixture in his African Inland Mission Church (AIC). Moi used the church leadership to further and strengthen his political grassroots for his presidential leadership support base. President Kibaki is regularly seen seated at the Cathedral, The Roman Catholic Church for his morning mass. Because Kenya is overwhelming 80% Christian, it feels best to have a president who acknowledges the deity of Christ.

The Railways: The arrival of the British settlers and the construction of Mombasa-Nairobi Railways was a significant event for the majority of tribes in Kenya to associate their newborns, especially the villages and towns the railways passed through. Suppose Kenyatta was not old enough to see the construction of Mombasa–Nairobi Railways; then we would assume that he must have been born after 1895 or vice versa. Machakos town was first established about the same as the British East Africa Trading Company, which later become the colonial power in Kenya and East Africa. The German East Africa was first to start to build Tanga to Moshi Railways in 1893 which took the Germans twelve (12) years to reach Moshi town in modern northern Tanzania. Germany, France and Britain were in competition in railway construction around the world. The British East Africa started late and led in the completion of Mombasa – Nairobi Railways covering 600 miles.

When World War I broke out in Europe, the Germans and the British were occupying East Africa colonies. The settlers had lived in harmony as neighbors, enjoying the beauty of Africa. *Kamau* evaded becoming a war recruit, and went to Narok where he worked for an Asian contractor until the war was ended. While living in Narok, *Kamau* began to wear a Maasai belt called "Kinyata" just like any other Maasai warrior, no one would have guessed otherwise. As a graduate he understood written and spoken English, a language skill that was needed to work in government offices, as teachers, and government owned corporations, manufacturing plants, farm managers, and Asian store keepers. Five (5) years after the war ended *Kamau* assumed a new name, Kenyatta. From this time on **Leadership** will refer *Kamau wa Ngengi* as Jomo Kenyatta because he had acculturated himself with the Maasai art, language and tradition.

During his stay in Narok, he married Grace Wahu who bore him his first two children, Peter Muigai and Margaret Wambui. His first daughter, Margaret Wambui, who he so dearly loved, assumed his mother's name Wambui. Margaret Wambui, later in her adult life became the first Mayor of the city of Nairobi and was appointed the first Permanent Secretary in United Nations, in New York. Jomo Kenyatta bought land outside the city of Nairobi, large enough to build a house and garden-shamba for his family's upkeep in Dagoretti. Grace Wahu lived in Dagoretti until her death. Jomo Kenyatta opened a small family store under the name Kinyata Store. He also got a job as a water meter reader for Nairobi Municipal Council, under his old supervisor, John Cook.

From his city job Kenyatta was hired by Kikuyu Central Association as Secretary. It is best to say that Kenyatta's new job got him interested in local politics; he helped KCA officials to file a land case with Hilton Young Commission of which their case was denied. KCA regrouped and filed their case with London Colonial Office. In the meantime Jomo Kenyatta began to build popularity with his Kikuyu tribe. He became the editor and publisher of the Muigwithania newspaper, a periodical that dealt with the Kikuyu culture in addition to new methods of farming.

In 1929, Kikuyu Central Association had gained political strength. The association dispatched Kenyatta to London in [1929-1930] to formally file grievances before the British Colonial office, in London to request the return of Kikuyu land in Kenya, which had been taken by force and given to white settlers. Kenyatta toured other European nations including Russia in 1930. The KCA appeal was rejected. While in London Kenyatta wrote his first article in a foreign land titled, "Give Us Our Land," a subject that attracted many Britons with great concern at a time when the British Colonial Office was recruiting settlers to farm in her East African colony. This was the beginning of Kenyatta's politics. It is safe to say that when Kenyatta's mission was no longer worth pursuing with the British Colonial

Office, he looked for other opportunities in London.

Female Circumcision: Kenyatta sponsored by the Scottish Mission, returned to Kenya to combat the practice of female circumcision, in addition to encourage the development of independent schools. Kenyatta's campaign on female circumcision remained a touchy issue among the native Kikuyu tribe, the Akamba and other Bantu tribes who have practiced female circumcision for generations.

Kenyatta returned back to Nairobi for a couple of months only to hand over his job at KCA. He returned back to England on May 2, 1931 and remained until 1946. During Kenyatta's second return to London, he spoke before the Morris Carter Commission and presented a list of demands to parliament for the loss of land grabbed by white settlers and economic opportunities for the native Kenyans. Kenyatta's petition was rejected. He stayed in England through the Great Depression; worked on Barlow's Kikuyu Dictionary and enrolled at London School of Economics under Professor Malinowski. Kenyatta published his first book, *Facing Mount Kenya* – under the name Jomo Kenyatta. After the release of *Facing Mount Kenya,* the name *Johnstone Kamau* died away from the public.

The name Jomo Kenyatta, originating from a Maasai word in rural Narok, became a household name from London to the rest of the world, until his death, August 22, 1978 as President of the Republic of Kenya. Kenyatta published his second book entitled: *My People of Kikuyu.* Kenyatta remained in England for a period of fifteen (15) years, traveling and attending several institutions: Quaker College, University College, and London School of Economics. This time triggered a permanent separation and disappointment between him and first wife, Grace Wahu. She was a woman who never enjoyed the lime light of being a first lady, and a woman who never enjoyed her married life with the man she once loved and bore him two beautiful children. (Daily Nation Newspaper)

Kenyatta moved on with a new life. He found a new love and married Edna Clerke, a governess of West Sussex, England. The couple had a child, *Peter Magana* Kenyatta. The name *Peter* was Kenyatta's old name at Baptism and the name *Magana* takes up Kenyatta's grandfather's name *Magana*, the medicine man. Kenyatta continued with his tradition for naming his children after his father and mother. It is interesting how Kenyatta continued to name his other daughters the name of his mother, Wambui: Margaret Wambui, first daughter of the first wife, Grace Wahu and Jeni Wambui, a first born daughter with the third wife, who died during child birth.

Kenyatta advanced himself with academic knowledge. He lived in Russia for some time. He returned back to London School of Economics to pursue a degree in anthropology under Bronislaw Malinowski. It is here Kenyatta published his famous book, *Facing Mount Kenya* in1938. Kenyatta, in his book described his Kikuyu tribe, and at the same time disapproved the destructive changes brought about by the British colonial rule in Kenya. His book received wide reception in Great Britain as a precursor of African leadership by establishing Kenyatta as the key spokesperson for his people in Kenya.

In the course of the fifteen (15) years period in London, Kenyatta had completed his education, published, gotten married and met other African leaders including Nkrumah of Ghana during the

Pan African Congress in Manchester in 1945. He also met Mahatma Gandhi of India in 1932, at Downing Street, Parliament, who also presented his political claim in search for democracy for the people of India. It was a period of great regeneration for the millions of men and women living under British colonial rule.

Return to Kenya: September 1946 Kenyatta returned back to his native land. He left behind his second wife, Edna and child, Peter. Kenyatta returned back to Kenya to pursue his political dream, to fight for the release of the Kikuyu land that had been occupied by the white settlers since the inception of the British Colonial rule in 1920. During Kenyatta's absence, the KCA had organized themselves into a political movement under the name Kenya Africa Union. When his native Kikuyu realized that Jomo Kenyatta had returned home; James Gichuru, the chairman of KAU stepped down to allow Jomo Kenyatta to become the leader of KAU. Kenyatta had earned the respect of his native Kikuyu before he left for England. He had represented KCA at British Colonial Office in London. There was another secret movement made of Kikuyu alone. Their mission was to fight the white settlers and kill anybody including their native Kikuyu who stood in their way.

The movement would best be described as a terrorist movement of the day, because of their secret agendas. The movement was unknown by the authority but had organized itself under the name Mau Mau. During the arrival of Kenyatta, both KAU and Mau Mau were full blown movements. The British Colonial administration in Kenya was unable to contain both the political movement and the Mau Mau movement. The newly appointed governor to Kenya, Sir Evelyn Baring authorized the state of emergency in Kenya in 1952.

The Colonial leadership in Kenya charged Kenyatta as the leader of Mau Mau on October 20, 1952. Kenyatta and his colleagues, namely Fred Kubai, (Kikuyu), Richard Achieng, (Luo), Bildad Kaggia, (Kikuyu), Paul Ngei, (Mkamba), and Kingu Karumba, (Kikuyu), were apprehended by the authorities and charged for instigation of the Mau Mau movement. The six men on April 24, 1952 were apprehended, charged and sentenced to seven years in prison at Lokitaung. Kenyatta received two additional years of restriction to a remote place in Lodwar in western Kenya. There are conflicting theories whether Kenyatta was the leader of Mau Mau. However, the majority of native Kikuyu never believed that Kenyatta was the leader. It is possible Kenyatta was not a leader of Mau Mau because he never seemed to have recognized the Mau Mau movement during his rule.

On August 21, 1961 Kenyatta was discharged and set free to return to his place of birth in Gatundu location. One would imagine that he would go back to Grace Wahu, his first wife, at Dagoretti, but he never did. Unknown to the younger generation of his day, Kenyatta re-established himself to his native Kikuyu and the rest of the country. Besides, he was jailed with a few more politicians from other tribes. The country political climate was ready for self rule; Kenyatta was the man to take the mantle of leadership. October 28, 1961 Kenyatta, by his own right was elected chairman of Kenya African National Union (KANU). British Colonial Office at Downing Street was ready to let Kenyans take back their country. Kenya was the last East African nation to receive her Independence on December 12, 1963.

KANU Delegation to London: KANU delegation, including

Hon. Martin Shukuku and other politicians went to London to rectify and craft the Lancaster Constitution, the hallmark and historic document that has guided and governed the peoples of Kenya for four decades. The Kenyan politicians were widely accepted by the British Colonial Office, in contrast to 1929-31 when Kenyatta first presented demands for the Kikuyu Central Association. Permission was granted for Kenya to have a self rule government. It was an historic moment for the people of Kenya. June 1, 1963, Kenyatta was sworn in as Prime Minister of Kenya. One year later he became the first president of the Republic of Kenya on December 12, 1964. From that date "Madaraka Day" became a public holiday in Kenya celebrated as a reminder for all working men and women of Kenya. Kenyatta rose to the occasion as a leader; history is kind to him because of the stability of his government. Unfortunately, Kenyatta died in office August 22, 1978 at 89 years of age (?).

Kenyatta is regarded as one of the greatest pro-African leaders of his day. Under his leadership, Kenya's economy prospered and rose to the zenith of her glory. The people of Kenya enjoyed similar economics and prosperity during Kibaki's administration 2002-2007. Kenyatta's leadership was intolerant of dissidents in Kenya. He outlawed all opposition parties in 1969. He fought the state supported Somalia gorilla war along the Kenya – Somali border, who wanted to annex part of Kenya. Similar to Idi Amin Dada, Dictator of Uganda, a Moslem, he too, wanted to annex a piece of Kenya and sandwich Kenya between Somalia and Uganda. Kenyatta defeated all threats against his leadership from within and from without.

Meeting of the president: I was a member of the Athi River singing choir under the leadership Mr. Philip Ndeto, who was both the headmaster and choir director for Athi River School. We had recently won the district singing competition using folk songs, contemporary and other church related songs. We were selected to sing for the president at his home in Gatundu in 1967. When we were marched into the presidential parlor to sing for the president, I stood at an advantage point of view, close to the president. Although I had seen the president on several occasions aboard trains going for his working holidays in Mombasa, this was the first time I saw Jomo Kenyatta close up. Even though I was standing very close, the man looked untouchable; his deep voice and big eyes were very commanding and intimidating. We performed so well that it resulted in the awarding of a music scholarship to Mr. Ndeto in music at Exeter, England. The last time I saw the president was at his official State House in Nairobi. This time I was not going to sing for him, or attend his political rallies. This time I went to pay my last tribute to a man who had been my hero and my president. Members of the diplomatic corps, luminaries, nobles, and citizens from all walks of life gave their honor to the death of Jomo Kenyatta the first president of the Republic of Kenya.

Kenyatta's sickness had been kept secret for some time, until when his illness leaked out to the public. The country's attorney general issued a stern warning to anyone who would speculate on the health or the death of the president was a punishable offense, possibly to dissuade any surprises among the presidential lieutenants. Regardless of the attorney general's warnings, Kenyatta's illness was in its advanced stages of his life, he suffered a long battle of illness. He finally died in the previous wee hours of the morning in Mombasa State House during one of his many working holidays.

Kenyatta never had a family reunion that received public attention like the one he had weeks prior to his death. Local newspapers and vernacular radio broadcasts the gathering of his family which included the Londoners, Edna Clerke and their son, Magana who had never been in the public realm until this time. Four Wives of Kenyatta: Mr. Kenyatta was not an exception when it comes to marriage in an African context. He was a respected African elder by his own right, one who lived a full term of life. He married four times with one marriage accidentally ended at childbirth; he was survived with a beautiful baby girl. Kenyatta remained consistent with the norms of the tradition of his tribe. Histories will be kind to Mama Ngina Kenyatta, the only First Lady the country ever had. She became the most famous wife, respected, powerful and the Rose of Kenya. After her husband's death, Mama Ngina retired quietly from the public life. However, she has remained an integral part of her son's political career, the Hon. Uhuru Kenyatta.

Kenyatta Family: Mrs. Grace Wahu was Kenyatta's first wife, they had two children: Peter Muigai Kenyatta, (1920) and Margaret Wambui Kenyatta (1928). His second wife, Mrs. Edna Clerke of London had one son, Peter Magana (1943) London. His third wife, Grace Wanjiku, sister of the late [Mbiyu Koinange] had Jeni Wambui (1950). His fourth and final wife was Mama Ngina (1961) bore Uhuru Kenyatta, Muhoho Kenyatta and Nyokabi Kenyatta.

Grace Wahu, the first wife of Kenyatta, the founding father of the nation, was the second to be laid to rest; we shall never know what were her thoughts and feelings about a man whose struggle for the liberation of Kenyans' Independence cost their marriage. Mrs. Wahu's death left Kenyans with the unfinished story of the

first family saga of the late first President of the Republic of
Kenya, Hon. Jomo Kenyatta. In April, 2007 Nation Daily Newspaper, published an alleged letter written by Jeni Wambui to her
father January 21, 1963 (probably at age 13 years old). Caution:
Leadership cannot confirm the authenticity of the mentioned
letter below.

> "Dear Daddy, many greetings from your daughter, Jeni. I
> should like to ask you something. Please daddy, do you trust
> me or you don't? If you do, why then don't you let me stay
> with Margaret? I should prefer staying there rather than stay-
> ing with Jan. If you want to know why I shall be glad to
> explain it to you sometimes." _{Nation Daily Paper, April 2007}

Suppose it is true, it can be argued that it is normal for any teenage girl or boy to want the affection, attention, and warm love
experience of a father. After the family reunion, Kenyatta told
the nation that everyone should always have a family reunion;
as though he knew that he was about to die and maybe this was
his way of saying goodbye to the peoples of Kenya. With due
respect, I can only speculate that it is during the family reunion
that Kenyatta disbursed his estate to his family.

Nairobi, August 22, 1978, the radio announcement, spoken in
Swahili, the official announcement on the voice of Kenya radio at one o'clock national news, the announcement was made,
"Mr. Kenyatta died peacefully in his sleep early this morning in
Mombasa. In public appearances yesterday, Mr. Kenyatta, 89,
appeared to be in good health so news of his death has come as a
shock to us all." I remember to this very day, my wife and I were
taking our lunch break while attending a Bible Institute Seminar within the compounds of the University of Nairobi, when

the shocking news came over the air waves. The announcement went on and on punctuated with a Swahili Christian chorus throughout the day and night for several days.

It was a shock, it is as though the air was filled with fear, and everyone was out in the city streets going in his or her own directions. Before the end of the day, people rushed to public transportation headed to their rural homes, that is, those who could afford to leave the city. People fled in all directions in fear of what could happen in the city, just like what happened December 27, 2007. Separated by twenty-nine years, both situations were based on the validity of fear of what could happen. On August 22, 1978 the fear was in their heart and minds only, but in contrast December 27, 2007 the same fears were actually realized, people died, there were fires, churches burned, businesses burned, villages burned and people were forced to run for their lives.

This time there was no transition of leadership, because of the failed and disputed presidential election, it left a leadership in crisis. It happened that I was in the city of Nairobi both times; first, I was a citizen minding my own business. The second time, I was in Nairobi running for a political office, because Kenyatta had inspired me during my nostalgic youthful days for public life. Like Kenyatta, I too left Kenya to North America for more than twenty-seven years for higher education for the sole purpose to prepare myself for public office.

After Kenyatta's death, lawless and unfounded rumors began to fill the city that Mau Mau would strike again and take up control of the country from whoever would be the leader if the leader would not be a Kikuyu. That was the public perception.

Immediately, there was silent fear that somebody or a group of people would pull the **unwanted** and perturb the peace and harmony that Kenyans enjoyed for a long time. The public had their perception of fear of Mau Mau, while those in the immediate Kenyatta's inner circle had their own perception of fear. Shops and offices throughout the country including the capital, Nairobi, closed for the day, one as a mark of respect and second as a sign of fear. World rulers including Her Majesty, Queen of The British Empire, sent a message of sympathy to Mr. Kenyatta's family and the peoples of Kenya.

Memories: During the time of writing *Leadership,* it is now thirty years since his death and I pen down my deepest sympathy with respect to a man considered by many Kenyans a the father of the nation of Kenya. Kenyatta is to Kenyans as to what George Washington is to Americans as the father of the nation. At the same time I am filled with joy to experience democracy at work in the nomination and election of Barack Obama, the first African-American born of a Kenyan father, as President of the United States of America.

That is when democracy and leadership is at its best. Senator Hillary Clinton was right when she said, "See you can be anything you want." I was inspired by Kenyatta's leadership ability, oratory and his charisma as a national figure. His speeches are still alive in the minds and hearts of many Kenyans, including myself. Kenyatta was my hero and a role model as a politician. I know I speak for many Kenyans who knew him and worked under him. He was a no nonsense leader. People respected him both domestically and around the world.

When he died, he was carried by the most elaborate carriage of the day. Since he died in office, Kenya government erected a monument where he still lays up to this day on the same road going to National Parliament Buildings and Nairobi financial district center.

Flash back: Most Kenyans, alive today, can acutely remember when they heard the news that Kenyatta had died in his sleep. It was as though, there was a sinister silence everywhere in the country. Questions resonated in the minds and hearts of many Kenyans. Who would carry out the enormous burden of the Harambee where he managed to unit all tribes to live and work together as one family? Who would carry the mantle of peace and prosperity that Kenyans so dearly enjoyed? December 27, 2007 a group of people from an enemy within shattered the peace and tranquility that Kenyans had cherished for more than four decades.

My first memories of Kenyatta came from my elders who worked at the Kenya Meat Commission in Athi River, who told me of their close relationship with Kenyatta's relatives. The Kikuyu worried that other tribes would take away what they had accomplished. Other tribes worried that the Mau Mau would rise again. The British and western investors who had remained behind were also worried. Everyone had reasons to be afraid, VERY afraid. There is no doubt that Kenyatta led Kenya through the most prosperous years in history. It is sad though that despite all this, his sunset years became tainted with what some saw as human rights abuses, corruption and favoritism on tribal lines. Like most incumbents in any government, he had been in power too long. In contrast, if Kenyatta had abolished tribalism like his counterpart, Julius Nyerere of Tanzania, Kenya would not have suffered along political tribal lines.

Tribal/Elder Ideology Vs Democratic Principles: Many political leaders during Kenyatta's era displayed various leadership styles. Some continued with the leadership style that they inherited from the colonial masters at the time of decolonization. Military dictatorship, Socialism and Communism and a mixture of Democratic principles both Elder and Warrior are leadership styles.

The later is a system that existed long before the arrival of the foreign traders: such as Persian, Indian, Hindus, Phoenicians, and Arab dynasties were regulars on the Indian Ocean before the birth of Jesus Christ. The majority of the Arab traders established trading posts signing local alliances with coastal natives as early as the 1st Century. The relationships between the natives, African and Arab, were based on trade agreements. The Portuguese traders (15th Century) remained along the coastal area of the Indian Ocean. It was not until the arrival of the French, German and The British Empire, the superpowers of the day late in the 1800s that brought colonization.

When the civilized societies — managed to penetrate interior Africa, they were faced with Elder/Warrior style of small African kingdoms just to mention a few: the Buganda, of Uganda, Chief Kivoi of Kitui, Wanyamwezi under Chief Mirambo, The Hehe tribe under Mkwawa, Zulus, Chagga, Haya tribe and Maasai. The warrior and elder style leadership began as far back as African existence. The African institution of leadership began to emerge, some with strong resistance to colonial dominance during late 1800s - 20th Century.

However, Elder/Warrior tribal leadership began to diminish slowly during the arrival of the British and German traders then into Colonies of Kenya and Tanzania. The British Colonial rule embraced it even further as they used the existence of tribal leaders, they corrupted tribes against one another and put tribes into a compartmentalization, for the purpose to divide and rule tactic. The Elder/Warrior style Leadership has different ideologies, often similar to democratic patterns of leadership. It is best described as a council of elders or assembly.

The Akamba tribe met out under a large tree or a corral within a homestead, where they discussed matters of clan policies, enemies of the tribe, discipline, compensation between one clan to another and other matters arising. Yet these different patterns are not necessarily new in Africa. In some ways they follow the patterns established by Africa's oldest great leaders of the past. These African leadership styles form elements of continuity between Africa's pre-colonial past and post-colonial present, the Elder tradition and the Warrior tradition. In North America, the Comanche Indians, Apache, and Navaho Native American Indians practiced a combination of Elder and Warrior leadership styles, during many of the white settlers' attacks.

Elder Leadership Style: The elder tradition is heavily patriarchal (fatherly) by definition. It is particularly strong where you still have the original first president of an African state, head of an institution, religious-Judea-Christian-Abraham, a tribal leader and the head of a single family. The notion of a founding father refers to one with privilege, not just in politics but in opinion formation, and is a major component of the total political picture. The elder (Mzee, a Swahili word for elder) leader is one who commands reverence and a father figure in many societies. He may prefer to withdraw himself from involvement in the affairs of the nation/institution and dominate the scene from a godfather position in the background. In a political participation the elder may choose to micromanage his affairs of state, delegate duties to his lieutenants, assistants and his generals who carry out the daily business of running the nation.

And so, to emphasize Elder/Warrior African leadership style against colonial rule had long existence before the arrival of the western influence. Former President Julius Nyerere of Tanzania is best described as the true African Elder leader by his own right, who deserves the mantle of one of the original African resistance leaders of our time. It is the character of the leader who decides the direction of the nation.

Kenyatta used all three leadership styles. At first, he used democratic process one-vote one-winner. To achieve Kenya's independence, he needed every tribe on board. Kenyatta tried a lone ranger style being sent by Kikuyu Central Association movement. He failed to convince the British administrators, simply because they knew that Kenyatta's success in his mission required the voices of all Kenyans. So in the very beginning of Kenya politics he was very committed to democratic ideals. He was visionary, one who saw a glorious image of Kenya during his youthful age and kept working at his dream until his inauguration celebration June 1, 1963. Within six months, on December 12, 1963 Kenya declared her independence from the British colonial rule of more than half a century. The event made millions of people very happy.

Similar to the election of the first African – American President Obama, slogans with words "birth of freedom" appeared all over American cities with messages of hope. For the African-American communities, Martin Luther King's dream had been fulfilled once and for all. The majority of Kenyans believed that they had finally reclaimed what was rightfully theirs. Unfortunately, KANU regime slowly turned a blind eye to other political parties. KANU regime ruled for over twenty-four years and turned out to be a bitter disappointment for the majority of Kenyans. Yes, there was order, peace and stability in the country, but only to a few individuals selected by KANU regime.

As soon as Kenya got independence, the Kenya politicians under the leadership of Kenyatta entered into a covert pact with the British to protect their interests in return for the inheritance of the system left behind. Early Kenya politicians failed to demonstrate the principle of democracy in a parliamentary system that founded the very government on democratic principles. Kenyatta exemplified being an elder leader, and ruthless KANU leadership acted as dictatorship of a democratic institution without control. It is sad to note that newly elected Kenya politicians carried on where the British colonial left off, the Birmingham guard change effect.

KANU administration continued to plunder public resources, and sometimes was worse than the masters themselves. KANU leadership took all for themselves. Tens of thousands of acres of crown land taken from the natives by the white settlers – magically belonged to a few politicians! This included millions of hectares of land set aside for the purpose for forestation, wildlife preservation, and protection of endangered trees, sea frontage and the prevention of soil erosion. The majority groups of tribes most affected were dwellers in Rift Valley. The Rift Valley Province is the nation's largest region and the bread basket for: wheat, corn, tea, coffee and other cash products.

In stark contrast, Julius Nyerere, first President of Tanzania ordered all crown land remain public property; in addition no person, including his administration and politicians were allowed to own more than necessary allocation of land left behind by the British Colony. As a result of Julius's presidential order, there were no land grabbers, the environment was protected and no individuals who got rich over night. Julius reigned for a number of years, and then became the first African president to resign from his presidency to pave the way for a new leader. Julius died in a London hospital as a free ordinary citizen. He was considered one of poorest among African leaders of his day. One of his close lieutenants said Nyerere, a devout Catholic member, never missed his morning mass prayers.

Kenya politicians had mastered the art of oppression. First they got used to being oppressed by the British Colonial Administrators. Tribal politician leaders turned against each other to oppress the very Kenya leaders who fought together against the one enemy — the British Colonial, by exploiting the ignorance, biases and prejudices of the African elder tradition, a trend that still sadly persists. "What is Kenya today after all?" Koigi wrote. It is an example of Kenya's ruthless past administrations and intolerance that comes out in Koigi Wa Wamwere's autobiography. He states how Kenyatta once drew his gun in Parliament intending to shoot the late Ronald Ngala for criticizing his government, and was only restrained by then Speaker, Humphrey Slade. What Koigi Wamwere fails to explain in a culture of Elder/Warrior, respect from subordinates, juniors, and family members, is expected and required. Failure to do so could result in severe discipline. It was a practice used in city and states including the Roman Emperors.

The Kings or Emperors were above the rule of Law. In Kenya, failure to obey an elder may result in severe discipline. Unfortunately, Hon. Ngala died a mysterious 'road accident' on Mombasa-Nairobi Road one weekend returning to his coast Province, Mvita Constituency. Many onlookers at the scene of the accident alleged that a swarm of bees entered into his moving vehicle, attacked and killed everyone on board! Similar horrific deaths like the famous Man-Eaters of Tsavo at the turn of the 20th Century took place along this route. Tens of hundreds of motorists have died in fatal road accidents on Mombasa-Nairobi Road since the construction of this fatal single two way lane road by the colonial administration.

It was paved in the late 1960s. Mombasa-Nairobi Road starts at Kenya's harbor of Mombasa stretching a journey of more than 1,000 miles to Kenya international borders. This single two way lane feeds the nations of: Uganda, Rwanda, Burundi, Northern Congo, Southern Sudan, Southern cities of Ethiopia and Northern cities of Tanzania with goods and services. Day in, day out, it is the busiest single lane road in the world. The Nairobi-Mombasa Road known to Kenyans runs parallel with Mombasa-Kampala Railway line built in 1895. That explains Hon. Ngala's death; it is as if the "spirits" were mad at the behavior of the young politicians. The power of the "spirits" is explained in detail elsewhere in **Leadership.** Kenya government collects millions of shillings per day in taxes from the nations listed above for the use of Mombasa-Nairobi Road; yet the government has failed to expand the road into a four lane road.

On another occasion, Hon. Tom Mboya was gunned down and shot dead by an unknown gunman while on a shopping spree inside a Batta Shoe store in Nairobi city center. The young politician, a mixed breed between the Akamba and the Luo tribes was a rising star in the newly independent Kenya. He may have stepped on the wrong toe within the KANU politicians. Another member of parliament, JM Kariuki was a wealthy and likable personality of his day; he was known by many Kenyans as a cheerful giver. His spirit of giving cost his life. Rumor has it that one day during a *Harambee* trail JM Kariuki out-gave then President Jomo Kenyatta in a *Harambee* fund raising event. This theory was never proven.

Leadership will treat the rumor as an allegation. After the death of Hon. JM Kariuki, it is widely known by many Kenyans, a rule was established within the ranks of KANU regime that no one should give after His Excellency, the President has given at a *Harambee* fund raising event. The practice has survived, left only to the invited guest of honor when invited at a Harambee fund raising event. The guest of honor is expected to give the highest amount of money at the close of a fund raising event. I encountered many such events.

By all means the word *"Mtukufu"* is not to suggest that Kenyatta was superhuman, he was ruling and living in a culture that expected him to be the father figure of the nation. It is a title that no one should read too much into. Besides, Kenya tribes never knew the British colonial rule would someday ever come to an abrupt end. Whereby, they would wake up one morning and find themselves with a leader or a King like Jomo Kenyatta. Kenyans were used to titles of her/his Majesty during the British rule since 1895 in East Africa.

Each tribe has had a title by which they named their own tribal leaders. To some a leader was a king, to some a chief, to some a lead elder among a group of elders, to some a great medicine-man, almost immortal human being, with power over life and death. To some a leader is a great warrior, one who ruled over his tribe, with power to punish those who failed to obey customary laws and culture of the tribe. Collectively, a mixture of tribes in Kenya each with culture and tradition, the peoples of Kenya, bestowed upon Kenyatta a title *"Mtukufu"*. Throughout his reign, Members of Parliament and ordinary citizens referred to Jomo Kenyatta as *"Mtukufu"*, a Swahili word that translates as "holiness", godlike, worshipful admiration. Jomo Kenyatta never requested to be called *"Mtukufu"* but like any other rulers of ancient times: he enjoyed the title to the fullest. The title "Mtukufu" is no longer used by any of his predecessors, the title was buried with the owner and ceased to be used when Kenyatta died.

From a western society perspective, the need for a father figure seems to end soon after one reaches the magic age on the 18th birthday, a dominate sense of "me," a sense of individualism, the role of father and mother ceases to dominate the lives of young adults past the 18th birthday. There are many disadvantages and advantages based on this theory. It is a feeling of individual freedom from parents, a sense of disconnection between children and parents. Some children have taken the practice far to the extreme and some the opposite. Those who leave home never to return home, live a fugitive life of guilt, sometimes ashamed to face their ailing parents, only to return when the parents are feeble and want to take over what is left for their inheritance.

Some leave home but keep a close watch over their folks with appreciation of their parents and who they are in their lives. Female children seem to keep better watch over their parents regardless of their whereabouts, than male children. Therefore, western leaders should learn to understand the anthropology-sociological practice of the diverse cultures of Africa when it comes to leadership. It must be explained that Kenyatta ruled Kenya with a mixture of western democratic principles and his native ways of leadership. In fact, **Leadership** gives credit to Jomo Kenyatta's leadership which came at a time when no known Kenyan had enormous experience with first the British traders who later took the country to the level of a Colony under the British Empire, like Jomo Kenyatta.

Therefore, Kenyatta capitalized on the Elder/Warrior tradition and perfected his leadership style of the Kingdom of Kenya politics. Kenyatta, who died in office, was the leader and chairman of the KANU party, the leader of government and the President of the Republic of Kenya. The two institutions were one and the same, similar to Islamic state governments as mentioned elsewhere in this publication.

One key example, Kenyatta Conference Center is a skyscraper building located in the center of Nairobi financial district and was built by taxpayer's money for the KANU party national headquarters. KANU offices were scattered throughout the nation, some offices are still visible in many rural cities and urban towns in Ukambani. For example, in Machakos Town Constituency, it has a large compound dedicated to KANU although some greedy leaders within the district have since taken some of the KANU property under their wings. It took Kibaki government to separate what was KANU's property and what were government assets. That may have been so in Nairobi city center but not outside the capital where KANU still control a large amount of real estate.

Mr. Duncan Ndegwa, then, first secretary to the Cabinet, and retired governor of Central Bank of Kenya, reports in his book that most ministers held the president in such fear that instead of helping him find solutions to the problems confronting the young nation, they looked up to him to provide solutions, thereby, enhancing the African elder tradition. Ndegwa fails to mention that Kenyatta was feared-respected by the majority of his politicians outside his tribe.

Based on the capacity in which Kenyatta ruled Kenya, no living person would oppose Kenyatta and see the daylight, including Ndegwa himself. At least there was Hon. Jaramogi Odinga, then Vice President, who resigned from government in 1966, it was clearly emerging that the country had a president who was not going to tolerate any kind of opposition. Jaramogi Odinga would later write a book titled, *Not Yet Uhuru.*

Did Jaramogi Odinga know what the rest of Kenya politicians who worked with Kenyatta failed to know? In a democratic principle, opposition parties are encouraged to maintain a balance of views and the direction of a nation. That was not the case with the KANU regime after 1966 until its collapse in 1990s. Moi allowed a multiple party system to take its course in Kenya politics. Kenyatta never hesitated to remind everybody that he was the boss. Therefore, to suggest that other politicians could help "Mzee" Kenyatta find solutions is only wishful thinking.

Time and again, in parliaments of the third world democracies, dissidents find themselves in plenty of trouble. The freedom of expression by a citizen is always limited, and sometimes punishable with a mysterious disappearance of person(s) only to be found dead by bystanders. That includes those who put in print their opinions like **Leadership** for exposing political exploiters of the public funds, the rule of law, and the misuse of democratic principles to uneducated political masses of Kenyans. In 1975 Hon. Martin Shikuku found himself in a lot of trouble when in Parliament it is alleged that Hon. Shikuku, said that Kenyatta's leadership was in attempt to kill Parliament the same way KANU party had killed other political parties. Hon. Martin Shikuku rattled the snake!

Supported by the Deputy Speaker, Marie-Jean Seroney, within a matter of days, the two honorable politicians were arrested by the police outside Parliament buildings; they were led off to an unknown detention without trial until 1978 when they were pardoned and released by President Moi in the early days of his presidency. I had the privilege of meeting Hon. Martin Shikuku at the Parliament building, September 2007. He appeared both mentally and physically fit for his age. He is one of few law makers who stood firm on democratic principles during Jomo Kenyatta's regime. He is one of the early legislators who travelled to Lancaster House, London to rectify the Constitution of Kenya.

The application of Elder/Warrior African leadership style with added values of democratic principles, honesty and integrity is the only way forward for African leadership to establish her moral authority in a global world. Africa leadership must address ways to solve many of Africa's problems of healthcare, foreign debts, repatriation of African brain power, and Africa's artifacts scattered everywhere in museums of the nations of the North.

Leadership predicts that a united Africa will someday emerge with one federal system of government of Africa. When that happens, it will be an enormous power that will force the nations of the north to reckon with it. The continent has abundance of raw material, natural resources, oil, diamonds, uranium and tourism. A unifying Africa will compete successfully in a global market in the 21st Century and beyond.

Politics in African democracy continue to be characterized by two opposing trends: One, in some places, democracy is gaining ground by strengthening a series of discussions. There is hope for African leadership being realized by a host group of democracies in Africa like Kenya and others. In the majority of African democracies, citizens enjoy limited electoral, multiparty, freedom of speech, and limited greater civil liberties than any time in recent history.

However, there are few democracies in Africa, who are in the process of improving their democratic leadership style. It is safe to say that throughout Africa, leadership is threatened by poverty, political will-power, ethnic conflict, drug traffic, terrorism and corruption. The scary task that lay ahead of African leadership is a system that takes apart a democratic system and replaces it with tribal values, dishonesty and deceit, a system that provides the needs of the few. It is actually the Kenyans who have contributed to the predicament by standing as passive observers by allowing politicians to have the freedom to do as they please.

It is amazing that some members of parliament campaigned for amnesty for groups of people who instigated riots which resulted in destroyed businesses properties, burned church buildings and destroyed public government properties. Ethnic violence is a powerful system used by few politicians, armed and dangerous if not controlled to enhance their political career at the expense of the innocent citizens. However, that should never be an excuse for citizens to sit back as passive observers. One advantage Kenya citizens have is a democratic system that still plays by the rules, and is repeated every five (5) years.

Violence in Kenya: The history of the British Colonial rule in Kenya gave birth to the present federal government. The British Colonial rule established laws by which they used to exert control over tribes. Copying the British, the first two Kenya administrations used KANU as the one party system as a means to control and maintain power in the office of the President. Opposition parties were outlawed a few years after independence, politicians who could not agree with the KANU leadership were either detained without trial or died an unwarranted death.

Citizens lived the life of fear with no freedom of speech except during one of the four self regulated parliamentary commissions: The Hon. Kiliku Commission (1992), Akiwumu Commission (1999) and Waki Commission (2008), Kenya Human Rights Commission, journalists and other numerous independent writers. Politicians in opposition who showed no colossal danger to the presidency were lured with political perks, political government positions, and sometimes allocation of state owned properties to support the ruling party, and the presidency. Moi used the blessing of African Inland Church as a political platform to lure the Christian church to support his presidency. It is safe to say that the man, Moi, by average was a good man, except the men and the women who surrounded him.

The epic story of Kenya tribal hatred is perceived by many tribes to have started within tribes, the majority tribes send mixed signals as though they were entitled to Kenya leadership. Early in

1978 a few politicians rocked the boat in an attempt to stop Moi from succeeding Jomo Kenyatta's presidency. One unsettling episode is when a Police Provincial Commissioner stopped then Vice President Moi's motorcade, the instance occurred while Moi was in route from a state business tour in Uganda. This is the notion that, a lower ranking government official had no business to stop a man of such a high position. No one knows if the officer acted alone.

It is paradoxical that when Moi finally became the president of Kenya, the unnamed Police Commissioner, in fear, escaped by the night for refuge to a neighbor state of Sudan; months later, Moi asked the officer to return home. The officer was never punished. Moi was accorded as it is written in the constitution of Kenya, that he would become president when Kenyatta died. Knowing that he was terminally ill, it was not by accident that he chose Moi as his Vice President. This is the one man Kenyatta trusted so much to replace his leadership. Kenyatta had previously tried a vice president from his own tribe.

Since a few groups of anti Moi people could not change the constitution, their solution was to assassinate Moi. The failed attempted coup of 1982 against Moi marked the beginning of all future violence that Kenya suffers in the cycle of every five years. The seed of hatred between tribes was planted in the minds of men and women and to all those who would seek the highest office in the land. For reasons unknown to the majority of Kenya tribes, Moi got wise. He established a strong defense force of informant militias and used his high ranking government officials who served him with information to determine "who's who" in the political arena, especially the new rising political stars from the Kikuyu, Luo, Luhya and Akamba tribes. However, Moi was never successful to isolate the Luo tribe, because of their strong and amalgamated Luo Council of Elders which has continued to guide the tribe into a political muscle.

I once interviewed one of the Luo Council of Elders for my book. He stated that, Honorable Raila Odinga, shrewd Luo politician, must always check with the LCE in the matters of political issues. The Luo tribe has always remained united in matters of national politics, perhaps better than any other tribe in Kenya, following their counterpart, the Kikuyu.

With the establishment of the militias, KANU's political machine spread out strong throughout the country, in the effort to maintain KANU leadership. The Akamba tribe *a population of more than two million (census 1989)* was by far the greatest supporter of KANU leadership under the late Hon. Mulu Mutisya. Kenyatta and Moi presidencies used Akamba who were the loyalists in military manpower, the nation's government workforce, and their votes without any retribution to their lands. When the two administrations ceased to exist the Akamba people were dropped like a hot potato. To date the Akamba lands remain some of the poorest lands in Kenya. The history and current state of the Akamba tribe is very troubling; it is about a people standing at the crossroads of her economic and political survival. The deforestation and the depletion of the soil nutrients can hardly support her natural resources. The failure of vision and lack of leadership in the past millennial has cost the tribe dearly, to be dependent on the national government for local physical planning, and as a result plunged prey to political handouts.

Akamba tribe is known worldwide for their charm and attractiveness of the said wood carving skills; Akamba people are the brand name for the wood carving industry in Kenya. One time I was in the home of a Texas legislator, who proudly, shared with me the ecstasy of ownership of a group of zebra and giraffe wood carvings of the Akamba, given to him as a Christmas gift in the late 1950s by a missionary. The Texas law maker was not aware of the deforestation in Kenya preventing the Akamba their acclaimed wood carvings of past millennial.

The lands suffer soil erosion; there is not sufficient clean drinking water reserve for one million people and their domestic animals, they have a poor health care system, no reputable national education system, no rural electrification and are without infrastructure. And yet the Akamba lies within reach of Tana River and Athi River; these rivers pour billions of gallons of water into the Indian Ocean. Tana River is the nation's supply for hydroelectric power.

President Theodore Roosevelt, in his book *African Trails* (1910) hunting around the Kapiti Plains, pleaded with the British Colonial rule to build water tanks on hill tops; that request was never fulfilled until to this day. However, during the Kibaki first administration, the Akamba experienced the best years since independence, century old roads were paved, shortening daily commuting between rural towns and the nation's capital city of Nairobi into a matter of hours; it reduced highway accidents almost by half. The dry land supplies the nation with 1/2 of construction materials, quarry stones and sand harvested in the Akamba land.

The politicization and explosion of violence in Kenya first occurred soon after the legalization of the multi-parties of the 1990s. The decision not to punish perpetrators was left up to the political leaders of the day. The rule of law was not allowed to take its due course. Thus, perpetrators have led to a culture of thieves and killers like the old American Wild West, notorious gangs led by Billy the Kid and Jesse Wales and others, the era that man did what was right in his own sight, the survival of the fittest which was based on how fast a cowboy could pull the trigger. The tribal violence in Kenya was cemented and entrenched in the lives of political leaders who use politics to achieve the end means. The notion, that violence in Kenya must be revisited by all concerns to forge for a new way of life as one nation of more than (forty-two) 42 tribes is very troubling.

The growing power of the Members of Parliament has two or more factors: the Parliament is the only institution where one can get away without the rule of law, government fraud and the ability to access public resources for self and political cronies. There are no checks or balances of politicians, because they run and dictate the government departments they legislate. They are simply warlords of their tribes. It is commonly held that certain ethnic groups have been marginalized from returning to their ancestral land, which was taken by force by the colonial settlers during the British rule in Kenya, after independence, and bought by non-ancestral land owners. And also there is arising perceived misallocation of the national cake to every tribe.

In the case of the power surrounding the executive branch of the "Presidency" the checks and balances associated with democratic ideologies deliberately appear fragile in Kenya. High ranking government administrators in civil service, Judiciary, and Parliament understand the enormous power invested in the Presidency, irrespective of the law of the land. At the end of the day the president determines the menu of the matters of the state. In times when a country has a weak or strong Presidency, the state may easily fall prey to the inner circle of power.

One of the weaknesses of the Kibaki administration and his inner circle is that they failed to exert control over the country to prevent ethnic atrocities that were rumored by community leaders in the Rift Valley; and elsewhere in the country months prior to the general elections and after the disputed presidential elections of December 27, 2007. His inner circle secretly and dividedly failed to unite the country and was overwhelmed by negative feelings of marginalization to take a center stage of his presidency which fueled the post election violence, which resulted total 1,500 killed and over 650,000 displaced people.

The Kibaki kitchen table advisers appeared disconnected among themselves, while the President was afforded council by the religious leaders, who foresaw signs and forewarned the post violence during the remnant months of 2007 general elections. Some media radio outlets incited the people of the Kalenjin tribes regardless of whose president [won] PNU/ODM, the Kikuyu would be barred from Rift Valley. (Waki Commission 2008)

Historically, most all elections with exception of the first two elections held during Kenyatta's presidency, are viewed by the majority of Kenyans as contingent of the executive branch whose power influences public institutions, judiciary and the country election commission which was perceived by the citizens as unable to conduct elections fairly. Akiwuni report (1999) states that members of the provincial administration and the law enforcement understand clearly sometimes it was in the best interest of the individual safety not to uphold the rule of the law, which results in mixed signals on the part of the President or

Members of the Parliament.

The notion that, on a political class everything does not flow from the rule of law but it is a matter of the president's acquired power to disseminate his personal decisions. In a democratic state no citizen is above the law. The rule of law of the land must always take precedence. Therefore, marginalized groups of tribes would want to band together into a political party movement, to acquire the seat of the presidency for one of their own at any cost.

There are unemployed and uneducated majorities who by no choice of their own accept to join tribal militias to continue to fuel tense political differences between the tribes; the said militias were managed by political groups. The militias in Kenya can be compared with California and Texas gangs of the 1980s and early 1990s. The state legislator of Texas was forced to pass a state statue to combat youth street violence. These were the years when a minor could shoot and kill in public streets of America and get away with murder without adult court trial because they were covered by state child laws. In most states a minor is a child under age seventeen (17) and are immune from adult judicial court. Therefore, unless Kenya judicial law is allowed to exercise the law of the land, corruption, fraud and politically motivated perpetrators will remain immune until the public decides to change their voting behavior as to who they want for their leaders. Lawmakers are above the law. They are never tried for their crimes.

To solve Kenyans' widening gap of unemployed youth is to extend the retirement age from the current 55 years to 65 years; this will enable parents to work longer to allow their youth in primary, high schools and colleges to hang around a little longer at home while they continue to receive parental stipend until they find employment. Late retirement will increase jobs availability for youth and the older generation. This method will reduce the number of the nation's unemployed youth rooming in towns and cities of Kenya. In addition, it will reduce unwanted pregnancies of young mothers.

Since the discovery of the internet, the world community is more than ready to team with emerging democracies like Kenya to open textiles shops and other manufacturing products for export to industrialized nations. There is an increasing interest among businesses in USA to relay "Call Centers" in the third world. Call Centers are currently located in many English speaking nations of the world. Kenya as an English speaking nation, could easily tap into the Call Center market opportunity for her unemployed population. The majority of American companies continue to solicit nations of the third world for a cheap labor due to the rising costs of goods and services.

Kenya militias are so hard to root out because they are mixed within the state law enforcement. Sometimes Special Forces are used to furnish more unwarranted killings within specified tribe or groups. The militias of 2007/8 were complex because they recruited themselves into groups of tribal militias and gangs with names like: Mungiki, Taliban, Chonkororo, Kamjeshi, Baghdad Boys and others. There are no official leaders known to these groups except the Mungiki gang, the most recognizable gang since the 1980s. According to Waki Commission, the group is described as a cultural religious [cult] group which grew into a shadow government in many city slums of Nairobi. The groups are known to single out particular tribes or a community to carry out their operation to collect payment dues from citizens who needed protection for their business and personal body guards. Gangs like the Chicago Mafia, New York Mafia and Italian Mafia of Crete of the 1950s. Kibaki government outlawed the group "Mungiki" in mid 2007. They continued to operate under their alleged leader Maina Njenga. He was apprehended by authorities, and thrown into jail after government crackdown. It is alleged that he still runs his outfit from his cell. (Waki Commission 2008)

The truth of the matter is that the people of Kenya accept to be bribed by politicians for their right to vote. Once politicians rise up into leadership, citizens may not expect more from politicians because they sold their votes in exchange for a bowl of soup. Therefore, citizens of Kenya voted for politicians who are not obligated to fulfill a campaign promise given during their campaign trails. Once the trade of the right to vote is sold, there is no love bond between politicians and citizens until the next election.

It is morally wrong to the millions of people who knowingly accept bribes in exchange for their voting rights. For example, the aftermath of the disputed presidential elections resulted in 1,500 people killed; over 650,000 people displaced. Who should be responsible or blamed? Kenya has experienced corruptions, scandal after scandal from past and present administrations because citizens have continued to accept political bribes, and continue to vote for politicians in terms of where they come from instead of local and national issues that affect each citizen. Civil and parliamentary elections are based on clan versus clan, and national politics are based on tribe versus tribe. Integrity and honesty suffers when clan hood and tribe hood become a gold standard of leadership.

Once a politician is defeated at the polling box, he/she should never attempt to illegally crunch power to self and incite a message of hatred to those he leads. The change in political leadership in Kenya is yet to be realized, because the majority of Kenyans continue to live under a ferocious political life circle. With the purchase of power, a politician becomes untouchable, and leads to lack of accountability, integrity, honesty, corruption and deceptions. In such a state there is no democracy when power is bought from the city and villages of Kenyan population. Politicians should view themselves as loaned to the national office from their constituencies, parliament as an institution should never be used to enrich 210 MPs, but rather to enhance development, infrastructure, and the distribution of national wealth to all Kenyans. When citizens exchange money for a vote, the politician in this case, the buyer uses the purchased power as absolute to maximize for self interest.

The Four Commissions 1992-2008: The nation has had four Parliamentary Commissions that reported on the loss of life through explosions of violence since 1992 to 2008. The Kiliku (1992) reported 779 deaths, and 654 injured. The Akiwumu (1999) report took a long time to be released to the public. The Ndugu Commission failed to mention the numbers of deaths or injuries during the tribal violence of the early 1990s. The Waki (2008) was by far the most closely watched Commission, because it affected two principal leaders of the Coalition Government. The Commission was afforded the shortest amount of time to report its findings. The Commission reported 1,133 deaths and 655 injuries limited the months between December 27, 2007 and February 2008. The Waki (2008) failed to report the loss of human lives prior to December 27. The Waki (2008) categorically, states, "Because of the failure to obtain additional 60 days extension of time, the Commission abandoned its original plans to conduct public hearings and investigations."

Therefore, the total number of deaths and injuries reported by any of the three Commissions are unreliable concerning the total alleged human loss, because of the limitation of the time frame, instruments, money and the failure to be afforded with the state institutions availability. Second, previously, the Commissions had not been afforded with the whistle blowers protection Act. In spite of this, during the Waki (2008) Commission hearings, the August house passed a Witness Protection Act 2008 to help speed the hearings process, but it was too late in the game. The Commission feared the Act had not been tested.

Third, the Commissioners are not guaranteed safety after their findings. The Waki (2008) took a no name mention rule based on the histories of the previous Commissions reports.

A number of perpetrators were identified responsible for the violence, but the state never took any measure to persecute the alleged perpetrators. The state failed atrociously to address the predicament of the families' victims, and/or provide mental or financial assistance to the families of the victims. In their final remarks the Waki (2008) said that, "the impunity has become the order of the day in Kenya." The hallmark principles of the democratic ideology states that, no persons, or a tribe is above the law. Therefore, the perpetrators should have their day in court. The Waki (2008) findings were handed over to the President of the state, with a sealed envelope of the alleged perpetrators. Additional material was forwarded to the Panel of Eminent

African Personalities who helped in the creation of the Coalition Government. I was rigged out of an election in Machakos Town Constituency. I fought hard against tribal Euphoria and refused to compromise with Islamic ideology. Speaking from personal experience, voter registration is an easy way to steal any election. It happened to me December 27, 2007.

Why Kenya Matters? Kenya is considered by the International community as one of the stronghold states of Africa. All major powers have diplomatic missions in Kenya to watch over their best interests at heart. China has become one of Kenya's trading partners since Kibaki administration. Other Nations of the world have pretty much maintained their status quo. Nairobi serves as the hub for trade and a humanitarian center for peace-keeping for war-torn Somalia, Rwanda, Burundi and Southern Sudan.

United States Embassy in Nairobi houses the largest personnel for US strategic missions around the continent. United States budget is estimated over $6.6 billion per year for the entire continent. That is a lot of cash! Kenya is one of America's very most important nations in Africa.

Moi regime kept a strong diplomatic relationship with US and Britain. Whereby, US Navy ships and other US humanitarian flag ships were allowed to dock at Mombasa port. Strategically, US Air Force was also allowed to land and take off from Kenya airstrips within a moment's notice. For this arrangement US has kept a tight fight against war on terrorism from Kenya's Indian Ocean shorelines. A failed Kenya regime-leadership would only worsen the situation for the nations of Northern Congo, Uganda, Somaliland, and Southern Sudan as safe havens for terrorist groups.

During Kenya general elections of 2007, Bush was in office. He refused to endorse any presidential candidate with ties to Muslims. A Raila administration was perceived by Bush administration, that it would have been soft on terrorism. Therefore, Bush forced the two principals to share a Coalition government. When Obama was elected US President, whose late father was Kenyan born; it was considered a sign that there would be a richer Kenya – America diplomatic relationship. However, many Kenyans have not welcomed the notion that Obama has not visited a nation that he claims as the birth place of his father, Barack Senior. *Leadership* is in agreement with many US experts on Africa foreign policy, that Kenya is America's indispensable partner.

America in the 21st Century: At the dawn of the New Year 2008, oil reached its highest at $100.00 per barrel. At the gas pump, prices were soaring to the highest prices since 1970s.

Senator Barack Obama became the first bi-racial African-American man ever to win Iowa Caucus, whose biological father was of a Luo tribe of Kenya. On a cold morning, Obama declared that he would free America from the yoke of oil, if elected president; he pledged to end the war in Iraq and bring the troops back home. The tyranny of oil does not only affect the Americans, but the rest of the world is fully dependant on oil. Without available alternatives to oil, the entire world will continue to suffer with increasing national budgets which must be allocated to purchase oil. President George W. Bush once told his fellow citizens that "America is addicted to oil," it was a serious accusation that unless America changes her consumption behavior, greedy oil executives will continue to rip apart the American consumers with high gas prices.

Lee Iacocca, a former CEO of Chrysler Corporation, a leader who rescued Chrysler from the verge of crumpling, even in his retirement, he has not stopped creating new ideas for Leaders. Lee's new book, *Where Have the Leaders Gone?* comes at a time when the majority of Americans viewed Bush's administration had a failed foreign policy on Iraq and Afghanistan states, where thousands of lives were lost during his presidency. The terror wars caused a downward spin of a domestic economy failure on Wall Street. Corporate greed and poor judgment in Washington, in cases of Fannie Mae and Freddie Mac, resulted in the mortgage crisis. This has resulted into a corporate bailout by government. The government bailout was a contagious effect of economic failure — in America and around the industrialized nations of the globe. The Government bailout was against the capitalistic principles of market, the notion of let the market take care of itself.

I once interviewed a retired oil executive of one of the major oil companies; he said that oil companies do not interfere with the individual politics of any nations. When asked "why," he said that, an oil company mission is to extract oil; they buy leases from government leaders plus protection of their interest. Therefore, oil gurus coupled with greed and corruption influence high gas prices and price gouging, environmental leaders, policy makers on world global warming, and erode weak democracy. The executive further stated that the best oil executives prefer to work with dictatorship governments of the world; because they are easily corrupted, compared to democratic governments whose leadership changes with the mood of the voters every so many years. It is a no brainer, majorities of the people are aware that oil producing nations of the world are located in the Middle East, South America and Africa, whose governments are not necessarily democratic governments.

The recent turn of events led to Lee Iacocca to say, "Am I the only guy in this country that's fed up with what's happening? We got a gang of clueless bozos steering our ship of state right over a cliff, we've got corporate gangsters stealing us blind." Corruption has now become an HIV of greediness among the leaders, politicians and the corporate executives of the modern world. The medical community is able to contain HIV through medication. The governments of the world use national laws to control corruption and greed in joint effort with United Nations to combat corruption and drug trafficking. The state of California has once considered legalizing the trade of marijuana.

The American Politics Were Played Like a Betting Card Game: During the American general elections, I was not sure which side each American voter was on, regardless of their political persuasion. The majority of American voters were concerned about the loss of millions of domestic jobs. The slogan "change we can believe in" is what the majority of Americans wanted to hear. What did the *change* mean? The real change was an attempt to move America from the foreign wars to domestic issues. McCain was right, "America first."

America was built on capitalist economy (Capitalism) ideology, not on a socialist (Socialism) ideology, where government taxes all, distributes the wealth from the ten percent of the nation's wealthy to the poor classes. Let's explore the fundamental difference of Capitalism vs. Socialism: Socialism ideology attracts large social programs funded by government. Socialism and Communism ideologies create a two tier class society, the rich and the poor. When a socialism political machine anchors its deep roots into a society; government takes control of everything while the large business sector remains in line with government bureaucracy.

Corruption and payback to the "good old-boy" network becomes a way of life, at last, deceptions turn into a chronic disease that is very hard to root out. This is exactly what happens in third world nations. Some greedy politicians tend to steal from the public coffers through scandalous state contracts. The majority of voters are left in fear, unable to demand a change through their elected officials. This creates a wide gap between rich and poor.

What got America into a Change mode may not be the same reasons Kenyans voted in their last general elections. The people of Kenya did not vote for the best alternative candidates, from the grassroots, civic, parliamentary to presidency. The people voted along tribal lines, each for their own candidate. The weak candidates were swept by the machinery of theft done by career politicians' greed to remain in power. The pay back was Killings, theft and deceit. In sharp contrast, in America, citizens voted on issues affecting their pocket book, the loss of domestic jobs and the war on terrorism. All the above were part of the paradigm shift change in American politics. In American democratic primaries, citizens had three choices, a chance to change the tides of the American politics and make history with a female or African-American, or keep a traditional white male president. Right from the beginning of the presidential race, Democrats and Republicans rejected the idea of a woman president.

The American Right Wing dwelled too much on politics as usual; they forgot to man their grassroots politics with wind of change. They took the minority votes for granted. Unfortunately, the Republican Party had no idea that their presidential candidate, Senator John McCain, would deal a Sarah Palin as a wild card into the political race! Too late in the political game somebody in the Right Wing began to think politics. Meanwhile, the Democratic Electoral College burgled Hillary from the Democratic presidential nomination. The Democrats had sealed the bid. The Right Wing could not believe that an African-American would make a presidential cut. Besides, this was not the first time an African-American presidential candidate surfaced in the American politics.

The Right Wing concentrated too much time on Hillary, and missed the real target, Obama. American voters were tired of the loss of domestic jobs and the rising gasoline prices. They turned to the democrats, who presented two minority choices of a male and a female candidate. The Republicans with Senator John McCain, thought they would end up against a female Democratic presidential candidate, Senator Hillary Clinton for president. Those who heard my speeches in the states of New Mexico, Minnesota, Oklahoma and Texas, I warned Republican voters about the DEM's game plan. The threat of the continuation of Bush administration foreign policy through another Republican president was derailed.

The slogan "change we can believe in" was the core issue in the American presidential politics. Well, think again, together with Hillary's eighteen million voters, she was tossed like silage of hay from a moving fast wagon, to the political mucky ground. Despite the fact that she laid unconsciously, mystified, still recovering from her political and emotional injuries, she was rejected. In a disguise of a political game plan, the Democrats leadership refused to honor her hard work in exchange to be VP running mate. Now, maverick, Senator John McCain, RNC presidential candidate brought a game changer VP Sarah Palin; young, beautiful and an experienced mayor and governor of a great state, she could not get a good rap from the main stream liberal media outlets in fear of overshadowing their candidate, Senator Obama.

The Democrats got into a state of confusion, wondering if they would lose women votes to a Republican presidential candidate, Senator John McCain. At that time, Democrats wished that they never had thrown away Senator Hillary. The Clinton's presidential episode has similarity of viciousness, and cruelty, like the animal kingdom found in the rich open grassland of East Africa, the home of the lion-*Simba*. The male lion, king of the animal Kingdom, seldom goes for a kill.

It takes a female lioness the hard work to hunt, stalk instinctively and in a cooperative fashion with another lioness; fans out quietly to attack the very best, fattest zebra of the herd. When the prey is within the vicinity of no escape, the female—lioness sprints and leaps at the speed of 36 miles per hour. With its enormous jaws open, equipped with canine teeth, powerful forelegs grab the prey by biting the nose and suffocate the zebra to its treacherous death in a matter of minutes.

When the job is completed, the male lion, king of the wilderness stretches out its claws, digs into the ground ready for action, majestically, roaring, strolling, with every gait growling, hissing and paw swiping as it approaches the midday lunch. After the meal is over the family takes a nearby nap, calm down, greet each other affectionately and life continues. And so, then the

Democrats got what they wanted, her 18 million women voters! They were like the male lion that goes to eat for what he never killed. The Right Wing was left in a cloud of white dust, wondering. In the meantime all minorities composed of African-American, Hillary voters and newly naturalized citizens converged to take the presidency away from the Republicans. That was the Democratic presidential trap.

In any election whether in North America or a third world nation, there are many issues to consider but when a society gets in voter fraud, drug trafficking, abortion, corruption, same-sex marriage, and embryonic stem-cell research, human cloning, wrong economic ideologies, and fraud in public assets; people are forced to think again about their elected officials. Martin Luther King said, "Don't judge someone by the color of their skin but by the content of their character." Mr. Huntley Brown said, "I don't know Obama. I can go off his voting record. I can't vote black because I am black; I have to vote Christian because that's who I am, Christian first, black second." This is a great lesson for Kenyans. They should vote issues, not vote based on tribes.

According to the national Journal issued for the years 2007 and 2008 Obama was voted the most liberal senator. He earned himself a decoration title of the most liberal when he was a state legislator in Illinois and in the U.S. Senate. In a short period, he advanced himself very quickly in the pinnacle of the American political machine to a Democratic Presidential nomination. At 11:00 PM Eastern Time, Obama with a strong lead became the first African-American and forty-fourth, USA President at the turn of the 21st Century. At that moment I turned on my desktop computer, filed what would become part of my continuing story. Many years into the future, grandchildren, will read my entry. Every person around the world will never forget where they were, November 4, 2008 when a new chapter of history was being made. However, the elected president requires prayers because he is faced with the most enormous economic burden in the history of America. American people were no longer concerned about the affairs of the following world leaders: Chavez, Castro, Ahmadinejad, Hamas and other Arabs state supported terrorism. They were concerned about their pocket book, while foreign policy took a back seat in the presidential election. Now that American voters have spoken — American Democrats or Republicans should not be concerned about whether a president of the free world should be a female, black or yellow; it is about protecting a century old American democracy regardless of who may be in power. This is what the American dream is all about, a good agent for self independence, creation of individual wealth and survival of the free market. The separation of the church and state is paramount and encouraged. In Matthew 22:21, Jesus commanded His followers, "Render unto Caesar the things that are Caesar's, and unto God the things that are God's." So, Hillary Clinton is right, "You see, you can become anything you want." The phrase cannot subsist in a socialistic state but only in a capitalistic state.

January 20, 2009, high noon, 12:00 PM Eastern Time, President Elect Obama was sworn in as the 44th President, the first African-American of the United States of America and the leader of the free world. [However, the oath of the presidency was reaffirmed again in the morning in the White House, January 21, 2009 because the Chief Justice had fumbled the words of the oath.] The official police count reported by Washington, DC was that over 2 million Americans attended the inaugural ceremony.

Just like in Kenya, a year later, Kenyans in the Diaspora joined the rest of the millions of Americans glued into their TVs and laptop computers to witness history in the making of a candidate born of a Kenyan father and a Luo tribe. From his book, "Dreams from My Father," Obama provides a brief history of his Kenyan born father, who came to America as a student in the early 1960s, and met Barack's white mother in the great state of Hawaii; during their short lived romantic relationship a baby boy, Obama was born. Similar to the events of Egypt, Moses and Joseph saved their people, the Hebrews from starvation and forced slavery from the Pharaoh dynasty. Will Obama presidency have an effect on his African roots? During the writing of **Leadership** many critiques argued and disputed whether Obama was U.S. natural born or US citizen by naturalization. Obama's birth certificate case was argued in a Pennsylvania court. January 9th 2009 United States Supreme Court declined to listen to the case Berg vs. Obama.

"Since the Supreme Court has now prevented itself from acknowledging the question of whether Barack H. Obama is or is not an Article II "natural born citizen" based on the Kenyan/British citizenship of Barack Obama's father at the time of his birth (irrespective of whether Barack Obama is deemed a "citizen" born in Hawaii or otherwise) as a prerequisite to qualifying to serve as President of the United States under the Constitution — the Court having done so three times and counting, first before the Nov 4 general election and twice before the Dec 15 vote of the College of Electors — it would seem appropriate, if not necessary, for all Executive Branch departments and agencies to secure advance formal advice from the United States Department of

Justice Office of Legal Counsel as to how to respond to expected inquiries from federal employees who are pledged to "support and defend the Constitution of the United States" as to whether they are governed by laws, regulations, orders and directives issued under Mr. Obama during such periods that said employees, by the weight of existing legal authority and prior to a decision by the Supreme Court, believe in good faith that Mr. Obama is not an Article II "natural born citizen". December 18, 2008 11:21 PM

The Decade of Deregulation: During the midterm of George W. Bush administration, American voters changed Washington's controlled House of Representatives and Senate with a majority of Democrats who pledged to weed out the greedy oil executives. Well, think again. The Democrats, they too, failed to deliver their promise to the American people. Simply, their agendas were politically lobbied and redirected by the force of greedy oil executives and special interest. Once again, the oil companies took their front row seat and continued to rake in more profits. For example, special interest groups rewarded lawmakers who voted in their best interest and received perks for their campaign kitties.

During the deregulation decade of the 90s, history repeated itself. In 1870 through the1880s John D. Rockefeller established Standard Oil Company. He controlled 90 percent of the entire refinery and 80 percent of oil products, a portion of America's crude oil output and kerosene. The Standard Oil Company was associated with unethical business practices, bribes, and anything illegal. To remain in business was the order of the day. Numerous court cases were filed against the company. These practices went on for a long time until Government used the

Sherman Antitrust Act to break up Standard Oil monopoly.

President Theodore Roosevelt never wanted business to control government. Later, the Federal Trade Commission was established by congress to control business influence and antitrust violations. By 1970s Exxon, Mobil, Chevron, Gulf, Texaco, BP and Shell formed an oil cartel. The new "Big Seven" controlled the world's largest oil market. Oil producing nations act as their own oil cartel but still NEED the Big Seven to extract and transport the sale of oil to the end users.

In the states, the years between 1991-1999 federal regulators allowed more than 2,600 oil corporate mergers in the nation's history of oil industry. America saw the mega oil companies re-merged again breaking the Sherman Antitrust laws; Exxon with Mobil, Chevron with Texaco, Conoco with Phillips, and BP with Amoco and Arco. The reestablishment of the mega oil mergers was as a result of the deregulations in the US. The merger allowed each oil company to drill, refine and sale their product without a middleman direct to the end users. The newlywed oil companies are able to manipulate the supply and inventory to boost their profits. Six out of ten oil companies in the world are American controlled corporations, the most of which are the most profitable businesses on the globe. In 2007, Fortune Magazine reported ten oil companies took $167 billion in profits.

There is no doubt that these mega oil companies can influence any major policy in any regime in the world. One case in point, ExxonMobil reserve reported in six continents pumps twice as much as the nation of Kuwait. During the last eight years and especially after the deregulations, oil companies have skimmed billions in profits. And so, Lee Iacocca has every reason to be mad at Washington. He argues that it is "not the fault of the Republicans or liberal Democrats." That would be an academic, sluggish argument. He further argues that he has never been a "commander in chief." Lee understands a few things about leadership from the top, down to the consumer.

A Leader Must Show Curiosity: There is a saying that states, "Curiosity killed the cat." The 'care killed the cat'. By 'care', an English Playwright recorded in1598 by Ben Jonson's play *Every Man in His Humour.* The expression is normally used when somebody is asking an unwanted question. A show of curiosity means that a leader must be a good listener of his subordinates — the "Yes, Sir" individuals within his inner circle and to his critics outside the box. He must read veraciously, because the world is a big, complex place. Thomas Jefferson wrote, "If it were left to me to decide whether we should have a government without newspapers, or newspapers without a government, I should not hesitate for a moment to prefer the latter." A lack of intellectual curiosity simply means that a leader is one who is not aware of what is happening around him and the community in which he lives. It is the mark of good leadership to stand for the rights of people in the community within the society.

Elsewhere, *Leadership* addresses why a leader must continue to read new studies on leadership. As the society changes, so are new ideas that emerge with every generation. As much as we had unfinished challenges during the 20th Century, as humans we will continue to discover new ideas to deal with the new challenges of the 21st Century and beyond. Lee says, "If a leader never steps outside his comfort zone to hear different ideas, he grows stale. If he does not put his beliefs to the test, how does he know he's right?" That means that a leader must be creative, go out on a limb, and be willing to try something new, think outside the box, and reach out for new ideas. Thus leadership is all about managing change—whether one is a lawmaker, leading a company, nongovernmental organization or a local church. With times and winds of change, a leader must be creative.

Character Develops over Time: Experts in the fields of psychology and behavioral research do not agree when a person's character is formed. There is no available research data suggesting the exact time when a person's character begins. However, out of the many behavioral therapy sessions of observation I had with dysfunctional teens that I carried in many years of my case work load at Texas Department of Protective and Regulatory Services, Brookhaven Boys Center, Solomon Youth Centers and Jefferson Home for Children, these sessions of therapy confirmed a valid indication of a person's character. I also found that character does not happen overnight, it takes a long time to build in the life of a person. One other thing I found, behavior can come in the form of strength and weakness.

We often hear that he/she has a strong character, the drive, determination, self-discipline, energy and the will within a person's character, these are the adjectives of a person's way of life that tend to attract people to a leader. The opposite of the strong character reaps negative assumptions, because an individual may not know what they want in life. Their portfolio of life is usually dysfunctional and disorganized; therefore, such an individual character is not committed or consistent about life. He/she is not capable to attract people.

People deserve a person with an honorable character and vision they can trust to guide the organization, private or public office.

A moral authority of a Leader is Honesty and Integrity
www.muumandu.com

These are the men and women leaders who engage their entire life in good leadership.

A successful leader is one who manages to sell his vision to his followers; when that happens, people will put their trust and confidence in his leadership. Korn-Ferry International, a reputable executive search company, conducted a survey on what organizations want from their leaders. The study showed that people want leaders with good morals and are capable to convey a vision for the future of the organization. It is the character of a leader that wins people's trust and loyalty that ensures continual commitment in any organization or a group of people. When a leader sets the stride and displays a good sense of character, poised with values, ethics, honesty and integrity, people will be attracted to their leadership. Our master teacher, Jesus Christ instructed us that whatever we do for the least of these, we are also doing for Him. So, let us as leaders glorify our God by serving our neighbors and those whom we lead. God help us all as we lead by example in every situation we are.

Abstract

The Man and Just Wars: The Akamba tribe was first enlightened to the Word of God in mid 1840s by Dr. Krapf. They generally have an ethical and moral basis on which they form their opinions because of the exposure to the Word of God. In addition, they are vulnerable because of the scarcity of the natural resources. The tribe's lack of aggression in leadership jeopardizes their political advancement in Kenya's political arena. Therefore, the town provides a creditable opinion about the Akamba tribe.

The Machakos town is located fifty (50) kilometers east of Nairobi, the first British Colonial headquarters and the capital city of the Akamba tribe who commands a population of more than 2 million. The city is conveniently located in the valley surrounded by three densely populated hills. The dwellers of the city are the descendants of the early Akamba traders who founded the city over a hundred years ago. Modern Machakos town has numerous scattered tribes here and there transferred here by government jobs, military police and other central and local government services.

The city utility services are not sufficient due to the poor ecosystem. However, the hills provide minimal water supply when the rains come, but the rain water is washed away to the seasonal rivers down to the gullies. The town is the home of the four prestigious Akamba Provincial schools: Machakos Boys, Girls High School, Technical High School, Machakos Teachers College and provincial general hospital, all government public institutions. Until recent decades Machakos served as the only Akamba District until Kitui District was annexed from Machakos District because of the size of the District, and thereafter, more districts were added.

Akamba tribe is crucial in Kenya national politics, because of their size and political association with her neighbor tribes: Kikuyu, Embu, and Meru, who have similar if not one and the same traditional value systems. The tribe had a presidential candidate during the last Kenya general elections, December 27,

2007. When an Akamba elder was asked why he voted for a candidate that had little chance to win a presidential election, the man said, he voted for the candidate simply because he was Akamba tribe. However, Akamba élite living and working in the metropolitan cities of Kenya voted for the incumbent President.

The tribe does not have scarcity of land, but it is a land with poor soil erosion, without adequate water supply and experiences shortage of food every other two years. Her economic pressure has lagged behind in public infrastructures since Independence. Akamba leadership is not aggressive enough to address her economic pressure within the region.

The Akamba tribe was widely used in both World Wars by The British Empire; war stories are told by some of my uncles who fought in Burma. Today in Machakos town, there is a display of a war memorial located at the main entrance of the city's roundabout. The war veterans were included in the new formed government of the new Republic of Kenya soon after Jomo Kenyatta was sworn in as the First President of Kenya. They were not publicly involved with Mau Mau uprising except those who lived along the Kikuyu borders. They were the favorite tribe mostly hired by the British Administrators both in government and private sector.

Machakos town has its international connection that dates back to Ted Roosevelt, the American president who visited the British Administrator at the turn of the 20th Century during his safari hunting in Kapiti Plains outside the city limits.

A team hired by *Leadership* conducted an unbiased poll between May to August, 2007, five (5) months before the Kenya general elections, December 27, 2007. The survey targeted the Akamba tribe living and working in cities and municipalities located in the following areas: Machakos Division and Kalama Division; the teams contacted every town and trading post in Machakos Town Constituency.

The selection of the poll takers were hired from a designated group of university students from Daystar University, located in Athi River and Nairobi University to maintain intellectual balance. Both young men and women were sent out in pairs of two to various rural towns and trading posts in Machakos District.

Leadership was particularly interested in three questions out of eighteen (18) questions which spark the discussion below: (1) What is the current trend of tribalism in our country (Kenya)? (2) What is your opinion on the fight on tribalism in Kenya? (3) Do you think that some media and elected Members of Parliament encourage tribalism? The opinions generated issues on Land and Tribalism.

Native Africans are the modern tribes of Kenya who long ago wandered from central African forests of the modern Congo to the present modern Kenya; the dwellers of the mountains, hills and plains of Kenya. The people of Kenya are organized in tribes with sub-tribes within a major tribe as a result of being acculturated into a tribe because of cross-tribal marriages and other customary laws.

A majority of native Africans governed themselves through chiefdoms, Council of Elders and Kingdoms, some until to this day. One is the Swazi Kingdom of the modern Swaziland, in Southern Africa. There are other remaining tribes who still rule by proxies like the Zulus and Buganda of East Africa.

The rest of the native Africa has adopted western style governments of: dictatorships, military rules and democracies. Even though, credit to some Africa leadership, there has been a decline of the extent of the military rule style governments, including a few Africa leaderships still practicing dictatorship government through the influence of one party ideology; they too, are on the downward spin. Kenya is one of the best practicing, developing democracies there is to be admired in Africa. However, the tribal issue still remains on the political negotiating tables all over Africa leadership. The world continues to experience the power of tribal misbalance as it did during the Kenya elections, in Rwanda and other atrocious killings that went on during the writing of **Leadership** in countries of Darfur, Sudan, Middle East and other hot spots around the world. Ω

Distribution of Africa Tribes

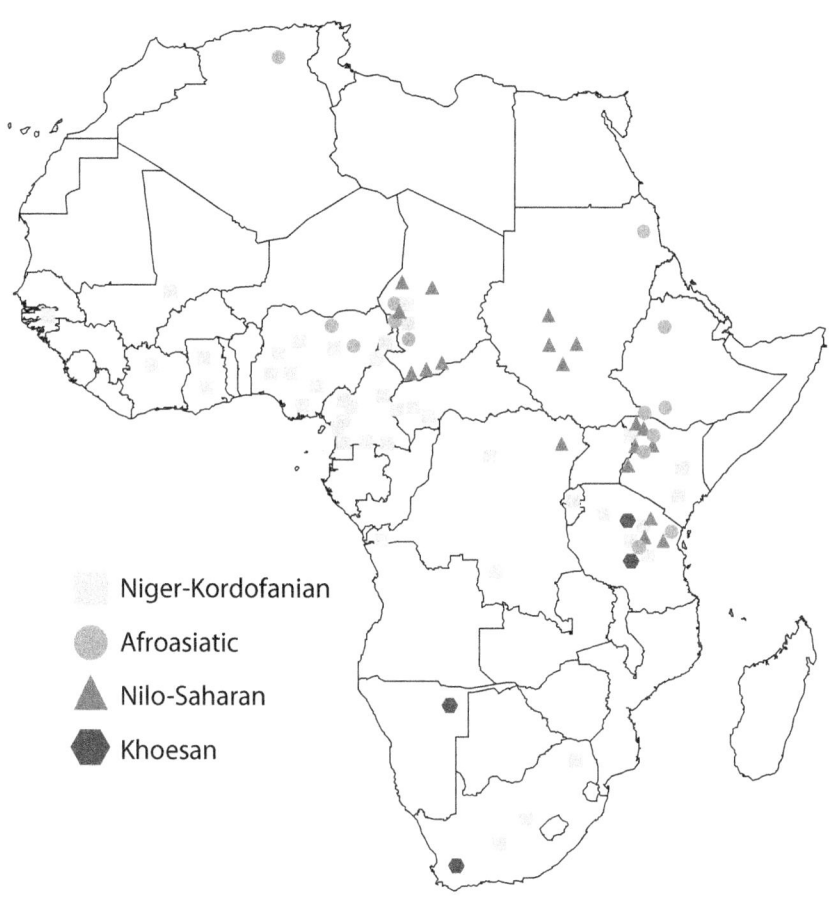

Niger-Kordofanian

Afroasiatic

Nilo-Saharan

Khoesan

10:1126/Science
1172257(April2009)
Map used with permission
©2009
Figure 1

Conflict

"Conflict may not be a problem in itself - it is rather what we do with the unsolved conflicts that come to haunt us and our societies." Page 82

Corruption in the Coalition Government

How far does the culture of corruption go in Kenya, Africa and the rest of the industrialized nations of the world? Is it perpetuated by bigwig politicians, government officials or does it start with citizens? Let us explore corruption as a chronic disease:

President Mwai Kibaki was born in 1931 into the Kikuyu tribe, the largest in Kenya. He was educated in Uganda and Britain before joining the struggle for independence for Kenya during early 1960s. He was elected to Parliament in 1963 and remained one of the longest continuous serving lawmakers in the country. He was a respected economist of his day. Kibaki served as finance minister under Jomo Kenyatta and vice president under Moi in the 1970s and 1980s.

After the death of Kenyatta, Kibaki disagreed in principle with KANU leaders and formed his own political party in 1991, the Democratic Party. After two unsuccessful bids for presidency Kibaki joined other political party forces and defeated Uhuru Kenyatta, the son of the first president Jomo Kenyatta in a landslide election victory in December 2002. Kibaki campaigned on the platform to fight against corruption and restored Kenya's economy in less than five years.

Kibaki won a parliamentary majority with National Rainbow Coalition (Narc) Party. The victory marked the end of 40 years of KANU one party state. It was Kabaki's third presidential try of which he won. The constitution barred his predecessor, Daniel arap Moi, from running for a third term.

Despite the tough talk about graft, Kibaki government became mired in major corruption scandals. It was Ntonyiri MP Maoka Maore (KANU) who broke the Anglo Leasing Scandal to parliament on April 20, 2004. The scandal was never fully resolved but there were a few honest MPs who were exonerated and resumed their Ministerial positions with no member of parliament ever charged. The alleged corruptions implicated former and current ministers into scams involving shadowy deals and large sums of public money. Despite President Kibaki's pledge to tackle corruption, some donors estimated that up to $1billion had been lost to graft between 2002 and 2005.

The president was thwarted over another key policy when voters rejected a proposed new constitution in referendum 2005. Mr. Kibaki had portrayed it as a modernizing measure while his critics argued that if the referendum had won, it would have left too much power in the hands of the presidency. However, Kibaki continued to guide the country into economic recovery during his first term in office. Economic growth in 2006 was 6.1%, compared with 0.6% when he took over. That was very remarkable.

February 2008 political veteran Mwai Kibaki had no political choice, but to enter into a power-sharing deal with his rival Raila Odinga after both claimed to have won the December 2007 presidential election. It was Raila's third time of his presidential bid. President Kibaki was sworn into a second and final term as per the Constitution of Kenya as president prompting a wave of unrest. Opposition said polls were rigged. Months of negotiations resulted in a coalition government, which was sworn into office in April 2008. Presidential elections led to widespread unrest, denting the country's reputation for stability. A power-sharing government was now in place.

Prime Minister: Raila Odinga, the son of first Vice President J. Oginga Odinga, during Jomo Kenyatta administration, and the leader of Orange Democratic Movement was sworn in as the first prime minister in April 2008, fulfilling a key step in a power-sharing deal aimed at ending a violent political crisis shy of his presidency. More than 1,500 people were killed and more than 650,000 were displaced following the elections in the previous December, which both Odinga and President Kibaki claimed to have won.

With the violence escalating, the rivals agreed in February to share power - but then wrangled for weeks over how to divide up their Coalition cabinet. Eventually 40 cabinet ministers took up their positions, 20 each from Kibaki's and Odinga's camps. Kibaki's party retained the key finance and internal security ministries.

The Coalition Government was first negotiated on February 28, 2008 between two presidential candidate leaders of PNU Kibaki and ODM Odinga. It is an event that should never have happened if the Electoral Commission of Kenya was not corrupt. That was a failure of a national institution, empowered by the Constitution to decide the rightful leader of the nation.

Therefore, without a referee (ECK) each principal was left without an alternative but each to claim victory on December 27, 2007 at the cost of more than 1,500 deaths of innocent people while in the process of the disputed presidential election whereby more than half a million men, women and children were displaced.

The Coalition Government resulted into one of the largest governments since inception of the Republic of Kenya. Two years into the Coalition Government, the Coalition dragged her feet, backed by her cronies in the national Assembly with agendas to reform; it had all the signs of a failed state. The people of Kenya appeared to have been ruled by two separate governments in a Republic. The citizens remained in a state of confusion, sometimes without basic food, water and rationed electricity in major urban cities and towns.

Corruption as it was known in Kenya, continued to be business as usual in the corridors of state run corporations, government Institutions, Parliamentarians and Executive branches all over the world. Call it graft, fraud or bribes; it is still illegal. One of the resolutions of Nairobi Accord 2008 was to prosecute those who committed post violent criminal offenses.

Therefore, the Coalition Government, torn in half, opted to forfeit a tribunal court to its expense, in favor of the Truth Justice and Reconciliation Commission. TJRC lacked power and mandate to indict, to punish any criminal offender. In other words the Commission would only sweep old criminal acts and offenders under the rug.

One would argue, why did the Coalition Government settle for TJRC? Some of the MP big wig politicians were members of the 10th Parliament who were the masterminds of the post-violence offenders; they risked criminal indictment and faced jail time with International Court at The Hague. Those opposed to the Tribunal Bill supported a TJRC, a substandard of the original Tribunal Bill as required by the ITC. In the national Assembly approximately 38 members of the small parties' forum affiliated to PNU endorsed the Tribunal Bill under the leadership of Hon. Imanyara, Imenti South Constituency.

Consequently, they were too few in number to enforce a change among other 210 MPs. The enactment of a Tribunal Court by Parliament would have pursued justice for post-election violence offenders' masterminds and their followers. The crimes committed by the seating and former MPs would have dethroned the big wig politicians from participating in all future general elections.

There were secret bribes during the 10th Parliament that went on, initiated by the big wig heavy weight MPs who bought protection of censorship from other MPs. The practice was a reflection of what happened during the countrywide political campaigns of general elections of December 2007.

In addition, the Ufungamano Joint Forum of religious leaders and Bishops said, nothing short of a special Tribunal Court will be acceptable by the civil society as method of dealing with post-election violence offenders and suspects.

Now, the re-appointment of the Anti-Corruption Commissioner and his assistants was by far a poor choice made by the incumbent President Kibaki. The president should have known that PNU lacked sufficient votes in the 10th Parliament to support his executive appointment. In sharp contrast the Kibaki scenario can best be compared to President Obama who tried to pass a healthcare bill with a majority of Democrats in both houses.

In the course of the span of more than two governments, the Attorney General, who is the state advisor and prosecutor, had yet to issue an indictment on any suspect. There were no criminal indictments which were issued to any ONE big wig politician or jailed for corruption since the establishment during the first term of Justice Rigera's tenure.

The Anti-Corruption Commission was established in 2003 during the first term of Kibaki administration. *Leadership* borrows a leaf from Rigera that he investigated and forwarded the cases to the Attorney General. There is an unanswered question that remains in the minds of the men and women of Kenya; indeed, it is immoral that the Attorney General had not prosecuted.

In sharp contrast, Kenya Anti-Corruption Commission should have learned from the Israelis authorities for indictment of a former Prime Minister Ehud Olmert on corruption charges.

This was the first criminal indictment ever filed against an Israeli prime minister. The Israeli Prime Minister, Olmert had a history of corruption going back to (2006) the days when he was a Jerusalem mayor, a cabinet minister, and to top it all off, when as Prime Minister of the Israeli government.

There were two cabinet level ministers in his administration who were sent to prison for corruption and bribes. Avraham Hirchson, former Finance Minister, sentenced to five years, and another cabinet minister was sentenced to four years. One would argue that Israelis have always had in their childhood upbringing and in their immediate memories the teachings of the legendary Ten Commandments, on which Jewish culture and worship of the Torah imply they were taught integrity and would not stoop to corruption. "Thou shall…"

The Justice Ministry of Israel sends a clear message to the governments of the world that it is possible to indict a Prime Minister, President and Cabinet Ministers of any government of the world. If the Israelis can prosecute their politicians, **Leadership** finds it hard to believe that the Attorney General in collaboration with Kenya Anti – Corruption Commission could never have caught even ONE big fish for a trial.

However, to his defense, Ringera, the Anti-Corruption director said, "I am not complicit in corruption and I am not corrupt." He investigated 498 cases of Anti-corruption and prosecuted 382 of which 316 cases were forwarded to the Attorney General. Among the cases included a number of Ministers, MPs and government administrators from the 9th and 10th Parliament. The following classic scandal of Ken Ren, has been a running epic since the 1970s, my nostalgic days in high school. A year earlier, 1969 the world applauds the landing of Neil Armstrong on the moon, the Vietnam War is over, and Lyndon Johnson is President. The aging first President of Kenya, Jomo Kenyatta is still in office.

The scheme of Ken Ren was entered into as a joint business enterprise with an unknown American businessman or persons with officials of the government of the day. The phantom chemical fertilizer factory was intended to be built in Coast Province in 1970s. Unfortunately, the mentioned chemical plant was never built. The legend of the matter was debated somewhere in Europe which ended up in arbitration. The phantom account was referred to BAWAG of Austria and DECROISE of Belgium against the tax payers of Kenya.

The Ken Ren scandal was resuscitated again and reported to the public by then Hon. Raila Odinga, ODM presidential hopeful, against the then incumbent President Kibaki in 2007 during presidential general elections. The scandal resurfaces every 5 years during presidential elections, and never seems to be settled; three governments have come and gone.

One would only ask why the scandal has lasted so long. The project was reported to be worth 4.3 billion Shillings which has continued to be paid out of the consolidated treasury funds for more than thirty years. The incumbent President, Kibaki was then the nation's Minister of Finance, this implies Kibaki must have had inside knowledge. Wouldn't the buck have stopped with him?

Nevertheless, Hon. Raila of Langata Constituency had prior knowledge that he would end up in a Coalition Government by the virtue of his new title as Prime Minister. He automatically, inherited the classic Ken Ren corruption scandal of the ages like all his predecessors.

Entering into the second year of the Coalition Government, numerous donor nations including the U.S. began to weigh on the progress of political status, the proposed national reforms as promised by the two principals before the country's future general elections. These sentiments bore concerns to the peoples of Kenya and Kenya Community Abroad who remit millions of foreign currency to their families at home.

The United States is the largest donor nation to Kenya behind England, and perhaps the largest donor nation through her enormous International NGOs program initiatives operating in Kenya. The U.S. - Kenya has a bilateral strategic relationship in the region to fight the War on Terror, Drug Trafficking and Piracy on the Indian Ocean, the horn of Africa.

Therefore, bad governance in Kenya jeopardizes the loss of her economic muscle and benefits she gets from numerous International agencies operating in Kenya as a contour aid to the surrounding member nations of East and Central African, landlocked nations with relief programs and other humanitarian initiatives.

The Obama Administration (2008 -) picked Kenya relations where Bush Administration left off. The state department undersecretary for African affairs issued the following warning to the Coalition Government in Kenya:

First, Coalition must bring to justice the perpetrators of the post – violence offenders before future general elections in Kenya.

Second, Coalition will be held responsible, to reform the national Police and the judiciary system in Kenya. Coalition Government was mandated by the Nairobi-Serena Accord to have a Constitutional review before the future general elections.

Third, USA further stated in a letter issued to the Coalition Principals and other 15 unnamed persons of interests connected to the opposition of the enactment of the Tribunal Court and the perpetrators of the post tribal clashes.

Fourth, USA would intervene with other world community

donors to sanction donor projects ear - marked or proposed for Kenya.

Leadership takes the position that a Coalition Government was forced onto the peoples of Kenya by the failure of ECK. The will of the people was compromised by the greedy politicians and the external power brokers. Two years later, the Principals were not heroes to anybody, but, only to themselves. Parliament is not about representation, but selfish representation and stuffing of one's pockets.

Mars group of Kenya reported September 2009 that 468 children die every day from preventable diseases. *Leadership* calculated 168,480 children would die in one year! While the MPs and their immediate families are considered a special class of people, raking in more than 600,000 Shillings in salaries and benefits for a five year term from heavily taxed Kenyans.

In the days of Robin Hood of England, the classic story is told that he stole from the rich and distributed to the poor. The negotiated Coalition Government turned out NOT to be a driven democratic choice by the peoples of Kenya, but rather, it was a dictatorship of two rapacious principals.

Kenya Media enjoys a more diverse and liberalized media scene than any other African country, with a large middle class providing a base for substantial advertising revenue. In early 2009, media outlets went to the streets and condemned President Kibaki's decision to approve changes to the media law, which they said would limit press freedom. The amended legislation gave officials the power to control broadcast content on grounds of national security. The **print media** was dominated by two publishing houses, the Nation and Standard. Over 80 percent of the Kenya population relies on the **broadcast media**, particularly radio, for news broadcasts in different vernaculars. Until recently the liberalization of broadcasting had a limited impact outside Nairobi but some private networks now have wide coverage of much of the country. TV viewing is mainly limited to urban cities. Few Kenyans are regular internet users, because of the lack of rural electrification and the cost of internet access.

The book *Leadership* started by quoting the flawed accounting system at the UNITED NATIONS. A probe of the Iraq oil-for-food program faulted the former U.N. Secretary-General Kofi Annan, the Security Council and some United Nations member states for "egregious lapses" that allowed corruption and incompetence to cripple the operation, according to a preface of the final conclusion. The United Nations is the very organization that the entire world looks up to for trust, guidance and leadership in world matters.

UN leadership failure to properly manage the $64 billion program was a central focus, but there was no new "smoking gun" linking him to an oil-for-food contract awarded to a Swiss company that employed his son, Kojo, said one official with knowledge of the final report, speaking on the condition of anonymity, because the report had not been released. In the eyes of the business world, it was the appearance of evil, corruption of nepotism, for a company to both hold a United Nations contract and employ the son of the Secretary-General of the United Nations.

The Independent Inquiry Committee's final report said the program succeeded in providing minimal standards of nutrition and health care for millions of Iraqis trying to cope with tough U.N.

sanctions imposed after Saddam's 1990 invasion of Kuwait. The program was successful and the corruption was successfully hidden to high top officials. To my knowledge, no one was ever linked to such high corruption.

Turning to the United States, leader of the free world democracy, she is not immune, corruption is identified on a daily basis in government, corporations and politics. In 2006 during Bush administration, corruption of greed was identified in an incident in the Department of Interior. An article published in a major media outlet stated, "Dirk Kempthorne Left behind a Lovely Bathroom at Interior Department." It was alleged when Dirk Kempthorne took over as Secretary of the Interior in May 2006, he was appalled by the appearance of the interior of his office bathroom. The office had no shower, refrigerator or freezer, vital staples of any adequate executive room. Dirk Kempthorne misappropriated non-budgeted government money to install unwanted appliances at the cost of $235,000 to the taxpayers. It is mockingly selfish greed to believe one needs a shower, refrigerator or freezer as vital staples in a government, public executive room. This is a blatant example of the arrogant misuse of the American tax payers, a behavior found in many third world governments, such as the use of high end dollar vehicles for government officials.

Returning back to Africa, Nigeria contributes to about 10% of Shell's global oil production and is home to some of its most promising oil reserves, yet the country is steeped in poverty and conflict. The country has continued to lose the war on hunger; something is not right. The money is going somewhere but not on the basic needs of human life, food, shelter, education, and environment. Time and time again, Nigeria's top government leadership, from the president down, has been inflicted with high end corruption. It is safe to say, when one thinks of Nigeria, the first thing that the majority of people inside and outside the country think is corruption.

In a neighbor country of Cameroon citizens report how they have to pay a bribe for a doctor's consultation. Cameroonian government like the majority of other African countries provides a socialistic medicine for her citizens. Imagine that students must pay a bribe to teachers if they have to pass their national exams. In Zambia the country's president was alleged to face corruption charges committed during his administration.

Kibaki promised he would get Kenya out of corruption when elected President. December 31, 2002 Mwai Kibaki was sworn the third President of the Republic of Kenya. His famous campaign pledge "Corruption" would cease to be a way of life in Kenya. He was widely received by many Kenyans after twenty four years of President Daniel Arap Moi. Corruption and bribery in public offices were widely practiced by politicians and government administrators. Kibaki said,

> *"Corruption will now cease to be a way of life in Kenya and I call upon all those members of my government and public officers accustomed to corrupt practice to know and clearly understand that there will be no sacred cows under my government."*

Kibaki pledged to revive the economy. Nevertheless, corruption under Kibaki government during his first term took a new turn when his government ministers entered into fictitious ghost government contracts that got Kenya government into billions of dollars of credit loans to unknown creditors. There is no time soon that Kenya will ever know where the money went. However, there were a few honest individuals, hardworking, sincere and committed men and women working to protect the interest of Kenya. That led to 6.1% economic surge.

In a democratic state, citizens have the power to put politicians into power and they also have the power to remove them from power. Citizens must learn to vote for issues that only affect their daily living and the best candidate who can represent and implement their needs. They have a person and a place to have their problems solved. When bribery is used as a means to elect a candidate, democratic principles are jeopardized. It is imperative for citizens to vote their conscience otherwise the consequences will come back to haunt them. When people of integrity are elected to power there will be a change in national policy and the way government does its business.

For the majority of African societies, corruption has gone from an act of acceptance of bribes to a complete state of mind and to some a way of life. It has progressed like chronic malaria sickness, from the poor attempting to "make ends meet" to the rich wanting more and more as though it is a sense of entitlement for someone in a position of authority.

Corruption in many parts of Africa starts with the law enforcement that breeds their behavior into the poor and rich citizens. For the majority of many honest people working in governments across the sub-Sahara Africa, sometimes they are put under peer pressure by their unethical colleagues, and are considered as traitors, fools, stupid and despised for not taking public funds or government property.

Grassroots civic education is a must to win the war on corruption and deceit in these societies. To Kibaki's credit his leadership established a public system to collect tax from sales of big domestic items; the practice will eventually reach everyone who enters into "mom and pop" small rural businesses into paying sales tax. Every person in Kenya is required by law to have a pin before one can transact a business which is amiable to government agencies. It was the leadership of the president to introduce these noble changes to the society. When such measures are introduced to the public, it will only be a matter of time when good people with good moral conduct will be elected to the political power that in turn will lead to better practices of good will.

A massive campaign of continuing civic education on corruption to refuse to pay a bribe in these societies will someday bear fruit. Many governments of the north like USA public or private employees normally expect to be paid a salary that exceeds the basic minimum wage required and sometimes many times over to meet the rising cost of living. Most American companies pay out by weekly pay checks on every Friday.

Wage earners have benefits, such as health insurance, paid vacation, paid tuition for continuing education for the update on technological changes and safe working conditions. Unfortunately, such basic tenants of public employment may not be assured by the majority of African public employees. Such practices contribute to the solicitation of forced bribes just to survive a weekend. There is no doubt; there are people who will always be greedy until they depart from this life. It is something else when ordinary people are faced with the choice of taking a bribe and surviving, or the choice to not take a bribe and starvation.

People should never be faced with such immoral conditions. Some greedy lawmakers in Kenya would rather fill their pockets with bribes and corruption while their citizens die of hunger and starvation. December 2008 - Kenya Anti-Corruption Commission (KACC) accused seven current and former MPs of taking illegal allowances worth $250,000 and in other public held corporations such as NSSF, billions of Kenya Shillings were misappropriated by directors and those in high government positions.

Having said that, corruption is also added to the pressing challenges that include high unemployment, crime and poverty; most Kenyans and in other parts of Africa, people live below the poverty level of $1 a day. Mother Nature with her seasonal droughts does frequently put millions of people at risk. However, the lucrative tourist industry in Kenya bounces back and forth because of the flow of tourists originating from frigid climates of Europe's winter to summer like climates of the tropics. Tourism is here to stay in Africa; governments of the south must plan well to accommodate their poor citizens with the highest of income for the country's best hard currency earners ahead of horticulture, tea, coffee and fresh flowers available to the florist shops and stores across Europe.

So many reforms would be necessary to restore integrity in the political system and business enterprises in Kenya and elsewhere in the world. Many people have become disillusioned on whether corruption will ever end. I am afraid to say that no ideology promises an end of corruption. But corruption can be minimized and controlled in public and private institutions to a point, until it becomes a way of life. It is possible if it is well manicured by a few honest politicians and the leaders of any state on earth. When corruption is minimized in Kenya and or other nations of Africa, poverty, Aids, ethnic cleansing, crimes and drug trafficking will take a second seat in public life. Corruption in most nations of the north is controlled by the rule of law, which is what has lacked in many of the third world nations.

The Profile of Kenya Political Machines: The golden age of Kenya was between the 1960s and 1970s. As soon as Kenyatta died, the history of Kenya degenerated into decadence, backwater of political intrigues, moral-insurrection, famine, killings, diseases and political back stabbings. In spite of this, Kenya is considered by the majority of the world community a stable country. The good news is for now the nation has no known internal insurgents operating inside or outside the country. Kenya leadership has historically promoted the spirit of nation-hood of one nation since her independence. However, the biggest source of internal unrest is half-century old tribal clashes, born during the colonial days and worsened soon after the country's independence. The country's politicians have never managed to abandon tribalism.

The tribal clashes have historically resurfaced every five years since the Multi-Party System was introduced in 1992. The System's first general elections were held in 1992 and 1997 when an unknown number of deaths went unreported and more than 35,000 people were displaced. The worst ethnic clashes occurred several months leading up to and after Kenya general elections of December 27, 2007 when more than 1,500 were first officially reported killed and 350,000 people displaced from the Rift Valley, the country's food basket and other outlining providences. However, the number of deaths increased to more than 3,500, and 650,000 people were displaced. Other DIP escaped to the nearby country of Uganda for safety. The Displaced population led to national unemployment and a shortage of food crisis.

Small mom and pop retail stores were destroyed. Mom and pop stores are integral businesses that are owned and operated within the community. They are the country's largest provision for daily, fresh produce. The mom and pop retail kiosks offer a shopping alternative to consumers living within the neighborhoods. While the proliferation of huge retail stores are strategically placed in smaller towns and metropolitan cities of Kenya they continue to thrive as they serve the upper and middle class Kenyan.

The community shambas *(equivalent to small ranches of 10 acres of land in rural west Texas)* were not plowed. Large seasonal agricultural fields of corn, tea, coffee and wheat grown for the nation's cash crops were not fully planted due to lack of man power. Export and import goods and services came to a halt due to apparent insecurities and the apprehensive future of the country at the time.

The unscheduled mother nature rains failed, devastated large and small scale farming with the consequential struggle for a day's meal, while the rich and the privileged few savored their bacon. The country's leadership was ambushed by the consequences of the disputed presidential elections that led to the outcry of citizens with short supply of maize, the nation's staple food. In the midst of the nation's maize shortage, some greedy politicians working with unscrupulous government administrators and opportunistic business-entrepreneurs took advantage of the situation and entered into government scandals of contracts for maize with dubious deals, which in turn led to corruption of the maize commodity meant for the hungry citizens. Such practices are brought about by the poorly managed nation's institutions, the politicians and the incompetent practices of the Rule of Law of the land.

It is very important for the future governments to develop a national emergency policy to handle the nation's food supply when the country undergoes imminent, unexpected, unwarranted political outcomes and natural disasters. It is common knowledge that the lack of global food supply does not occur overnight. The world has experienced food shortages since 4,000 B.C. back in the days of the Hebrew slaves in Egypt. For decades Kenyans have always known about the annual rainfall seasons guided by the monsoon winds. The short rains occur in October through December; every farmer knows exactly what and when to plant. The long rains occur in the months of February through early May of every year, leading to cool climates for the months of July. Kenya and other East African countries rely on the fabulous tropical climates for domestic and agricultural cash crops.

The climate is not about to change any time soon, regardless of what the environmentalist may say. However, the human encroachment destroying natural trees, rivers, forests and vegetations should be stopped and the environment left alone for the beauty and enjoyment of man and wild life. The challenge in Kenya and other African states is how and when political leadership machines will ever practice good governance. The political machines must find new techniques to circumvent perpetual food crisis every time the rains fail. The leadership in power must manage well the available natural resources afforded by mother-nature with a balanced climate year round, some for farming and some for pleasure as found in tourism.

In the United States, the Department of Transportation stores salt in strategic places within the city limits to be used during the frigid months of November – March of each year. Every local government has long known that the roads would become slippery because of freezing ice causing accidents, in every American city and state. In addition, United States has set aside money for disasters during the summer months for torrential rain falls that hit the southern sea board, California for its wild fires, and the western states like Texas for its dust storms and tornados.

Every government including Kenya has a department of planning and management — which is referred to as the Ministry of Planning. Citizens expect by the nature of the word (PLANNING) every planning expert and government technocrats are housed in this department. Yes, there is always room for errors and improvement by every government of the world. But it appears that Leadership in African states fails to see the obvious.

There is a fallacious premise made by the majority of Kenyans who continue to dwell on the idea that Rift Valley Province will remain to hypo enough food supply for Kenya's growing 38 million plus, and this idea should be abandoned. Kenya's growing population in itself should serve as an alarming warning; every inch of The Rift Valley continues to be subdivided between families until there will be no more land to go around in a matter of a few decades. Rift Valley was adequate for settlement before the 1960s and 1970s when the nation's population was less than 15 million.

About the same time, U.N. reported the atrocious reality of food shortage in the world; that followed the decades of 1970s - 2000. The world grain producers drastically declined as the monsoon rains did not come, causing severe famine in the sub-Sahara.

The late Michael Jackson, an American entertainer, will be forever remembered for leading a campaign for hunger, "We Are the World," where millions of dollars were raised to combat hunger for the peoples of Ethiopia, only to end up in the hands of a military government.

Kenya has extensive open lands containing good nutrients and a manageable underground water base, good for drilling for sizable commercial farms. The majority of Eastern and Northern Provinces are severable lands out of the rest of the public lands, compared to the used up soil in Rift Valley and Central Provinces due to over production of grain and the increasing human population. It is only a matter of time when nutrients in the soil of Rift Valley Province will be depleted and there will no longer be enough land to farm. It is safe to say that Eastern and Northern Provinces should be carefully considered as the future home of the growing population of Kenya. Due to the increasing technology, leadership in Kenya should redirect national resources to the arid lands for future food supply and energy to power and support the growing rural cities and metropolitan cities of Mombasa, Nairobi, Nakuru, Eldoret and Kisumu, which are commercial urban centers located strategically along the nation's transportation road and rail systems of Kenya.

The nation's capital of Nairobi infrastructure was built for a maximum population of 200,000. To date the city is surrounded by modern high rises unable to cope with the city's water pressure. The transit system is poorly managed, incapable to meet the basic needs of the city dwellers, daily commuters working in various government institutions, foreign missions to Kenya and other nongovernmental international agencies located in the financial district of Nairobi.

The local government and municipality leaders of the city of Nairobi must consider a transportation solution. The government planners and engineers must look to their colonial rulers' master plans that produced one of the most efficient transportation systems the world has ever seen, the tube and subway systems of London, German and other European cities. All Europeans depend on well-organized transportation systems that were developed so long ago to fit the needs of the daily commuters from city to cities connecting to other European city and states.

The second place to look for major transportation solutions is the transportation systems of North America. United States has one of the best transportation systems available anywhere in the world. Outside the city limits of any state of the United States, a motorist would be challenged by one of the fastest moving long hauling trucks on the interstate highways traveling more than 80 miles per hour. These truckers cover long distances on wide open roads from the eastern states to the western sea board carrying goods and services from one state to another 24/7.

The United States road transportation system can support these massive, never ending capitalistic trade routes. Texas alone, is larger than Kenya, with a population of over 25 million people. Texas has an estimated 25,000 state highways and over 5000 bridges and these numbers increase every year. It is amazing to watch any metropolitan city of the U.S. moving millions of autos between 6 AM and 9 AM and 3 PM and 7 PM with almost zero accidents compared to the inadequate transportation systems of Nairobi.

The Kenya national transportation road system between rural towns and villages connecting the national urban cities of Kenya has never sufficiently been serviceable with connectivity to assist the populous rural Kenya trading centers to the metropolitan cities since Independence. It is true there were signs of improvement during the years of 2002 – 2007; perhaps it was due to some western donor nations contracting for national projects. Kenyans living in the Diaspora ask why the government at home is so imprudent to the point that local business contractors are not reliable and are untrustworthy.

During the first part of January 2008 I visited an old friend in rural Kenya. He had grown sweet apple-like golden mangoes intended for sale to a buyer in Mombasa. He told me he had waited for days for his regular buyer. Unfortunately, the buyer failed to come on time due to the political crisis during the disputed presidential elections of December 2007. Ships at the Mombasa national harbor were delayed to unload and load millions of tons of goods to and from the international communities. Millions of shillings of the county's income were lost.

The unthinkable happened. The small scale farmer could not sale or transport his mangoes and produce, partly because of the country's political unrest, and partly because he had no capital to haul his best ever crop to the market place. The sweet tasting apple-like mangoes were getting spoilt on their natural trees; birds of the air, family members and perhaps unexpected visitors were gifted with a few mangoes before they decayed back to the soil. He is an example of the tens of hundreds of such small scale family shambas whose crops were ruined into devastation because the national leadership was thrown into disarray as a result of two individuals fighting for power.

Malawi, a nation of about 13 million should serve as Africa's leadership role model. Mr. Mutharika, equipped with hybrid seeds and fertilizers purchased with the country's money, distributed to 1.3 million farmers, who were permitted to purchase the seeds and fertilizers for one third of the market value, whilst ethnic clashes in Kenya were slaughtering each other by the cover of night.

In sharp contrast, the Malawians harvested 3.44 million metric tons of maize. The country's national deficit went from 44% to 18% in surplus! In 2008 Malawians had reached 53% surplus and exported corn to Zimbabwe, a country larger in land mass with a large reservoir of natural resources compared to Malawi, a small democracy landlocked and sandwiched between surrounding democracies of Tanzania, Mozambique and Zambia. That was the mark of governance and Leadership. National Geographic, June 2009

The Speaker of the National Assembly was categorically unsuccessful when he failed to unite the two principals, President Kibaki and Prime Minister Raila to come to terms. The principals and their allies failed to compromise, which resulted in the abolition of the chair of "House Business Committee," historically reserved for the Vice President of the majority party in parliament. The Speaker temporarily crowned himself the chairman of HBC until further notice; it might as well be for the life of the 10th Parliament. However, the Speaker was not alone. There are other neighboring democracies like Tanzania whose House Business Committee is chaired by the Speaker of National Parliament.

What is Kenya's relationship to the world community? The immediate concern from the world community is the vulnerability caused by Islam Fundamentalist terrorist aggressors. Kenya's future is not immune to terrorism; it happened to her and can happen again. In fact, acts of terrorism to any nation serve a great concern to the citizens of the world.

Kenya Islamic communities are the major inhabitants of the coast. They are largely viewed by the world community as potential providers for sleeper cells along the vast, immeasurable, over 1,000 miles of coastal strip of Somaliland to southern cities of the islands of Kilwa Kivinje, in Tanzania. Somali communities have historically crossed the porous Kenya/Somalia eastern boundary which runs hundreds of miles from the Indian Ocean to the tip of southern Ethiopia's unmanned border.

During the first term of Kibaki administration, it is estimated half of the Kenya judicial-senior judges were investigated. The majority of the judges resigned rather than face tribunal investigations. The most recent notable extrajudicial cold blood killings occurred in 2009 during the life of the Coalition Government. Four people associated with investigating the killings were themselves murdered on the streets of Nairobi by unknown assassins. The killings included human rights lawyers, Oscar Kingara and John Paul Oulo, who were assassinated driving to an afternoon meeting at the Kenyan National Commission on Human Rights in March 2009.

According to Prof. Philip Alston, Special U.N. Reporter, he told the U.N. Human Rights Council that during the investigation of the extrajudicial killings, Kenya's police were a "major stumbling block" for probes into the killings. The Prof. further stated on June 3, 2009 that, "Attacks on those who document abuses do not absolve a government of its obligation to investigate, prosecute and punish those responsible for extrajudicial executions." The nation of Kenya is engulfed with multi-ethnic entities with tribal leadership who tend to affect the law enforcement carried out in the country.

In many cases alliances to more than one tribe is common in Kenya. To manage criminals within a country of more than 42 tribes, each with a set of customary traditions and issues of moral code is difficult, for many Kenyans are unable to perceive in their minds and hearts right from wrong. Every so often, it is very problematical for government agencies to implement what could be easily accepted by one tribe over another tribe.

Criminal injustices are sometimes based on the poor, inadequate respect for the government and the law makers who should live as an example before their constituencies. When the law makers do not withhold themselves from crimes of corruption and the use of state institutions which foster one's criminal activities, what can a regular citizen expect to do? To a larger extent the war on corruption can only be minimized when citizens are well-informed on basic civic education on the role and responsibility of each individual inhabitant. There should never be a person above the Rule of Law. Sometimes in Kenya, it appears to be the case. WikiLeaks/www.wikileaks.org

Corruption breeds crimes and vice versa in the majority of Kenya run state corporations. The majority of criminal activity leads to corruption embedded in the daily activities of the highest office down to middle management of state government administrators and the politicians who run the state held public corporations, who maintain close relations with criminal gurus within a country like Kenya. Therefore, historically, a corruption is seen by some as acceptable ethics as long as one is stealing from the government. Kenya is yet to bring to justice the criminals of the Anglo leasing and Goldenberg scandals of the previous administration before 2002.

The Coalition Government of 2008-2012 failed to implement a tribunal court simply because a majority of the perpetrators were one and the same in the government. However, due to international pressure, Kenya Parliament voted in 2009 to send the criminal perpetrators of the clash killings of 2007 and 2008 to The Hague, World Court. In sharp contrast, in the United States when a law maker is caught up into criminal acts he/she hides behind the provision granted by the Constitution of the United States and for the purpose to save one's own skin he/she will take what is known as the "5th Amendment" afforded by the Constitution of the United States, which means you cannot testify against yourself. That does not mean criminals are above the law. They are still prosecuted to the full extent of the Law.

In sharp contrast, law makers, government administrators and other high profile criminals in Kenya will use bribery to save their own skins. Average Kenyan voters have no concept that their constitution affords them the luxury to elect and form a government every five years. Some voters have never enjoyed the good will of leadership from their representatives since Independence.

There is a false assumption by some citizens from remote and rural parts of Kenya who assume that members of national Parliament join politics to embezzle government institutions to enrich themselves. Therefore, with such a premise, corruption becomes an outgrowth of tribal social tradition and beliefs, because the majority of the people of Kenya view themselves as a country of tribes. In 2003 a survey by the Kenya Anti-Corruption Authority revealed 65 per cent of Kenyans come to work with the intention to steal from their employer. This premise can only be changed by the Principle of Democratic Ideals, good governance and the practice of the Rule of Law. Ω

EPILOGUE

D uring one of the many tours I made to Kenya, I visited the home of an old friend and teacher, a retired elementary principal during my nostalgia days of my youth at Athi River. When Sunday worship came, I was amazed by the order of the morning worship services at a local indigenous church. It had not yet adopted the contemporary worship like the majority of the rural churches I visited. They sang songs of Negroid spiritual type music of the old south and like the old gospel music, of the churches located along the Bible belt zone of North America. Men and women wrapped their beautiful vocal cords around gospel songs they sang in voices of tenor, soprano, alto and male bass, all without a family of instruments.

I could feel and hear the music pitch falling in the right places of the music notes, the spiritual gospel songs were presented in their vernacular, the way it was intended to be at the beginning of time. I left the village, with tears, knowing that it is only a matter of time, before the old ways of worship will soon be replaced with a contemporary worship, soon after the guardian elders of the church pass on to the eternal land of their ancestors. Yes, change in culture; change in Africa Leadership is inevitable.

Finally, brethren, whatsoever things are true, whatsoever things are honest, whatsoever things are just, whatsoever things are pure, whatsoever things are lovely, whatsoever things are of good report, if there be any virtue and if there be any praise, think on these things. Philippians 4:8 21st King James Version

A moral authority of a Leader is Honesty and Integrity
www.muumandu.com

If you have mastered material provided in this book – you are on the way to becoming a successful leader. You are in the process of changing your organization. As a leader you are giving direction to the lives of those who are and will become leaders - so they in turn will influence the lives of others. A leader may never know his impact until lives are changed. But that does not mean you are to perform every task by yourself. You are to delegate certain tasks to the best qualified person according to their ability, skills and talents.

Once tasks are completed to your satisfaction, you must always give praise and recognition; otherwise you may become a burden and even an obstacle to those you lead. You are in charge. **This is my story. Ω**

WORD MEANINGS

Aaron: used his **communication** skills to support his brother, Moses.

Apartheid: was a political segregation system used in South Africa (1948-1990s) that separated the original black people of South Africa and white and gave particular privileges to those of European origin.

Asante: a Swahili word for thank you.

Boma: a Swahili word for homestead.

Circumcision: is a ceremonial practice of man/womanhood for both boys and girls in Kenya and other parts of Africa.

Deborah: encouraged Barrack to end Canaanite tyranny.

Diakonos: Greek word for "Deacon" translated as minister and or servant.

Eusebius: wrote fifty years after the death of Jesus and witnessed the destruction of Jerusalem by the Romans.

Ethics: Greek word *ethos*, Ethics the study of morality: [Latin word **moralis**]: What is right and wrong. The words are used interchangeably – ethics is an individual character; while morality refers to relationships between people. A moral function of a person is when he/she develops an argument on moral issues whether good or bad.

FBI HQR: in Washington, DC, More is stolen everyday with a flick of the pen than the point of a pistol-paraphrased.

Goliath fall: Goliath was boastful, proud, and arrogant. He thought that he was indestructible. Pride comes before the fall. The giant literally fell dead at the feet of David.

Graft: The use of dishonesty, illegal means to gain money or property by an official in a position of power.

Harambee: Swahili word for pull together.

Jehoshaphat: destroyed idols and taught God's law.

Joseph: was an **administrator** in Egyptian leadership.

Josephus: was a Jewish historian writer (37-101) A.D. Witnessed destruction of Jerusalem (70) A.D. by Roman General Vaspasian, his writings covered Roman emperors, Kings and Jewish customs.

M.D.: A medical doctor is a carpenter of a human body.

"Mo": is ancient Egyptian word for water.

Mdozi: a Swahili word for boss.

Mzee: A Swahili word for elderly person aged with wisdom.

Nanobots: are small molecules equal to the size of a blood cell.

Nanotechnology: A precise manipulation of a single atom and molecules used to create larger structure/smaller. These nano-technologies are used by both scientists and engineers to design and produce useful products.

Nehemiah: demonstrated leadership skills when he led his fellow Jews to rebuild the Jerusalem wall.

Philo: wrote during time of Jesus and His earthly Ministry.

Stole: [1]Ecclesiastical scarf usually worn, embroidered scarf made of silk or linen, worn by various members of the clergy.[2] A draped robe worn by women of high standing in ancient Rome.

Shifuta: is an associated/nick name in Swahili for the word terrorist.

Transcendentalism: A system of philosophy that regards the processes of reasoning as the key to knowledge of reality.[2] Transcendentalism is a system of philosophy especially that emphasizes intuition or divine.

Vass: A discussion of various issues of current events that cross the minds of people, such as politics, economics, and tribal relations.

Vision: "The power to perceive what the eye cannot see, natural, intellectual shrewdness." Webster Dictionary

Contributors

Bruns, Lois, retired school teacher, contributed additional valuable family history and oral histories of Pipestone

Kapten, Stanley, his noble thinking and reason contributed additional material on Corruption, Dallas, Texas

Nyangena, Kenneth O., a student in Kenya contributed additional valuable material on Mzee Jomo Kenyatta

Bibliography

Allen, James E., <u>Nursing Home Administration</u>, 3rd Edition, Springen Publishing Company, NY, NY, 1997

Anderson, John. <u>The Struggle for the School: The Interaction of Missionary, Colonial Government and Nationalist</u>

Andrew J. Dubrin, <u>Minutes Guide To Leadership</u>, Macmillan Spectrum, Alpha Books, 1997, New York, NY

Arnold J. Toynbee, <u>A Study of History</u>, Oxford University Press, N.Y. N.Y 1962

Aubrey De Selin Court, <u>Herodotus The Histories</u>, Easton Press, 1996

Barbara Mertz, <u>Temples, Toms & Hieroglyphs, A popular His-</u>

tory of Ancient Egypt, William Morrow, Publ.1964

Bruce, Chilton, Abraham Curse, A Roots of Violence in Judaism, Christianity and Islam, Doubleday, 2008

Cantalupo, Ch. (Ed.) Ngugi wa Thiong'o: Text and Context, Trenton, NJ 1995

Carlton J.H. Hayes, James H. Hanscom, Ancient Civilizations, The Macmillan Co. N.Y 1963

Charles M. Bakewell, The Republic Plato, Charles Scribner's Sons, Dallas, 1928, 1956

Chenevix Trench, Ch. Men who ruled Kenya: the Kenya Administration, 1892 - 1963, London 1993

Chester Bowles, Ideas People and Peace, Harper & Brothers Publishing, 1958 New York

Chruden/Sherman, Managing Human Resources, 7th edition, South-Western, Dallas

Colin Legume, Africa a Hand Book, Praeger Publishers, New York

David Barton, The Myth of Separation, 5th Edition, Aledo, TX 1992

David R. Hawkins, M.D., PhD, Power vs. Force, The Hidden Determinants of Human Behavior, Ray House, Inc, Carlsbad, 1995 CA

David D. Van Fleet, <u>Contemporary Management</u>, Houghton Mifflin Company, Boston, Massachusetts

Edmond Morris, <u>Theodore Rex</u>, Random House, NY 2001

Elgin Groseclose, <u>Money and Man</u>, 4th edition, University of Oklahoma, Norman, OK

Ernest Hemingway, <u>The Snows of Kilimanjaro and Other Stories</u>, Charles Scribner's Sons, New York, 1961

F. Gerald Ensley, <u>Persons can Change</u>, Abingdon Press, 1963, NY

Freeman & Taylor, <u>How To Pick Leaders</u>, Magazines of Industry, 1950. USA

Gatabaki, Njehu (Ed.) <u>Twenty years of independence, 1963 - 1983</u>, Nairobi 1983

George A. Rothrock, Tom B. Jones, <u>Europe: A brief history</u>, Volume One, Rand McNally 1975

George L. Morrissey, <u>Management by Objective and Results in the Public Sector</u>, 1970

Githieya, Francis K. <u>The freedom of the spirit: African indigenous churches in Kenya</u>, Atlanta, GA 1997

H.W. Crocker III, <u>Robert E. Lee On Leadership</u>, Three Rivers Press, New York, New York

J. Clifton Williams, <u>Leadership Quest</u>, Leadership Press, Mc-Gregor, Texas

Jacques Thiroux, <u>Ethics Theory and Practice</u>, 5th Edition, Prentice Hall, 1995. USA

James Currey, <u>General History of Africa Vol. 4 Twelfth to Sixteen Century</u>, UNESCO Publ. Paris, France, 1997

James Currey, <u>General History of Africa Vol.5 Sixteen to Eighteen Century</u>, UNESCO, Publ. Paris, France, 1999

John Naisbitt, <u>Megatrends</u>, Warner Books edition, 1982, New York

Joe Aldrich, <u>Lifestyle Evangelism</u>, USA, 1993

Joseph Epes Brown, <u>The Sacred Pipe</u>, Penguin Group, New York, 1953

Joseph T. Glathaar, <u>General Lee's Army from Victory to Collapse</u>, Publ. Free Press, NY,NY,2008

Judge Waki, <u>The Waki Commission</u>, 2008

Kenneth Scott Latoourette, <u>A History of Christianity</u>, Harper & Row, 1953 New York

Kenya, <u>Ministry of Planning, Millennium Development Goals</u>, NRB, 2006

Kershaw, Greet. Mau Mau from below. Athens, OH 1997

Kihoro, Wanyiri, <u>Politics in Kenya</u>, Centre of African Studies, Edinburgh University 1992

Kirsch, Jonathan, <u>A Life of Moses</u>, Easton Press, Norwalk, Connecticut

Kivuitu, <u>Election Handbook</u>, 2001

Lee Iacocca, <u>Iacocca An Autobiography</u>, Bantam Books, NY, 1984

Lee Iacocca, <u>Where Have the Leaders Gone?</u>, USA, 2006

Leaf, A. (1973), <u>Getting Old</u>, Scientific American, 229(3)

Levtzion & Pouwels editors, <u>The History of Islam in Africa</u>, Ohio University Press, Athens, Ohio

Likert, Rensis & Likert, Jane, <u>New Ways of Managing Conflict</u>, McGraw-Hill Company, NY

Likimani, Muthoni, Passbook Number F.47927: women and Mau Mau in Kenya. New York, NY 1985

Maas, Maria. <u>Women's groups in Kiambu, Kenya: it is always a good thing to have land</u>, Leiden (Netherlands) 1986

Maloba, <u>Wunyabari. Mau Mau and Kenya: an analysis of a peasant revolt</u>, Bloomington, IN 1993

Mark Sherman, <u>Personality: Inquiry and Application</u>, Pergamum Press. 1979. New York, USA

Marianne and Gerald Corey, <u>Groups Process and Practice</u>, Brooks/Cole Publishing Company, CA 1992

Mathis & Jackson, <u>Personnel/Human Resources Management</u>, Fifth Edition, West Publishing Co, St. Paul, MN

Maughan-Brown, D., <u>Land, Freedom and Fiction: History and Ideology in Kenya</u>, London 1985

Messey, Robert F., <u>Personality Theories</u>, D.Van Nostrand Company, NY

Michael Allin, <u>Zarafa</u>, Random House, New York, 1998

NACP Secretariat, <u>National Anti-Corruption Plan</u>, NRB, unknown

Narang, Harish. <u>Politics as Fiction: The novels of Ngugi wa Thiong'o</u>, New Delhi 1995

New King James translation was used for the Bible references unless otherwise indicated

New American Standard Bible, (NASB) by The Lockman Foundation, Copyright 1960,1962,1968,1971,1972,1973,1975,1977, CA

Pearce II & Robison, JR, <u>Strategy Management</u>, 2nd edition, Richard D. Irwin, Inc. Homewood, IL

Roberts Fagles, <u>The Iliad</u>, Homer, Easton Press, 1998

Roberts Fagles, The Odyssey, Homer, Easton Press, 1998

Schermerhorn, Hunt & Osborn, Managing Organizational Behavior, John Wiley & Sons, New York

Sharon Drury, Leader-Member Exchange Theory (LMX), In-group/Out-group, used with permission, August/2005

Solomon Kimuyu PhD, Policy and Procedure, Solomon Home for Children, Inc. Manual, unpublished, 1995

Stephen L. Carter, Integrity, Basil Books Division of Harper Collins, 1996 (pages 4-22)

Steve Christopher, PhD, Leadership Development Class, used with permission, Livermore, CA, unpublished , July 2005

Stewart Gordon, When Asia was the World, Publ. Da Capo Press, USA, 2008

Sturges F. Cary, Arrow Book of Presidents, Scholastic Book Services, New York, 1968

The Holy Bible, Authorized King James Version (AKJV) Copyright 1975, by Thomas Nelson Inc., Nashville, TN

The Holy Bible, Revised Standard Version (RSV) Copyright 1946-1952 by Thomas Nelson & Sons, New York

Theodore, Roosevelt, African Game Trails, Charles Scribner's Sons, 1909, 1910

Thiroux P. Jacques, <u>Ethics theory and Practice</u>, 5th Edition, Prentice-Hall, Inc, New Jersey

Thomas B. Smith, <u>If It Is To Be It's Up To Me</u>, Possibility Press, USA

Tom B. Jones, <u>From the Tigris to Tiber, An Introduction to Ancient History</u>, The Dorsey Press, 1969

Tom Peters and Nancy Austin, <u>A Passion for Excellence</u>, Random House, NY, 1985

Unknown, <u>Enterprise in the Development of Formal Education in Kenya</u>, London: Longman, 1970

Unknown, <u>The History of Pipestone County</u>, Taylor Publishing Co, Dallas, July 1984, Dallas

Victoria Davis, <u>The Wars of the Ancient Greeks</u>, Publ. Cassell and Co, London, 1999

Watson, <u>Think</u>, Autobiography of Watson, 1969 (page 108)

Welch, Soldier & State in Africa, Northwest University Press, US

Will Durant, <u>The Context of Plato, The Story of Philosophy</u>, Pg. 5-40, Simon and Schuster, NY, 1953

Ibid., Aristotle and Greek Science, Kant, German Idealism, Pg. 41-71, Pg. 192-220

BIBLE COMMENTARIES

David C. George, Layman's Bible Book Commentary, Ephesians Vol. 21, Broadman Press. , Nashville, TN, 1979

Davidson, Stibbs, & Kevan, The New Bible Commentary, The Inter-Varsity Fellowship, London, 1954

Exell and Leale, Genesis and Exodus, The Preacher's Complete Homiletic Commentary, Funk & Wagnalls, NY

McGee, J. Vernon, Genesis, Exodus, Thru the Bible, Vol. I, Thomas Nelson Publ., Nashville, 1981

Peter V. Ross, A Digest of the Bible, Prentice-Hall, Inc. New York, 1938

C. Simpson, Introduction and Exegesis of Genesis, The Interpreter's Bible, pg 458-464, Vol. I, Abingdon, TN 1980

Id, Beare & Wedel, Ephesians, pg 597-749, Vol.10, Abingdon, Nashville, TN, 1980

William Barclay, Daily Study Bible Series: Acts of Apostles, Luke, Timothy, Titus, Ephesians & Galatians

ENCYCLOPEDIAS

Crystal, David, <u>Park, Mungo</u>, pg 722, The Cambridge Biographical Encyclopedia, 2nd Edition, Cambridge Univ. Press, UK, 1998

Edwards, editor, <u>Plato, Aquinas, Augustine, Hume, Kant, Aristotle, The Encyclopedia of Philosophy</u>, Vol.1 & 2 198-206, Vol. 3 & 4, 78-89, 305-323, Macmillan Publishing, 1967, New York

WEBSITES

www.Wikipendia.com

www.marsgroupkenya.org

www.news.bbc.co.uk

www.sciencemag.org

MAGAZINES

Business Weekly, July, 1984, (pp. 24-30)

Time Magazine, "Teddy," USA, July 3, 2006

Van Biema, David, "The Legacy of Abraham," *TIME*, page 64, September 2002, New York

JOURNALS

Achenbach, Joel, <u>The God Particle</u>, NATIONAL GEOGRAPHIC, page 90-105, March 2008, Tampa, FL

Draper, Robert, <u>The Black Pharaohs</u>, NATIONAL GEOGRAPHIC, page 34-59, February 2008, Tampa, FL

Fay & Nichols, <u>Ivory Wars</u>, <u>Wildlife Haven</u>, NATIONAL GEOGRAPHIC, pages 34-77, March 2007, Tampa FL

Jeffery, <u>David</u>, <u>Renaissance Michelangelo</u>, <u>Holy Land Map</u>, NGM, pages 688-712, December 1989, Tampa, FL

Jenkins, Mark, <u>Virunga Gorillas</u>, NATIONAL GEOGRAPHIC, pages 34-65, July 2008, Tampa, FL

Gugliotta, Guy, <u>Maya Mysteries</u>, NATIONAL GEOGRAPHIC, pages 68-109, August 2007, Tampa, FL

Quammen, Wainaina, Kotch, Mendel, & Fuller, <u>Africa, Special Issue</u>, NGM, pages 2-122, September 2005, Tampa, FL

Salopek, Paul, <u>Lost in the Sahel</u>, NATIONAL GEOGRAPHIC, page 34-67, April 2008, Tampa, FL

Sloan, Christopher P., <u>Origin of Childhood</u>, NATIONAL GEOGRAPHIC, pg 148-159, November 2006, Tampa, FL

END NOTES

1. United Nations, Independent Inquiry Committee, <u>Management of the Oil-For-Food Program</u>

2. The Associated Press, <u>Death of Idi Amin, former president for Uganda,</u> 2003

3. Samuel C. Certo, <u>Principles of Modern Management,</u> WMC-Brown Co. publisher, 1983, Dubuque, Iowa. Pg 319

4. bid., pages 318-323

5. Mrs. J.H Worcester, JR, <u>David Livingstone</u>, Moody Press, Chicago, Illinois, page 103

6. Samuel C. Cero, <u>Principles of Modern Management,</u> WMC-Brown Co. Publisher, 1983, Dubuque, Iowa. Pages 343-348

INDEX

Aristotle, 21, 50, 51, 88, 135, 136
Asante, 219
Asbestos, see (MDGs Kenya), 261, 262, 263
Assyrians, see (Early traders Indian Ocean), 236
AT&T, 20, 124
Athi River, 85, 163, 259, 296, 298, 302, 322, 323, 328, 344, 369, 401
Athi River Baptist Church, 262
Augustus Caesar, 45, 102, 360

B
Barack, 226, 227, 282, 294, 327, 353, 361
Beyond the Sahara, 137, 142, 143
Bible, 4, 6, 13, 33, 46, 51, 63, 66, 88, 98, 99, 105, 112, 122, 129, 157, 180, 218, 255, 258, 324, 401
Blue Nile, 3, 234
British poet, Jonathan Swift, 138
Brother Joseph Mukasa, 123

C
C.S. Lewis, 128
Caliph, 237
Campus Crusade for Christ, International, 122
Catholic Martyrs, 123
Chagga tribe, 85, 233
Charismatic leaders, 7, 8, 9
Charity Ngilu, see (Place of Women in Society, Kenya), 289, 290
Chester Bernard, 34
Chief Kivoi, see (Akamba history), 175, 177, 178, 179, 329
Chief Justice, see (USA), 360
Chinese, (Indian Ocean), 137, 236, 251
Chreia, 111

G

H

K

L

O

P

U

V

Vision, 7, 14, 38, 42, 45, 46, 47, 71, 89, 90, 96, 104, 109, 119, 162, 261, 306, 343, 365, 366, 405
Visionary, see (envision), 34, 45, 109, 331

W

Waki Commission, see (Kenya Parliament), 209, 210, 341, 346, 348, 349, 350, 351
Walter Rodney, 166
War Between the States, see (USA history), 119
West Texas, 42, 50, 59, 70
What is my responsibility? 7
What is your definition of leadership? 89
Why? What happened? 167
Wildlife Preservation, 141, 143, 157, 161, 163
Winston Churchill, see (WW II), 8
Win-win, see (Problem solving), 82, 83, 84

Y

Years of 1946-1960s, British East Africa, 169
Youth, see (Kenya), 267, 270, 347, 348, 401
Youthful(ness), 306, 326, 331
Youth street violence, see (Kenya), 347

Z

Zanj, see (Zenj Empire, Dominion Zanzibar), 143, 237
Zebra, see (Kenya wildlife), 163, 178
Zipporah, see (Jethro's daughter), 9
Zulus, see (South Africa), 38, 329, 370

CPSIA information can be obtained at www.ICGtesting.com
Printed in the USA
BVOW08*2210060316

439317BV00007B/28/P